In this lively and moving memoir U Kyaw Win, one of Burma's most outspoken opposition leaders, vividly brings home the heavy toll exacted on his nation and family by a half century of rule by a succession of incompetent, brutal and swaggering military dictators. Once one of the most prosperous nations of Southeast Asia, by the beginning of this century Burma earned a UN classification as one of the poorest members of the international community.

In unfolding the story of his family Dr. Win also unfolds the troubled history of modern Burma. We see through his eyes a nation ruled by fear by a military clique whose loyalty is kept in place by material rewards and special privileges while the Burmese people sink deeper into poverty and despair. But the Burmese picture is not one of unremitting gloom.

In fresh detail accompanied by insightful analysis, Dr. Win expounds on the popular uprising of 1988 which, though in the end bloodily suppressed, came close to overthrowing the regime and gave rise to one of its most powerful and determined opponents, Aung San Suu Kyi.

He also recounts the regime's unprecedented use of force against Buddhist monks protesting a rise in fuel prices which aroused such popular hatred of the regime that it forced upon the military leadership the need for change. For the past few years that process of change has been underway. Burma is gradually opening to the outside world and its harsh totalitarianism is easing.

Burma still has a long way to go and it remains to be seen as to how accommodating the still dominant military leadership will be to the reform process. As Burma stirs favorably it would be remiss not to take our hats off to Dr. Win for a consuming and for the most part lonely five decade long struggle for Burmese freedom. At eighty-two he can let up a bit, secure in the knowledge that he has contributed greatly to breaking the Burmese log jam.

—**BURTON LEVIN**
American ambassador to Burma, 1987–90

I spent three years in Burma in the 1960s as a junior member of the British embassy, and returned there 25 years later as ambassador. I was at my post during the uprising of 1988, and its aftermath, so vividly covered in the book. The author with Riri his Indonesian wife describes a huge range of experiences and events throughout these years, his objective to make Burma's vicissitudes known to the widest possible audience and to point the way to the future. He managed to involve the great and sometimes the good in his efforts, in the U.S. from ex-President Carter downwards and in Burma all the main players. While his father did his best to give Ne Win and the army the benefit of the doubt he rejected their claims from the outset. I can only add that U Nu once told me emphatically Burma was two thousand times better under the British, two thousand times.

—**MARTIN MORLAND**
British ambassador to Burma, 1986–90

My Conscience

Margt Barrie

My Conscience

An Exile's Memoir of Burma

Be blessed.

Win *31 July 2016*

U KYAW WIN

Foreword by Sean Turnell

RESOURCE *Publications* · Eugene, Oregon

MY CONSCIENCE
An Exile's Memoir of Burma

Cover art by Han Win depicts the eleventh century temples of Bagan, Burma. The Irrawaddy River and Shan Highlands are in the background.

Resource Publications
An Imprint of Wipf and Stock Publishers
199 W. 8th Ave., Suite 3
Eugene, OR 97401

www.wipfandstock.com

PAPERBACK ISBN: 978-1-4982-8271-0
HARDCOVER ISBN: 978-1-4982-8273-4
EBOOK ISBN: 978-1-4982-8272-7

Manufactured in the U.S.A.   07/15/16

To the memory of my Father,
The Reverend U On Kin, 1894–1980
And my Mother,
Daw Sein Thit, 1896–1979

Contents

Foreword
The Song of U Kyaw Win

A COUNTRY'S COLLAPSE INTO the brutality and arbitrariness that is the hall-mark of dictatorship brings with it many victims. Most apparent of these is the population ruled over in such a State, whose lives and freedoms become as precarious as their economic prospects. Less obviously apparent is the fracturing of the lives of the people who are forced out and away. Often constituting an especially enterprising and courageous cohort, these exiles suffer individually, but so too do the countries from which they have made their escape, and to which they could have contributed so much.

This book tells the story of one such principled exile from Burma, U Kyaw Win. Son of a Burman father and a Karen mother, U Kyaw Win personifies the diversity that can and should be Burma's strength, but which all too often has come to be the exploitable source of ethnic and religious chauvinism, division, and repression. Such iniquities have all been too apparent in recent times in Burma, alas, but countering them has not just been a key part of U Kyaw Win's past. As he puts it, the quest for "a vision of a larger inclusive social reality" over the "constricting impulses of ethnicity" remains the central task for true Burma nationhood in the twenty-first century.

Today the cause of Burma has become well known and even fashionable. It was not always so, and for many years U Kyaw Win's voice against the atrocities and injustices in Burma was a lonely one. From demonstrating on the sidewalks of San Francisco in the mid-1970s (when Burma was in the mere spring of its fifty-plus years of darkness), founding and publishing *The Burma Bulletin,* undertaking relief work for Burmese refugees in the wake of the bloody events of 1988, to organising Daw Aung San Suu Kyi's honorary degree from American University, what U Kyaw Win calls his song has been one of *metta* (loving kindness) and *garuna* (compassion).

U Kyaw Win modestly describes his lifelong effort as being simply to brighten the corner where he is. As an individual motivation that is a fine

goal, but it also brings with it the considerable virtue of bringing enlightenment to the rest of us.

Sean Turnell
Associate Professor of Economics
Macquarie University
Sydney, Australia
28 December 2015

Acknowledgments

I HAVE RELIED ON recollections of events and substance I remembered, experienced, and articles I published in *The Burma Bulletin* during its nineteen years' existence (1973–1992) to write this memoir. I have also relied on my letters to editors which were published in various periodicals, the speeches I made, and the interviews I gave.

My Woodstock School classmates Kenneth Bonham, Nirmal Chand, Ashoke Chatterjee, Gordon Hostetler, Ho Kang Liu, and Margaret Winfield Sullivan, helped me with material I might otherwise have forgotten or overlooked about our days in India and beyond.

Ethan Casey early on helped build the foundation and framed the architecture of the book by recording my dictation and turning them into many successive drafts.

My wife Riri and son Zali kept me moving on track as the writing progressed, sometimes giving me more advice than I needed or wanted, but patiently countenancing to the end. They helped me tremendously verifying my facts or otherwise refreshing my memory of events that might have gone into obscurity.

U Nwe Aung, from his perch in Germany, helped find our young compatriots Ko Min Hein and wife Ma Wutyi, who made assiduous efforts to obtain a copy of Sir Hubert Rance's historic telegram to Lord Listowel, from the British Library's archives to which Patricia Herbert, a former librarian there, pointed the direction.

April Lynn Htut, accompanied me to Carnegie Endowment for International Peace in Washington, DC and helped me research the name of the senior associate who, in 1975, had lent me his ear about the situation in Burma but whose name I had totally, and unforgivably, forgotten. April had just a fortnight earlier graduated *summa cum laude* from Bucknell University.

Christine Pulliam, public affairs specialist, and her scientist colleagues at Harvard-Smithsonian Center for Astrophysics identified the comet I had sited over Rangoon's skies in November-December 1948. I am vindicated.

My fellow survivors of De La Salle Institute, an orphanage in the Ir-rawaddy Delta jungles, during the trying World War II years, 1942–1945: Robert Anthony, Father Edward Evans, Brother Patrick Minus, FSC, Robert Murdock; and Heather, who lived with her parents Thomas and Ada Joyce at Sookalat Rubber Estates, six miles from De La Salle, shared memories of DLS and the Brothers of Christian Schools at Hnget Aw Zan village while we were traumatized by the war.

Burton Levin and Martin Morland, former American and British am-bassadors to Burma, respectively, and John Haseman, Colonel, U.S. Army (Ret), who was the U.S. defense atttaché to Burma from April 1987 through June 1990 provided me with their eyewitness accounts of the tumultuous uprising for democracy.

Walter Marciniak, Commander, U.S. Navy (Ret), former U.S. naval attaché to Indonesia, enlightened me on naval protocol. Walt, the old sea dog, has great respect for the Royal Navy despite its participation in wars in 1770s and 1810s.

U Kin Oung, another retired officer but of the Burma Navy, an activist in our homeland's struggle for democracy exiled to Australia, filled me in with many details from personal knowledge of the assassination of General Aung San and the godfather Ne Win era.

Ashin Gunissara, Gerald Holbrook, Mary Maxwell, and Kyin Kyin Nyein collaborated on the music to *Free, Free, Our Country is Free!*

Gail Fisher, Ashin Gunissara, and Ellen Scheffler contributed a tre-mendous amount of their talents and time with the photographic and other illustrations, which make the Chinese adage "A picture is worth a thousand words," come to life. (Ellen accompanied Riri and me to India as our pho-tographer where we were received in private audience by His Holiness the Dalai Lama for the second time in forty-four years.)

Professor Josef Silverstein, a distinguished Burma scholar and friend of long years shared the depth of his knowledge and wisdom.

Several others inside Burma, at great risk to themselves and to their loved ones, provided me with information during the darkest times when the military had sealed the country. Their identities must remain unrevealed for obvious reasons.

Professor Richard Soulen, a long-time friend and author several times over, helped me harness my thoughts and focus my writing.

Professor Sean Turnell of Macquarie University, who has done so much to help Burma's antiquated economic policies transition from the remnants of the Burmese Way to Socialism to an open market and equitable economy, for writing the foreword to this book.

Doris and Tom Baker of Filter Press, Palmer Lake, Colorado, provided pre-press services, which greatly relieved me of the technicalities of seeing this book to fruition.

Finally, to Susan Zingale-Baird, who snuck into my study while I was not watching and left a note on my desk: "Win, make time and write your story," before she returned to her job at the University of Pennsylvania. Here it is Susan. Thanks for the nudge. How can I not love you for that?

I shall forever be grateful to these and all others who generously gave their time and talents to help me tell my story.

U Kyaw Win
Boulder, Colorado, USA

The Dalai Lama and Win in Dharamsala, September 2014. In the meeting, the Dalai Lama signed the letter of endorsement for this book. Photo by Ellen Scheffler.

THE DALAI LAMA

MESSAGE

Burma and Tibet are not only neighbours geographically, but our peoples have ancient racial and cultural ties, reflected in some of our linguistic similarity. Our two communities are traditionally Buddhists although there are followers of other religions like Islam, Christianity, etc

In recent decades, Burma has had to go through much political and social upheavals and as a result the people have experienced much challenges. U Kyaw Win and his family have lived through that sad era in Burmese history. Even though he left for the United States quite early on, his parents remained behind, and through them and other channels, he had been following the situation in Burma with active concern and participation.

In "My Conscience: An Exile's Memoir of Burma", he tells the story of Burma, along with that of his own family, as their lives evolved with that of their country. He has written with a deep love for his country and there is much to learn from this book.

September 18, 2014

1

Home Again

WHEN MY MOTHER DIED in April 1979 and my father eleven months later, I was prevented from performing my duty to comfort them when they took their last breaths. I had been stripped of my citizenship by the Burmese military junta after it toppled a democratic government in 1962. Failure to perform that final duty is a wound in me that will never heal.

I tried for many years to return to Burma, but it was in vain. Every time I applied for a visa I had to complete a long form giving the military regime detailed information about myself and my family. Then in 2001, after living for more than forty years as an exile in America, I was pleasantly surprised to be issued a visa. General Khin Nyunt, the second most powerful man in the junta, had authorized it. Khin Nyunt was chief of intelligence at the time and widely feared, but he fell from grace three years later.

The regime was using the Venerable Dr. Rewata Dhamma, a Burmese Buddhist abbot based in England, as an emissary to coax democracy leader Aung San Suu Kyi and other opposition leaders into toning down their rhetoric. Early one morning in California, Dr. Rewata called me from Malaysia and said, "If I can get you a visa to Burma, will you go? I will speak to General Khin Nyunt."

"I will, Reverend," I told him. "But I don't want them to trap me."

"Don't worry about that," he assured me. He gave me the names and telephone numbers of two senior intelligence officers and told me to call them if I ran into a problem. I went into Burma with trepidation. I didn't know what to expect, but I was emboldened by the holy man's assurance.

During those forty years, I had been busy earning a living and raising a family in America. I had also been speaking out against the junta. When my wife, Riri, and I left Burma in 1961, I took a job teaching at the U.S. Army Language School (now the Defense Language Institute), at the Presidio of Monterey in California. I took out a mortgage in 1962, in order to provide a home for our first child, Zali. I became an American citizen in 1966, because being a stateless person was not an option.

THE JUNTA, MY NEMESIS

When U Nu, the Burmese prime minister ousted in the 1962 coup, came to California in 1969, I secretly hosted him. Earlier in London, he announced his intention to raise an army to overthrow the military regime. He did not believe it was wrong by Buddhist tenet to kill the killers.

I launched, and for nineteen years published, a quarterly newsletter, *The Burma Bulletin*, as a chronicle of the movement and a voice for Burmese living abroad. I took every opportunity to expose the brutality of the military led by General Ne Win that had forcibly sealed the country off from the outside world. When widespread unhappiness erupted into unrest in August 1988, the military responded by killing thousands of protesters. The effect was like the lid coming off a pressure cooker. The massacre, the ensuing movement led by Aung San Suu Kyi, and her National League for Democracy's overwhelming victory in the 1990 elections, which was nullified by the regime, had finally compelled the outside world to notice Burma. I had been a witness and a participant from afar in the country's tortured history throughout my exile. But things had turned out differently than I had hoped.

I went to Burma in November 2001. I was apprehensive. Before I went, I made sure that family and friends were aware that I was going. One person I told was Betty Jane Southard Murphy, a Washington lawyer with connections to the senior Bush White House and a loyal friend for half a century. B. J. said, "If you run into a problem, let me know." I also informed Denis Gray, the longtime Associated Press bureau chief in Bangkok, as well as Nick Williams Jr., the *Los Angeles Times* Bangkok bureau chief, and the

Burma Desk at the Department of State in Washington. Members of my church's prayer chain in Boulder, Colorado, lifted me up.

In the departure lounge at Bangkok airport were several Burmese, but only the women were dressed in native attire. They seemed cautious and reserved in their body language toward me; perhaps they suspected that I was associated with the military regime. By wearing Burmese national dress, which consisted of a collarless white shirt, a *longyi* or sarong, and a jacket called *taik pon eingyi*, I was making a statement of my cherished Burmese heritage. The *longyi* is of Indian origin, which the Indians call *lungie*. The *taik pon eingyi* [jacket] is of Chinese origin. Sandwiched between China and India, Burma draws from the cultures of both these giants.

I felt anxious and constricted, but I did not consider backing out. I vowed to myself that if I was interrogated I would tell the truth, but would not tell everything. I was not going to be intimidated.

Map of Burma

As the plane came to a halt on the tarmac in Rangoon, I spied an armed soldier standing at the foot of the stairs. He was just guarding the plane, but my heart skipped a beat. In Burma we have a saying that if a ghost senses your fear he'll frighten you all the more. (Superstitious Burmese believe in ghosts.) So I put up a brave front.

As the passengers disembarked, the lone Burmese monk on the plane nodded at me and asked, "*Dagah gyi* [benefactor]—what is your *zah ti* [origin, place of birth]?" "*Thongwa ba, paya* [Thongwa, Reverend]," I answered. The friendly exchange helped relax me.

In those days only a trickle of tourists went into Burma. I got into the immigration line for foreigners. There was a man, untidily dressed in a *longyi*, a short-sleeved shirt without a jacket, and flip-flops, scrutinizing the passengers. His eyes told me that he was military intelligence. When he spied me, the only person in the foreigners' line dressed in Burmese attire, he said, "Myanmar passport holders are the next line." I told him I didn't hold a Burmese passport.

When the young women at immigration noted my age in the passport, they became deferential. "Oh, uncle," the young ladies at customs greeted me. "Do you have any presents for us? We are poor." I gave them a few lipsticks. As I was collecting my bags, I spotted two young women waving frantically at me from the other side of the glass partition. I was expecting somebody to meet me, but I didn't know who would show up. When I got out of the secure area, I had to ask, "Whose daughters are you?" One turned out to be the daughter of a childhood friend and the other a relative. Neither had been born in 1961 when I left the country. Their fathers were long gone.

Outside the airport I saw soldiers standing guard in front of buildings. There were more cars. Forty years ago, privately owned automobiles had been few and far between; to get around, people had relied on public transportation and their own feet.

My plane arrived at 8:30 a.m. From the airport I made a beeline for Twante, my father's birthplace and my boyhood hometown, about twenty-five miles away from Rangoon by ferry and road. My first duty was to do homage to my parents at their final resting place. Images of long years past flashed through my mind's eye. Standing over their graves in the tiny church compound, I was emotionally exhausted.

Even though it was November, the heat and humidity were overwhelming. The Methodist school that my father had co-founded with an American missionary in 1919 still stood, but the football field was filled with dwellings. Private schools in Burma were nationalized in 1963, and the Methodist Mission had been broken up and occupied by squatters. The footpath behind the school had become a road, but the roads in Twante were little more than unpaved bullock cart tracks with bamboo-and-thatch houses lining both sides.

From my parents' graves I went to Shan Zu, the town's Shan quarter in the shadow of the Shwehsandaw Pagoda where a cousin's family lived. From their home you could hear the pagoda's tinkling bells. Twante had grown and was much more crowded than I had known it. In my day, you had to cross the Rangoon River on a *sampan* to Dalla and then take a bus to Twante, but the more practical route was by boat or *sampan* on the Twante canal. The road to the pagoda, which used to cut through bamboo groves and jungle, was now completely built up. Even though the town had grown, it had hardly developed. There was still no indoor plumbing, garbage collection, electricity, or telephones in most areas.

I ate lunch in Shan Zu, but I wanted to get back to Rangoon before dark. My family home in Twante was no more. I returned to Dalla and re-crossed the river on a filthy, ragtag ferry. I looked for life jackets on the crowded ferry. They were secured tightly in a difficult-to-reach place. I checked in at Yuzana Garden hotel, which in colonial times was the chummery [bachelor quarters] of Steel Brothers Company, a British mercantile conglomerate that was the setting of a Maurice Collis book, *Trials in Burma* (1938). A reception clerk later remarked that my voice sounded familiar. I kept mum. I did not want to let the cat out of the bag that she had indeed heard me on the British Broadcasting Corporation (BBC) Burmese Service in some interviews I had given and two pieces I had recently done on Cesar Chavez and the United Farm Workers and another on the American form of democracy. BBC shared several letters commenting on my contributions it had received from listeners.

The next day I called the U.S. embassy and asked to speak with Priscilla Clapp, the chargé d'affaires. The United States had withdrawn its ambassador from Burma after the 1988 uprising and conducted diplomatic relations with the junta at the chargé level, in rebuke. She was unavailable, but Karl Wycoff, the deputy chief of mission, was. I told him who I was and that I would like to see him. Apparently, the State Department had cabled the embassy to inform them of my coming. "I'll come to your hotel," Wycoff said.

When he arrived, I asked him whether I would be under surveillance. "Probably," he said. "They use about fifty people to tail a person they want to keep under surveillance. You won't see the same face twice." He said he hailed a cab from the street to come to my hotel instead of using an embassy car. He wanted to avoid being tailed. He spent about forty-five minutes briefing me on the situation in Burma. I wanted the embassy to know my travel plans up country. He gave me his home and direct office phone numbers, and the 24/7 number for the embassy's Marine guard station. I saw him one more time before I left the country. "If you run into a problem at the airport at departure, call," he said. "Someone from the embassy will be there within fifteen minutes."

An amusing incident took place while I was leisurely strolling westward on Merchant Street from Sulé (SOO-laye) Pagoda Road. A neatly dressed chap standing under a tree on the sidewalk made eye contact. A hand-scribbled sign in Burmese, "*Baydin* [astrologer]," was tacked onto the trunk. "How much do you charge?" I asked. It was about a dollar. "How accurate is your forecast?"

"*Hman thint tha-laut taw, hman ba deh* [it is as accurate as it can be]," he said.

"Do you refund the fee if you are incorrect?"

He pounced back, "You have to pay whether or not I am correct."

I was willing to do my tiny part to help alleviate poverty in my homeland. He asked for the date and time of my birth and the day of the week, and then scribbled some calculations in a little note book. "You come from far away. You are successful and prosperous there. You are a teacher. You have gone through several setbacks in your life, but you are a fighter. You have been victorious every time." His articulation of the Burmese language was polished, poetry to my ears. I went back to that same spot the next day. He was no where to be found. Could his have been one of those fifty faces Karl Wycoff, the diplomat, had said I would not see more than once?

Next, I went to Syriam where my three cousins lived. The eldest was Daw Mya Mya Lay, (elder sister, *Ma Ma* Mya, to me). At eighty-eight she was the most senior of my paternal bloodline still living. When I arrived at the front gate, she was standing outside the front door, calling out *ChoCho,ChoCho* (my familial name to family and childhood friends). I rushed to her and went down on my knees and touched the ground at her feet with my forehead and the palms of my hands. (This physical expression of deep respect rendered to one's parents, elders, and teachers, is of Indian origin.) I had not seen her in more than forty years. She, as the firstborn of my father's eldest brother, was a second mother to me (the lastborn of her father's younger brother) under our kinship system.

Many years ago, my mother told me that after my birth she became very ill and Ma Ma Mya and her sisters cared for me. Ma Ma Mya was twenty-one years my senior. On my subsequent visit, two years later, frail as she was, she insisted on accompanying me to Thongwa where our families had lived long ago. She pointed out the landmarks as the van drove us across paddy fields. She showed me my first home, which was still standing but in a very dilapidated condition, and the land where her's had once stood but had since been occupied by another house. I never saw her again.

On Sunday I attended the Methodist church on Creek (now Bo Myat Tun) Street where my father had been pastor for more than half a century. Aung Than, a boyhood playmate in Twante, was now the sexton, living behind the church. Word had spread that I was in Rangoon, so friends and relatives came to church to see me. One woman asked if I remembered her. "No, I don't," I confessed.

"When I was very small, you told me you would cook me and eat me once I turned five. You frightened me. I will never forget that."

"Did I say that to you? Well, I can't do that now, can I?"

Another childhood friend was Margaret, whose father *Saya* Tha Hto, was a teacher at the Methodist Boys' High School located at the corner of Creek Street and Montgomery (now Bogyoke Aung San) Street, before World War II. Margaret and I were dancing partners in a kindergarten recital and I had been made to sing to her:

> I will give you the keys of heaven,
> I will give you the keys of heaven,
> Madam, will you walk?
> Madam, will you talk?
> Madam, will you walk and talk with me?

She initially responded:

> Though you give me the keys of heaven,
> Though you give me the keys of heaven,
> Yet I will not walk; no, I will not talk;
> No, I will not walk or talk with thee.

But in the last stanza she relented:

> Thou shall give me the keys of my heart,
> And we will be married till death us do part;
> I will walk, I will talk,
> I will walk and talk with thee.

Margaret's father had become a leader in the separatist movement for the Karen (Ka RENN) ethnic minority in the late 1940s, in the aftermath of Burma's independence. She now lived in the Karen quarter in west Rangoon, in the former Irrawaddy Flotilla Company's residential compound. She introduced me to her adult children and grandchildren.

Mahn Ba Sein, my lone surviving maternal uncle, came from Pa-an in the Karen State. It was a five-hour journey by bus. When I reimbursed him for his expenses, he thanked me and said, "I will donate it to the seminary."

In his letters, he never failed to tell me that my parents had put him through high school, which had enabled him to become a police officer.

Younger people greeted me, saying, "I'm so-and-so's son" or "so-and-so's daughter." I was saddened to have missed their parents—my childhood friends or relatives, who had since passed away.

After the nostalgic visit to the old Methodist church, I went to Mandalay. A niece accompanied me, and it was the first time she had flown. The taxi driver we had arranged to meet at the airport initially missed us because he was looking for a foreigner, a Westerner. I was traveling on an American passport, and therefore was required to pay the higher foreigner's fare. But we eventually found each other. He drove us to Hsipaw, a distance of 145 miles, toward China and to Maymyo (now Pyin Oo Lwin) on the way back. In Hsipaw we went to the former *haw* [palace] where Inge Sargent, the author of *Twilight over Burma: My Life as a Shan Princess*, had lived.

When we got back to Maymyo, it was already dark. I wanted to stay at the Candacraig (now Thiri Myaing) hotel, but there was no vacancy. In colonial times the Candacraig was the rest house for officials of the Bombay Burmah Trading Corporation. It had only six spacious suites, each with an attached bathroom, a fireplace, and a sitting area. Margaret Bernard, the Eurasian front desk clerk, found us two rooms in another hotel. Her friend who worked there was afraid to take me in because I was a "foreigner."

In Burma, only hotels approved for stay by foreigners can legally accommodate them, and they have to report to local authorities. "He holds an American passport, but he's Burmese," she assured her friend. Shortly after I had retired, a knock on the door startled me. The clerk had told my niece that precinct security was on the phone and wanted to talk to me. I went to the front desk and picked up the phone.

"What's your name?" asked the officious voice. I told him my name. "Don't you have an English name?"

"No, I am Burmese," I barked back. (To the Burmese, all Westerners are English.)

"What is the country of your citizenship? What's your father's name? What's your mother's name? Where did you come from? Where are you going to? What is your occupation in *naing ngan gya* [foreign country]?" The questioning continued. He was gruff, and it made me uncomfortable.

I tossed and turned in bed that night, not knowing what to expect in the morning. My niece and I left the hotel very early, skipping the hotel's prepaid breakfast. We went to the botanical garden and around Maymyo where we saw the iconic Purcell clock tower before returning to Mandalay. A maternal first cousin was married to a Purcell, but I have been unable to ascertain whether this was the same Purcell. Their union produced Pearl and Ruby, who were orphaned when they were very little. Our maternal grandmother and extended family took them under their wings, and my parents sent them to the Methodist English Girls' High School as boarders. When World War II broke out, they evacuated to India over the rugged northwestern mountains. Ruby, the younger one, perished in the trek over that harsh terrain. They had been afraid to remain in Burma because the invading Japanese would have noted their semi-European features.

At the hotel in Mandalay, I joked with the front desk clerks about the $25 million bounty the United States had put on Osama bin Laden's head. "Is he hiding in Mandalay?" I queried, with tongue in cheek.

"Yes, that's him," they replied, nodding to a bearded fellow who had just walked out the door. You cannot help loving these witty young chaps.

Then we flew to the ancient city of Pagan (Ba-GAHN), site of thousands of temples, many in ruins. I had never seen its ancient temples. I saw four of the major ones. Upon return to the hotel in Rangoon, the reception clerks wanted my passport to photocopy for "someone" who had asked. The young ladies would not tell me who the "someone" was, but their rolling eyes said it all; I now had proof positive that I was under surveillance and had been tailed. When I returned after an outing, I was handed a telephone number to call immediately. A voice on the other end said, "*Sayadawgyi* [senior monk] U Rewata from England is here. He wants to talk to you." It took me by surprise, but I was greatly relieved.

"I need to see you, *Sayadawgyi*, where are you?"

An acolyte (military intelligence) said, "Come to No. 35 Inya Road." It was only a ten-minute taxi ride away.

The house was a big colonial-era mansion obscured by tall hedges. It was now a guesthouse of the junta, but I did not know it at the time. I made a little noise at the gate, and a young boy let me in and pointed to the entrance. I went inside. There was not a soul in the cavernous hall. Then a soft voice from the second floor told me to come up the wide double-banistered stairs. He showed me to a large reception room where the *Sayadawgyi* was seated on the dais. I was so happy to see him. "How are you? Is everything O.K.?" he asked.

"I am well, *Sayadawgyi*, everything is fine, thank you."

We chatted alone for several minutes until an acolyte came in and *shi-koed* (prostrated and paid homage) to the holy man. It was time for me to take my leave.

Two men drove me back to the hotel in a van. In small talk, I enquired about their families. When I told them I had been away from the country for more than forty years and remarked on the many changes that had taken place in my absence (which had made much of the area unrecognizable), they asked whether there was any particular place I wanted to see. They drove me by Heroes' Mausoleum, a restricted area. I was grateful.

I don't know whether it was by deliberate design or coincidence that brought the holy man to Rangoon while I was there, but to have seen him there was like having a security blanket. (The Venerable Dr. U Rewata Dhamma, a compassionate soul, died in his sleep on 24 May 2004, in Birmingham, England. He was seventy-four years old.)

I had brought a copy of *The Kenyon Review* for Aung San Suu Kyi, but she was under house arrest, held incommunicado. Former General U Tin Oo, chairman of the National League for Democracy, had weekly access to her and I needed him to take it to her. I found him at his home in Windermere Park one night after taking a relay of several taxi rides. *The Review*'s spring 2001 issue celebrated the centennial of the Nobel Prizes. Aung San Suu Kyi was featured on the cover jointly with Albert Einstein and Marie Curie. My son, Zali, had worked on *The Review* when he was a student at Kenyon College, in 1980–1984.

One evening I was received by British ambassador John Jenkins and his wife, Nancy, over drinks. The ambassador's residence, the former home of the general manager of the Irrawaddy Flotilla Company, was next door to my hotel. We had a nice chat about the situation in Burma and Nancy showed me the upstairs bedroom that Aung San and Ne Win shared during the Japanese occupation.

I had been in Burma only two weeks. I was saddened that the country of my childhood had been driven into such dire poverty, but the people refused to permit poverty to diminish their dignity. I am proud of my people. My visa permitted me to stay for twenty-eight days, but I chose to leave after a fortnight, not wanting to press my luck too far. I was so relieved when I reached the Bangkok Christian Guest House that I called Riri at home in California and my friends in Rangoon to tell them I was back in the free world again!

WHY THIS MEMOIR?

Thongwa, my birthplace

Entering the evening of my years, my thoughts often turn back to the beginning. Not a day passes when my mind does not wander back to my beloved Burma. So many things have happened that I did not want or anticipate, but which I have been forced to accept. I was born on Monday, 5 February 1934, in the town of Thongwa, in the Irrawaddy Delta. Thongwa is only twenty-five miles east of Rangoon as the crow flies, but it was then a journey of several hours by *sampan* across the Rangoon River to Syriam, and thence by road. I remember traveling to Thongwa by train as a child on a spur track that went north to join a main north–south rail line between Rangoon and Mandalay. That spur was later washed away by heavy rains, never to be rebuilt.

My first home in Thongwa was a teak structure with a corrugated zinc roof, a sizable main room, and three bedrooms. Most houses in Thongwa, as well as in Twante, where we moved when I was eight, were built of teak. There was no plumbing, electricity, or telephone. In all of Thongwa and Twante, there were only two telephones each: one at the post office and another at the police station. At night we stayed indoors, for fear of *dacoits* [robbers] and other intruders. Before we turned in each night, the family would hold vespers, which concluded with the singing of the hymn, *Abide with Me*. We slept on the floor.

Win's first home in Thongwa. Photo by Tran Nguyen.

Win's family, 1940

We were six brothers and one sister. I am the youngest. My eldest brother Ko Kyaw Nyein (Victor) was born in 1920. When we were living in Thongwa, sometime in 1941, after Pearl Harbor was bombed, he came running home across the paddy fields, yelling, "Take cover, take cover, Japanese bombers are coming." The first Japanese bombs fell on Rangoon on 23 December 1941. The apartment at 180 49th Street at the corner of Montgomery Street, we had earlier vacated, took a direct hit.

Ko Kyaw Nyein attended Judson College in Rangoon and roomed with my second brother Ko Tun Nyein (Wales) and another fellow named Nam Soon. All three studied chemistry, and Ko Kyaw Nyein tanned leather from cowhides, raised pigs, and made paper from bamboo when we moved to Twante before the arrival of Japanese troops in 1942. He was quite success-ful in these endeavors, but earned little money because wartime conditions were difficult. Occasionally he also taught at my mother's school.

When I was at De La Salle Institute, he would bring roasted lentils to eat whenever he visited. He had been selected by the prewar colonial gov-ernment to study abroad as a state scholar, but the war intervened. When the war ended, he was able to take up this opportunity and continued at the University of Texas, beginning in 1946, where he earned a bachelor's degree in chemistry. He went on to the University of Colorado and earned a master's degree in chemical engineering. Upon return to Burma in 1950, he worked at the Union of Burma Applied Research Institute (UBARI). He later trained and was ordained as a pastor at the Methodist church where my father had served.

After he retired he worked for the United Nations Development Pro-gramme teaching the people in Jamaica the latest brick making methods using modern technology. He later went to the Philippines as a missionary-teacher (chemistry) at a Methodist university. While in the Philippines, he also volunteered for the evangelistic Far East Broadcasting Company, doing translation and broadcasting to Burma. He died of hepatitis in California in 1997.

Ko Tun Nyein (Wales), born in 1921, contracted tuberculosis. In those days, contracting TB in Burma was tantamount to a receiving a death sen-tence. My parents sent him to Meiktila in central Burma because of its dry climate. That didn't help, so they sent him to a sanitarium in India. That would have been in 1940, when he was eighteen. I went aboard the ship with my father to bid him adieu. He held my hands when I placed my feet on his, facing forward, and walked me on the deck. I never saw him again. I was only six years old.

His ship sailed down the Rangoon River toward the Bay of Bengal. That was the last time he fixed his gaze on the sacred Shwedagon Pagoda's magnificence from the fantail of his steamer. How lonely it must have been for him to leave home to go to a foreign land.

After his hospitalization at a TB sanitarium in Ajmer, where one lung was excised, he went to New Delhi, where he eked out a living with the help of caring Burmese expatriates there. The renowned singer Dora Than É was one of them. From there he moved to Simla, where he worked for the Burma Christian Literature Society's exile office. His translation into Burmese of *Christ's Method of Prayer* by the Reverend E. L. Strong was published posthumously in 1948 in Rangoon. Because of the Japanese occupation of Burma, he could not return home and we had no contact with him. It was only when the war ended that we learned of his death in Simla, in 1944.

The Reverend George Appleton, the Anglican priest who buried him, confirmed it. I was with my mother at the Methodist English Church on Signal Pagoda Road in Rangoon when Reverend Appleton conveyed the sad news. She wept and he comforted her. This was the second time my parents had lost a child. It hit them very hard. It pained me so much to see my mother weep. I was eleven.

Reverend Appleton had evacuated to India as Japanese forces invaded Burma. For the duration of the war, he was chaplain to the exile colonial British Government of Burma in Simla. He was consecrated Archbishop of Sydney and later returned to England to retire in Oxford where Riri and I visited him in December 1984. He remembered Ko Tun Nyein well and told me about his days in Simla. I thanked him for pastoring my brother in his final days far away from loved ones.

The third sibling was May May Kyi (Constance), born in 1925. While the brothers were high achievers, the sister was modest in her outlook and ambitions. She became a happy primary school teacher. One thing she did well was to play the piano, and she always accompanied the church services. My brothers and parents were very protective of her. She died in 2006 in Rangoon.

Another boy, Charles, was born in 1926 but lived less than two years.

The next brother was Simon Kyaw Myint, born in 1928, who went on to become a surgeon. After he graduated from Phoenix College and the University of Arizona, he studied medicine at Northwestern University and graduated from there in 1953. He did his surgical residency at the Hospital of the University of Pennsylvania in Philadelphia under the tutelage of Dr. Isadore Ravdin, who as a brigadier general in the U.S. Army Medical Corps had served in Northern Burma under the command of General Joseph Stillwell during World War II.

Irwin Hla Shwe, born in 1929, graduated from Woodstock School, Ohio Wesleyan University, and the University of Colorado, and pursued advanced study at The American University, but did not complete the dissertation for his doctoral degree. He taught political science at Prince George's Community College in Maryland and retired from there on disability. He died in California in 2012.

I was the last born and the English name Father gave me was Willingdon, after Lord Willingdon, Viceroy of India at the time of my birth. We were a subject people under the British Crown and Father was a man of history; thus our names reflected colonial personages of the era.

There are no family names under Burmese custom. Each child is given an individual name. To the question how can one tell which family one comes from, the answer is simple. A well-bred person would always formally introduce himself as the son of so-and-so—both father and mother—to honor the family.

My father, the Reverend U On Kin, was a Methodist pastor. He was a dynamic preacher who was very passionate about the Church. After high school and a teacher training course, he taught school briefly before he went to India, to prepare for the ministry. He first went to Bareilly and later moved to Jabalpur when Leonard Theological College opened. He graduated from Leonard in its first class ten years before I was born. In 2001, I retraced his steps at Leonard.

The principal, faculty, and students received me graciously. I was asked to speak at an assembly, which I was honored to do. He was a voracious reader and writer, as well as an athlete and a classical Burmese dancer. He loved the American and British missionaries, often saying, "These are teachers of great learning." Learning is highly respected in our as well as in other Asian cultures. He held in high esteem the missionaries with whom he "worked in the vineyard," as he put it, but held in contempt the few who condescended to his compatriots.

He hated colonialism with a pitched passion. He was elected as a ministerial delegate to the quadrennial General Conference of the Methodist Church, which he attended five times at eight-year intervals beginning in 1932.

Father espoused social causes and was outspoken in the nationalist anti-colonialist movement. Twante, his birthplace, was a very small town. Every morning he walked the rounds, beginning at the market. We were a family of very meager material possessions but richly blessed in many ways. The family never even owned a bicycle, radio, or refrigerator, but did have a hand cranked gramophone that Father had brought back from abroad on one of his travels. He joined the *Dobama Asi-a-yone* [We Burmans Association] whose members addressed each other as *thakin* [master]. This was a direct rebuke to the ruling British, whose men demanded that they be addressed as "Master."

The basic aim of the *Dobama Asi-a-yone* was to rid Burma of British rule through nonviolent means. The politician Dr. Ba Maw and General Aung San, the country's great independence hero, were members of the *Dobama Asi-a-yone*. Dr. Ba Maw, the barrister, had unsuccessfully defended *Saya* San, who led a failed uprising against the colonial rulers. *Saya* San was hanged in Tharawaddy Jail in 1932.

Earlier, in 1886, the British had exiled King Thibaw to India after it annexed Upper Burma into its empire. In song and in speech, the wounds from these two events inflicted by a colonial power on the Burmans' psyche were still festering in the countryside. I was too young to comprehend the depth of its passion.

MY FATHER'S LEGACY

Father became a Christian at the age of twenty-two, after interpreting for two missionaries and being moved by their message. One of the missionaries was the Reverend Benjamin Milton Jones, at whose grave in Hong Kong I paused to pay the family's respects on my way to America in January 1952. This pleased my father. The Reverend Jones died en route home to retire, in 1939. Father dedicated his book *China as a Burman Saw It* (1939): "To the Memory of the Rev. B. Milton Jones who laboured 36 years in Burma."

I wish I knew which passage it was that Father had interpreted for the missionaries, because it was that scripture and its message that moved him to embrace Christianity. I have often wondered whether it might actually have been the passage about Paul's own conversion on the road to Damascus. Paul himself was a revolutionary. He proclaimed "I was born a Roman citizen," yet he was against the Roman Empire. Father was passionate about Paul—and Christ too, of course; Christ was the foundation of his life.

In 1939 the Methodist Church in India sent three clergymen to China on a mission of fellowship and goodwill. The Methodist Church in Burma was then administered as part of Indian Methodism. Father was chosen, along with the Reverend Shot K. Mondol of India and Bishop Ralph A. Ward, an American missionary to China. By that time Japan had occupied parts of China, and China had suffered immensely. The mission's purpose was to buoy the spirits of the Chinese people.

The team traveled from Rangoon by truck to Lashio and continued from there to Kunming in China on the newly constructed Burma Road. It continued on to Chungking, where Generalissimo Chiang Kai-shek had

moved China's capital. They were received by Chiang Kai-shek and his gracious first lady, Soong May-ling, who were staunch Methodists. Chiang Kai-
shek spoke no English, so his wife acted as interpreter. "When we left after
an hour and a half interview with them," my father wrote afterward in his
short book, *China as a Burman Saw It*, "we had no doubt as to the kind of
leadership this truly Christian couple, is giving to China at this time. China
is extremely fortunate in having them at the helm during this critical time
in China's history."

The team stopped in Chengdu where there was a large Methodist college, before moving on to Shanghai. Throughout their journey, they spoke
at churches and colleges, and visited orphanages, hospitals, and medical
schools. Reverend Mondol later became one of the early indigenous Methodists to be elected to the episcopacy. "Your father and I travelled together
from Rangoon, Burma to China by way of Quinming [Kunming] on the
newly constructed mountain highway, along with Bishop Ralph Ward and
his party," he reminisced in a letter to me dated 29 July 1980, three months
after Father's death:

> In some places your father and I had to share the same bed for
> the night. It was no easy trip, and life was rather rough in some
> places. During those three months we became very close friends.
> On our return he wanted to write a book, and he wanted to use
> some of the material that I had written for the *Indian Witness*.
> He was warm-hearted, courageous and fearless, and with a deep
> faith in God in dangerous situations, such as we faced in China.
> Your mother was a most gracious hostess, tender-hearted, and
> had a keen sense of humor.

Father wrote another short book, *China's Freedom and the New World
Order* (1940). Later he also wrote *Burma Under the Japanese* (1947) and
Cruising Down the Irrawaddy (1956). In his letters to me during the 1960s,
following the 1962 coup led by General Ne Win, he repeatedly mentioned
another book he said he was writing, with the intriguing title *The Vicissitudes of Burma*, but I never saw the manuscript and I don't know if he ever
finished writing it.

His books were a blend of first-hand reports on things he had experienced and witnessed and the sermonizing into which he was never able to
resist lapsing. He was a preacher by nature as well as long habit. Those books
display Father's mind at its best, both as a thinker and as a witness of the
world in which he found himself living. They are also relics from a period
when he was unambiguously free to write and publish what he earnestly

believed to be the truth. This was always his concern and the impulse he obeyed, as he wrote in *Cruising Down the Irrawaddy*:

> Ours is an age of mass indoctrination. Advertising, with its pressures toward conformity, dominates every medium of communication. Propaganda is skillfully used to create a mass mind. How can a fellow get past the propaganda to the truth? . . . We firmly believe that dictatorship, in whatever form, has within itself elements that ultimately lead to degeneration and decay. If Communism, Fascism, and Socialism imply dictatorship, though garbed in different dress, some day they too must pass.

Father gave his books away. He sent some copies to America, including Harvard's Widener Library. Because he wrote them principally for international readers, he wrote them in English. To Americans, China was a mysterious land, just as Japan had been before Commodore Matthew Perry landed there in 1853. In the two books on China, he was trying to tell his readers what was happening in China and the effects of Japanese imperialism.

At the same time he did have a message for his fellow Burmese. "Some day the present war, like all wars, will be over," he wrote in *China as a Burman Saw It*:

> The China-Burma highway should serve more significantly in times of peace than even for the present emergency. This is the time when leaders of China, both political and civil, and similar leaders of Burma should come closer together in mutual understanding of their own best interests and not allow this new commercial undertaking to be thwarted. Nationalism has its helpful place so long as it is not predatory. People of this worried world must come closer together in mutual helpfulness. It is timely for the people of China and the people of Southern Asia to know each other more. Another modern international trade route between that quarter of the human race living in China and the great population of Southern Asia is an important step forward.

Also, he frequently yielded to the urge to express wonder and admiration for the splendor of God's creation:

> In nature, in order to produce a splendid panorama, it calls for rhythm, co-operation, integration, symmetry, and a set-up of square deal; but in human relationships the tendency is to forget the humdrum valleys of common human living when one climbs higher and higher. . . . After all, life is truly measured not by the number of breaths taken, but by the number not taken;

in other words, by its breath-taking amazement by beauty or wonder which causes one to hold his breath.

It is poignant to read Father's books seven decades later, knowing all that came thereafter. The Allied bombings of Burma during World War II were, he wrote, "evidence that there are no more barriers, no more refuges, no more isolated area, evidence too that we can no longer sit snugly and serenely enveloped in a mythical cloak of isolation."

He wrote *Burma Under the Japanese* because the Russo-Japanese War of 1904–1905 had shaken the Western powers, and then Japan's aggression and brutality throughout Asia had stirred the entire world. A question cried out to be addressed: How could such a small country have done such things? Although in *China as a Burman Saw It* he had striven dispassionately to explain the Japanese point of view, he had paid a price for publishing that book. The *kempeitai* [secret police] had come to Twante. As he related after the war in *Burma Under the Japanese*:

> Well, here was Bo Mojoh ["Chief Lightning," the Burmese epi- thet for Commander Minami Suzuki] in Twante; and it fell to my lot, as Chairman of the Town Committee, to entertain him. During lunch he disclosed the purpose of his visit. It was to in- terview the Chinese detained in our school and to find out if they were followers of Chiang Kai-Shek or of Wang Ching-Wei.
>
> "Commander," I said, "What about me? I went to China on a Goodwill Mission in 1939. Since my return I have written two booklets somewhat against the Japanese Military."
>
> "Why did you write that way?" he asked.
>
> "Commander, I belong to a subject race under British rule and realize what it means to us politically, economically, and psychologically. When I witnessed your military campaign in China I laboured under the notion that you were launching a devastating war on China purely for territorial gain. Out of my sympathy for China and my love of freedom, I hated to see such attempts at domination. I therefore put the case for China before my countrymen."

Perhaps what had annoyed the Japanese were passages in *China as a Burman Saw It* like this one:

> Japan has thus built up an ideological case for war which is not necessarily ineffective in influencing the Japanese because it seems mythological to most Westerners. The main thesis of this case is that Japan is fighting to save China and, in the long run, other Asiatic countries as well, from the double threat of Soviet

Communism and occidental colonial exploitation. For many
Japanese this is just as valid a rationalization of their country's
career of conquest as Kipling's famous phrase about "the white
man's burden" was for western Empire-builders at the turn of
the present century. . . . The cry of "Asia for the Asiatics" is being
given such an illogical twist that the neutral observer wonders
how it can fool anybody. And yet he remembers that in the
words of Abraham Lincoln, "You can fool some of the people all
the time, but not all of the people all the time."

He later wrote *Cruising Down the Irrawaddy* because he wanted to
mingle with the common folk, feel their pulse, listen to their concerns, share
in their joys, empathize with their sorrows, and of course, enjoy the vistas.
His little book, which was dedicated to "Our *Bogyoke* [General] Aung San,
a martyr to the cause of the independence of Burma and to the memory of
our gallant soldiers and armed police who laid down their lives in defence
of Burma we love," told of his joy and excitement. "I swung down the Irrawaddy by mail boat," he wrote:

> I enjoyed the world of nature, finding in the flowers of the field
> more beauty than in the raiment of Kings. As the boat steamed
> down, I beheld the ever changing vast panoramas of mountain
> ranges and spiral banks, forests and precipices, unfolding hour
> by hour. Here, then, is a country offering great underdeveloped
> resources and a market of some millions of people.

He quickly reverted to his preacher's impulse to teach:

> Under their colonial policy and practice, the British tried to
> drive a wedge between the communities to ensure the continu-
> ance of their domination of Burma. It appears that they have
> succeeded to a remarkable extent, if the minority groups' desire
> to emerge out of the Union of Burma is taken as evidence.

But even amid some ominous signs, he could not suppress his own
optimism:

> At the moment of writing this brochure the upsurge of feelings
> suppressed for a century is almost gone with the wind, and the
> Burma-wide insurrection has reached its height. This is a good
> symptom, because it means that automatically the insurrection
> will begin to diminish, though it still continues to exert a dis-
> turbing influence on Government efforts at rehabilitation.

Father projected a strong voice and commanding personality in his books as well as in person. When he came into the presence of others, those around him felt the power of a dynamic voice. He was so compassionate and generous with the treasure he might have earned but gave away. There was an Indian king in classical times, named Vessantara, or Wethandaya, in Burmese. He was legendary for giving things away to gain merit. According to tradition, Wethandaya was a bodhisattva, one of the previous incarnations of the Buddha. If you say to a Burmese person, "Don't be a Wethandaya," he will know what you mean: Be not overly generous with what you don't have. Mother often accused Father of being a Wethandaya.

Mother was the practical one—the money manager of the family. She was always looking out and ahead to make sure there was food on the table and clothing on our backs. She was very thrifty and never wasted a penny. As principal, she made sure that the teachers were paid both in cash and in kind, often taking little or no salary for herself.

The school did not take in enough in fees to cover its costs. Many of the children's parents were farmers and fishermen and would pay in rice, vegetables, dried fish, chickens, ducks, eggs, pork, and other foodstuffs.

One day when we were living in Rangoon in 1940, she brought home shoes she had purchased at Scott Market for my brothers, Simon and Irwin, and me, along with something for our sister. She spent all of her wages she received from substitute teaching on us. She was so happy when we got our share that she rubbed her hands together, exclaiming, "All for my children, nothing for me." She was also generous to others.

Another time in Twante, just as our family was sitting down to eat, a Eurasian woman in tattered clothes walked by our home in the Methodist Mission compound. She appeared as if she must be hungry, and she was carrying a baby. Mother went out and invited her to the small table around which we ate, seated on the floor, to share our meal. Then, suddenly, Mother said she was not hungry and went without eating. There was not enough food for everyone.

Father had many friends from all of Burma's ethnic and religious communities. Whenever and wherever they gathered at social or religious functions, he was there. On Christmas Day, the town's non-Christian elders, dressed in their respectful best, would come to our home as a group to convey their felicitations. By the same token, Father would also pay them a call on their sacred days.

Deedok U Ba Choe, one of the seven shadow cabinet members who were assassinated along with General Aung San in 1947, was a billiard playmate of Father's in Twante during the war. The two would engage in long conversations expressing their anti-colonialist sentiments. U Ba Choe had contributed the preface to Father's book, *China's Freedom and the New World Order* (1940), in which he wrote: "U On Kin the Author in the first part of this booklet tries to explain this curious mentality of the Nipponese with respect to the present Sino-Japanese conflict and he has done it in an unbiased manner."

Father loved Burmese classical music. He loved to cook, especially goose curry, and he relished watching others eat his specialty. As a convert who had once been a Buddhist monk, he was well versed in the teachings of the Buddha. His sermons kept churchgoers spellbound. He garnished his sermons liberally with Buddhist concepts and vocabulary, such as *law-ba, daw-tha, maw-ha* [greed, anger, delusion] to the extent that parishioners often exchanged furtive glances as they wondered whether the man in the pulpit was a Buddhist monk in Christian clerical garb. He debated tirelessly with the monks in Twante and Thongwa, but he was always passionate about his God, Christ, the Apostle Paul, and of course, John Wesley.

The Buddhist monastery in Twante was in the compound adjacent to the Methodist Mission, and the abbot was a relative. Father was all too aware of how the Christian religion he had espoused set him apart. "It is hardly possible for a Westerner to realize fully the disastrous consequences of the destruction of the social status of a convert in a Buddhist community," he wrote in a testimonial titled *What Christ Did for Me*, published in a Methodist journal in India:

> Society demands that a Burman to be one must be a Buddhist.
> If he renounces his Buddhist religion, he alienates his national-
> ity as well as his social rights and all his relatives disown him.
> I soon went home with the purpose of telling the story of my
> Saviour. But when I reflected on how dearly my mother and my
> sisters loved me, I did not have the courage to break their hearts
> by telling them that I belonged to Christ.

In that book he went on to describe how he was shunned and abused by his family and community on account of his conversion. For my part, in my time, I never felt different or alienated from my peers because I am a Christian. I was born into the church, just as I was born into Burma. I drew great strength from my father. He was such an inspiring teacher, well loved and liked in the community. The respect that everyone felt for him extended to his children. I was proud to be his son.

I think that, in the back of his mind, one thing Father wanted to do was to show the Western missionaries that the Burmese people could be Christians on their own, both financially and morally. As he put it in *Cruising Down the Irrawaddy*:

The foreign missionary outreach of the Church has been criti-
cised as being merely a pious expression of the colonial expan-
sion of the Western powers. . . . [But] with the passage of time,
we have, according to the dictates of our conscience, chosen
Christianity as the basis for our lives here and hereafter. Hence
we become heirs of the spiritual heritage of this gigantic sweep
of the missionary enterprise.

He went so far as to foresee the day when foreign missionaries would
be asked to leave Burma, and he was right. In the mid-1960s, the Ne Win
military regime expelled all foreign missionaries, even including Indians
propagating Hindu doctrines.

Dependence on foreigners' money—*largesse* was the word Father liked
to use—created "rice Christians," local people who would kowtow in exchange for being provided for and given advantages. He also saw clearly
how foreigners' cultural myopia could be unhelpful and offensive. Another
term Father used often was *self-reliance*. "Now we have our autonomy," he
told me in a letter dated 3 June 1964, "we will wipe out all semblance of
Ecclesiastical Colonialism and operate our Church according to the spiritual genius of the East."

Mother was a Pwo Karen brought up in the Baptist church. When we
lived in Rangoon, she never failed to participate in Karen New Year celebrations held in Ahlone, in the western part of the city. I believe that my parents
met when they were both young teachers, but I never got to know much
about the circumstances in which they met, or what had attracted them to
each other. Father once mentioned to Riri that he had been attracted to my
mother because she wore her *htamein* above her ankles. By the time I was
old enough to start wondering in earnest about such questions, I had been
deprived of the chance to ask them about such things: I couldn't get into
Burma, and they couldn't come out.

As a pastor, Father's responsibilities included not only the church but
also the management of school and mission properties, as well as both the
spiritual and physical well-being of his flock. When he made home visits,
he carried with him aspirin, quinine, and tincture of iodine, which he gave
away to anyone who needed them. When the Japanese army occupied
Twante beginning in 1942, they took over the Methodist Mission house as
well as the school building. So, we had to relocate to the Karen quarter on
the far side of the football field, where we moved in with a teacher's family
and built a new bamboo shelter with a dirt floor. My parents continued the
school there.

Money was tight, and because of that, we were short of basic essentials. The family raised chickens, ducks, and pigs and grew vegetables like bean sprouts, gourds, pumpkins, onions, roselle, squash, and watercress. Of necessity much sharing and bartering for food took place. To earn some cash, my mother would buy an oxtail each day from the Muslim slaughterhouse. She would make it into soup and sell the soup at night at the only cinema in town.

The fat that was produced in the broth would be scooped up to fuel the small lamp that lit our house at night. Mother also roasted peanuts, which she made us sell around in town. "War is not romantic when you find yourself in the midst of it," Father wrote afterward. "The outstanding thing about life under war conditions was its magnificent simplicity," he continued.

TWANTE, MY FATHER'S BIRTHPLACE

Life in Twante during the war was one of privation. Healthcare was almost nonexistent. People relied on native healers, herbs, witchcraft, homemade remedies and the like—and prayer. The civil hospital, which was staffed only by a part-time physician, a compounder, and a nurse/midwife, and a couple of other volunteer helpers, was overwhelmed. Mother came down with Beriberi. The only remedy available was to eat brown rice. Three neighbor sisters, the eldest no older than eight, died of intestinal ailments one by one within a few days of each other, for lack of medical care. Inpatients had to have their families or other relatives or neighbors provide food for them.

My uncle *U-lay* Sitway, Father's younger brother, was brought to the hospital on a bullock cart from Shan Zu, the Shan quarter. He had been burned in a kitchen fire that had consumed much of his meager bamboo-and-thatch hut. It was so painful to see him suffering at the hospital, down the slope a quarter mile from our home in the Methodist Mission compound.

At *Thadingyut,* the day marking the end of Buddhist lent, my uncle's wife, Daw Chaw, came with Pauksi, their only child, to do obeisance to my parents. Uncle Sitwe was still in the hospital, incapacitated from his burns. I distinctly remember Daw Chaw in tears, lamenting, "Last *Thadingyut* Ko Sitway was with me. This is the first time I have come without him to *gàdaw* [do obeisance]. On his behalf, I beg you to forgive his transgressions as you do mine."

Security was of concern to everybody during that time. Father was constantly in the thick of things, as a community leader and particularly as agent for De La Salle Institute, which was run by the Christian Brothers of the Roman Catholic Church in a village called *Hnget Aw Zan* [Birdsong

Spring], fifteen miles from Twante. "I trudged to and fro sometimes covering 30 miles a day," he recalled in *Burma Under the Japanese*.

> I sweated out, so to say. I found myself amid air-raids lying face down as the planes passed directly over our heads with a terrific roar. While trudging across the thick of the jungle I was waylaid by robbers. I was attacked by cholera; kept under surveillance and harassed by military bullies, and hounded by the "thought" Kempetai. I was spied upon, gossiped about, and subject to all kinds of indignities.

Throughout the war there were robberies and killings, what we call *da-mya* in Burmese or *dacoity*, the Indian term, in English. Father made a tradition, every year on his birthday, of cooking a meal for prisoners in the local lockup. It is Burmese custom to serve others on one's birthday. One day, while walking alone along the road to De La Salle Institute and carrying a large sum of money (proceeds from the sale of kerosene oil that the Brothers refined from latex rubber), a gang of machete-wielding bandits accosted him. Their leader recognized him and asked, "*Sayagyi* U On Kin *m'hoke lah* [Are you not the rabbi U On Kin]?"

"Yes indeed," he replied, whereupon the bandits escorted him off their turf unharmed. The leader must have eaten one of his home-cooked meals while incarcerated.

The Japanese granted Burma independence from Great Britain on 1 August 1943 and put up the English-trained barrister-politician Dr. Ba Maw as the puppet head of state. His mantra was: *Ta thway, ta than, ta maint* [one blood, one voice, one command] within imperial Japan's Greater East Asia Co-Prosperity Sphere.

After the Japanese had retreated and the British returned to Burma, a frequent visitor to our home was a British police officer known to the townsfolk simply as "Sitoke." He was tall and stocky. Twante was a district headquarters, and he would make his rounds sidearmed with a pistol and accompanied by an unleashed Alsatian dog that obeyed his every command. He was never in uniform but always had a camera hung around his neck. Mother asked him to take her picture. He made her so happy when he brought her a copy of her photograph on a subsequent visit.

One day, outside our home, when Officer Sitoke came to call, a Chinese person kept pestering, "Does your dog bite? Does your dog bite?" Somewhat annoyed, Officer Sitoke uttered a command, and the dog roughed up the Chinaman without harming him. The man screamed bloody murder until the dog stopped on his master's countermand. Twenty-eight years later in America, I learned that Sitoke was Colin Tooke. Our name for him had been adapted from "C. Tooke." His Alsatian was poisoned and he himself died of a mysterious illness.

Officer Colin Tooke had been investigating the assassination of General Aung San and his cabinet. Although not directly involved in the official investigation, he suspected something was amiss, so he made an investigation of his own. After his sudden mysterious death, investigators found that the files he had maintained on his investigation had gone missing from his home. It was believed that he was poisoned. Author U Kin Oung recounts this in his book, *Who Killed Aung San?*

MY EARLY CHRISTIAN UPBRINGING

The Christian church, in its outreach, engaged in social services. Christian schools in Burma taught girls and boys. They operated hospitals, leprosaria, schools for the visually and hearing impaired, homes for the aged, orphanages, and other services like the YMCA and YWCA. Judson College, a Baptist institution of higher learning, was a jewel of Southeast Asia's academia before the military regime nationalized all faith-based and other private schools in 1963. Monks of the Hindu Ramakrishna Mission provided healthcare at the hospital they operated in east Rangoon, widely known as Gandhi Hospital. The Islamic community operated the Muslim Free Clinic.

The school I attended with my two brothers during the war was De La Salle Institute (DLS), an orphanage located at Hnget Aw Zan village, fifteen miles from Twante in the jungle. It was run by the Brothers of the Christian Schools, a French Catholic Order of lay teachers founded in 1724 by Jean Baptiste De La Salle. It followed a strict monastic schedule. The Order's official Latin name is *Fratres Scholarum Christianarum*. Brother Patrick Toner, FSC, an Irishman, was its director. There were about 200 boys—Burmans, Eurasians, Indians, Karens, and Shans—and about fifteen Brothers and half a dozen other teachers. English was the medium of instruction at DLS. A few Brothers who were too old to teach were cared for at the orphanage, which received an influx of Brothers who sheltered there from the war.

The school was the vision of the Frenchman Jean Vilderbert, FSC, who was affectionately known as Brother John to all, who founded the orphanage in 1921. The school's objective was to teach boys life skills, mainly farming, along with traditional school subjects such as Burmese, English, geography, mathematics, and science. The rubber plantation provided income to support the school. The plantations of Burma, Indochina, and Malaya produced considerable amounts of rubber latex for the British and French colonialists, until synthetic rubber was invented and the price of rubber slumped.

When I arrived at DLS in August 1942, the earth on Brother John's grave had only recently been turned, and Brother Celestyne was carving his name on a tall wooden cross to be erected at the head of his grave. My family's link with DLS and the Christian Brothers was itself a serendipitous happenstance. Simon and Irwin had attended Rangoon's St. Paul's High School when we lived there before the outbreak of World War II. Brother Patrick Toner was then its director. It was the premier Catholic school in Burma and the largest of the Brothers' nine schools in the country. The Christian Brothers schools taught boys only, while the nuns taught girls in convents.

One day Simon approached Brother Patrick's *chaprasi* [office door-keeper] at St. Paul's and asked to speak to Brother Director Patrick. "There is a small boy who would like to speak to you," he told Brother Patrick. "Send him in," said Brother Patrick. Simon asked Brother Patrick whether he and his kid brother Irwin could attend St. Paul's, explaining that their father was a Methodist pastor with little means who could ill afford the school fees. Brother Patrick looked Simon in the eye and said, "You pay six rupees and your brother pays four rupees a month." That was how the family's relationship with the De La Salle Brothers began.

When the Japanese occupied Burma in 1942, St. Paul's was shut down and the Brothers, like many citizens of Rangoon, moved to outlying towns and villages to escape the Allied bombing. The Japanese army moved into St. Paul's and remained there for the duration of the war. Rangoon became a ghost town and there was a lot of looting. The European Brothers at St. Paul's—Czech, English, French, German, and Irish—who could not or would not retreat to India, sheltered at De La Salle, from where they were one day brought to Twante to the courthouse to await transport to Rangoon. The courthouse was down the slope from the Methodist Mission on the road that led to the pagoda.

Father lost no time rushing there. "These are good, honorable, highly respected teachers. They are not spies. I vouch for them," he told the Japanese commandant. The group was not being fed, so he and members of his congregation cooked rice and fish curry for them. Among the group was the Thomas Joyce family, who had an eight-year-old child named Heather. Mr. Joyce was the manager of the rubber plantation in Sookalat, six miles from De La Salle between Twante and Hnget Aw Zan village. Because he was Irish, the family had been rounded up along with the European Christian Brothers. Mr. Joyce loved the Burmese people and chose to remain with his workers rather than evacuating. There were no eating utensils, so little Heather had to show these Brothers how to eat rice and curry with their fingers as the Burmese do.

The group was taken by boat along the Twante canal to Rangoon, where they were imprisoned at Insein, a northwestern suburb. The interrogations were frightening and traumatic, what with those intimidating samurai swords dangling from the captors' hips. Twenty-three-year-old Irish Brother Christopher Bennett was the youngest of the Brothers. He was deadly afraid of the Japanese soldiers. When they were freed to return to De La Salle, Brother Christopher ended up spending the entire three years of the Japanese occupation in mortal fear, only venturing out of his room to work in the foundry. Heather's mother, Ada, would occasionally go to his quarters to calm his nerves.

When the war ended, Brother Christopher made a swift exit from Burma, returned to Ireland, left the Christian Brothers Order, and earned a degree in agriculture from the University of Dublin. He worked for the government in some agricultural capacity and years later left behind a widow and five daughters.

When I visited Heather and her husband Ken in Ettalong Beach, Australia, in 2012, she related to me of a poignant incident that took place during the war in their Sookalat Rubber Estate home. A Japanese army sergeant would come and harangue them periodically. He would enter the house and look around. He may have been drinking. He was side-armed with a pistol and a sword dangling from his left hip. The rubber estate's workers would gather on the clearing in front of the house and squat down silently to bear witness until the bully departed—such loyalty! And courage!

I was a boarder at De La Salle off and on between 1942 and 1945, walking the entire fifteen miles each way through the jungle and the rubber plantation, but came home to Twante whenever classes were suspended. I remember a Eurasian boy named Johnny White, who was in the sick room when I was also a patient there. The closest person the orphanage had to a physician was a compounder who dispensed medicines and generally treated the sick. He was an Indian called Menon. In Hnget Aw Zan village lived a Dr. Peters and his family, war evacuees from Rangoon. Dr. Peters was an Anglo-Indian, a Licentiate Medical Practitioner (LMP), who helped out in the orphanage's sick bay.

Our illnesses were anemia, coughs, diarrhea, dysentery, fevers, intestinal worms, malaria, malnutrition, and skin infections. Johnny White had a bad case of the runs and he had soiled the rattan mat on his bed while I was myself dealing with the same issue in the latrine. Because my bed was momentarily vacant, he was moved to mine. When I returned, Johnny was moved onto the table that doubled as our dining table. He became delirious and kept muttering that he was in a dark chamber where his body was being gnawed by grotesque creatures. We were no older than nine, and the rest of us could only recite a few "Hail Marys" as Johnny's life ebbed away after Father Lawrence administered the last rites.

When I returned to Hnget Aw Zan village in 2013, I searched in vain for Johnny White's grave. Brother John and only a few others still had their faded tombstones intact. In the ache of memory, I could only pause in silence and swallow the lump in my throat. It happened so long ago and so far away in the harsh jungle.

The buildings at De La Salle were connected to each other by walkways that were covered by corrugated zinc roofs. They shielded us from the tropical sun and kept us dry in the monsoons. The main building was a long, two-story brick structure, with classrooms on the ground floor without partitions between them. Two parallel corridors that sandwiched the rooms and ran the length of the ground floor provided cross-ventilation. The Brothers' dining room was at the far end. Brother Patrick, being the director, ate alone in his private dining room. His personal cook was Anthony, a Tamil (South Indian). Whenever Father came to DLS, he would lodge in the guest room on the second floor and Brother Patrick would share his table. Father would leave some money with Anthony, who would give me a few morsels of leftovers or an occasional bowl of soup. The dormitory, sick room, and the Brothers quarters were on the second floor.

De La Salle Orphanage, founded by Brother John in 1921, is situated in Hnget-aw-san Village in the Twante Township.

De La Salle Institue. Photo from the 1950s.

In 1978 a violent earthquake leveled the main building. All that remains of DLS are the play shed, refectory, *godown* [warehouse], St. Theresa's Church, and the bungalow where single male teachers lived. De La Salle had no female teachers. The parish house still stood, but in a very dilapidated condition.

Brother Patrick and Father became close friends. The European Brothers were grateful to Father for speaking up for them when they were detained by the Japanese army. Brother Patrick also made him distributor of the kerosene the orphanage distilled from the rubber latex produced on the surrounding estate. He was compensated one percent of the sales for his services, but he donated most of it back to the orphanage.

Bales of smoke-browned latex were transported by bullock cart to our home on the bank of the canal that Father had built early in 1942; from there it was trans-shipped to Rangoon. Mother named the house Riverside Mansion. Father warned us that a time would come when he would no longer be pastor of the church and would have to vacate the mission house. Riverside Mansion accommodated Brother Patrick, the Joyces, and other DLS pupils and Brothers, who used it as a stopping place on their way to and from Rangoon.

Directly across the canal from Riverside Mansion was the fifteenth mile post, a substantial black-on-white rectangular sign that marked its distance from the Rangoon River. The canal, which had been dug in the 1920s, was twenty-two miles long. It linked the Rangoon River with the huge Irrawaddy, past Maubin (*Ma'u bin*) to the north. It is the longest canal in Burma and provided a vital shortcut. At high tide an occasional paddle wheel craft of the Irrawaddy Flotilla Company would navigate it. Because of its strategic importance, cargo vessels traversing the canal would be regularly strafed by Allied planes to deprive the Japanese of food and war materiel. On Mindadah Road, on the roof of a rather substantial house commandeered by the Japanese army, was a watchtower from which the canal's traffic was monitored.

One day an Allied plane strafing the canal flew a little too low and failed to clear the telephone/telegraph cable strung across above it. It crashed and the pilot's body was recovered. Father was called to conduct the burial in the public cemetery at the edge of town near the pottery kilns. Father wore his white clerical robe with a black stole and performed Christian rites at the Buddhist cemetery, at a ceremony attended by some town elders. When the war ended a team of British soldiers came to Twante, and exhumed the remains, and took them to Rangoon. They were guided to the site by a Mr. Mackay, a Eurasian who lived across the duck pond from our temporary shelter in the Karen quarter when the Japanese army expropriated our Methodist Mission house.

Another Allied plane was brought down in a distant paddy field across the canal. The tall pilot had bailed out but I did not see the wreckage. I saw the badly bruised pilot, being helped aboard a boat by Japanese soldiers and taken to Rangoon. He may have been beaten by his captors, as the Japanese soldiers were known to torture and even execute their prisoners of war.

Night strafings were the most frightful ones. Flares would be parachuted down from the planes as they circled over the targets and fired the cannons. The still night air exacerbated the sound of low flying planes' machine gun fire. When the flares lit up the canal and large swaths of bamboo-and-thatch houses, we could only pray for the planes to go away. On another cold night, an Allied pilot dropped an incendiary bomb on some homes along the canal near the jetty to lighten his load to evade pursuit. I don't think he meant to hit the homes; he meant to dump the bomb in the canal. The term today for what happened would be "collateral damage."

At least fifty bamboo-and-thatch huts rapidly went up in flames. The families fled to the field in the Roman Catholic Church compound behind the cemetery. Fortunately, no one was killed. Father rallied the community to give the families rice, cooking oil, dried fish, firewood, blankets, and anything else it had to share.

That night a Japanese army band rehearsed martial music below the school to receive a senior officer who was coming the next day. The soldiers remained in the barracks, oblivious to the suffering of the people who had lost everything, bereft of all compassion.

The years at De La Salle Institute were the worst of my childhood, but all my life I have held a respect for the spirit that piece of ground in the jungle has evoked in me. Scarred though I was by the adversities, both physically and mentally, the miracle was that I survived. The experience also hardened my mettle. I still maintain contact with my known surviving De La Salle schoolmates: Monsignor Gordon Anthony and his elder brother Robert, Father Edward Evans (Australia), Joseph Gabriel, Brother Patrick Minus FSC (India), Bobby Ledesma, and Douggie D'Silva (Australia).

When the war ended in 1945, I continued at the Methodist School in Twante until St. Paul's in Rangoon was ready to receive students in increments as furnishings became available. Brother Patrick had left Burma and the German Brother Fulbert became its director.

Upon instructions left behind by Brother Patrick, not a word was uttered about my boarding and school fees. This was the way the Brothers expressed their gratitude to my family; however, Father did regularly contribute whatever he could. Mr. Timmy Marshall, the school clerk, gave me a beautifully crafted receipt, using a pen whose nib he dipped into the inkwell between strokes whenever I took Father's contribution to the school. He always called me Willingdon.

With all the fighting and the general state of lawlessness during the transition, looters had stripped the school bare. When I arrived there in 1946, about 75 percent of St. Paul's and the football field were still occupied by the Burma Navy. Chinese carpenters worked at great speed making desks and benches for the classrooms. St. Paul's was paradise after DLS, where life was rugged—plagued by leeches, mosquitoes, and ticks. Food was scarce and there were too many mouths to feed. It was our chief craving. I do not remember a single night when we went to bed not hungry. We dreamed about food. We even invented a word for eating: "jabork." My own nightmares were of a bully snatching away a jackfruit pod from my hand before it reached my mouth.

All of Win's clothes fit into this box when he enrolled at St. Paul's as a boarder in 1946. Photo by Zali Win.

At St. Paul's I was a bugler in the band, and played football (soccer). I also had a Spartus 120 box camera that Simon had sent me from America. I earned some pocket money processing film in a tiny darkroom set up under the stairwell next to the study hall on the ground floor, through the kindness of Brother Felix, the boarding master. The dark room had no electricity, but I managed reasonably well developing films and printing photos using daylight shuttered through a small opening in the window.

My buddies Robert Anthony, Douggie D'Silva, Bobby Ledesma, and Patrick Minus from De La Salle days also continued at St. Paul's. Patrick was initiated into the Brothers of the Christian Schools Order and became a lifelong teacher. Even though he was born in Burma, he was deported to India in 1966 when the military regime kicked out the Chinese and Indians. Patrick had never been to India but since he had an Indian-Portuguese lineage, by way of Goa, he was branded a foreigner.

**Win (top row, fourth from right) was a Boy Scout at St. Paul's in 1949.
Brother Peter Mandel, the sub-director, is front row center.**

My favorite teachers at St. Paul's were Mr. Mariano (history), Brother Peter Mandell (chemistry), and U Hain Chong (Burmese). Brother Felix also taught English and penmanship. Mr. Machado taught physics. I was to visit Brother Peter once, and Brother Felix thrice in Illertissen, Germany, before they passed away. I remember U Hain Chong telling us, "Go abroad boys, go to a polytechnic school. Learn a skill."

There were also U Sein and Mr. Archie Rivers, who taught Burmese. Mr. Rivers, whose Burmese name was U Than Aung, would come to class impeccably dressed in Burmese attire. He later served as ambassador to India, under the U Nu administration. In 1974, as deputy minister of education, he showed up at the airport when former UN Secretary General U Thant's body was brought back to Rangoon from New York. That ruffled the dictator General Ne Win's feathers. Mr. Rivers lost his job.

The sternest teacher was Mr. Lazaro, who taught mathematics. He knew his stuff, but he scared us all. The only time I ever saw him crack a smile was when, in December 1951, upon my return from India, I went to pay my respects to my former teachers. Burmese upbringing teaches children to respect their teachers and to always honor them. Mr. Lazaro never caned me, but he did cane some students for not turning in their work on time. He was noted for the verbal thrashings dispensed liberally, such as, "You good-for-nothing fellows! You uncouth fellows!" Mr. Liard taught geography and told us about his wartime experiences in India's North-West Frontier. He was also the scoutmaster. Hearing him talk about his adventures made me long to ride the train through the Khyber Pass.

I was at St. Paul's on 19 July 1947, the morning General Aung San and his shadow cabinet ministers were assassinated. When we came out for recess at 10:30 a.m., I saw many people milling about at the corner of Sparks (now Bo Aung Gyaw) Street and Fraser (now Anawrahta) Street. Word had spread quickly that sound of machine gun fire had emanated from the Secretariat, which was directly across Fraser Street from St. Paul's. It was a dismal day. The sky was grey and dreary; the air was dank; there was a constant drizzle. My parents happened to be in Rangoon, and they came to see me in the evening. They were worried about what was going to happen in the country. What interested me more as a thirteen-year-old was whether school would be shut down for a while. It was not.

FREE, FREE! OUR COUNTRY IS FREE!

Free, Free, Our Country Is Free!

I was at St. Paul's on 4 January 1948, the day men of the Burma Navy at the barracks at the school broke out singing *lut latt pyi, lut latt pyi—doh pyay lut latt pyi* [Free, free! Our country is free!] at 4:20 in the morning while merchant ships in the Rangoon River belched out their fog horns. Even though the school was on break between Christmas and New Year's, I was permitted to remain in the dormitory together with some other boarders whose homes were distant. I was also a participant in the celebratory exhibitions of physical drills and sporting events at the Burma Athletic Association grounds (now Aung San Stadium), which required my presence in Rangoon.

The Royal Navy's *Birmingham* had come to Rangoon to convey Sir Hubert Rance, His Britannic Majesty's last proconsul in Burma, to England. It was docked at the Brooking Street jetty. The cruiser held open house, while its band entertained appreciative crowds in Fytche (now Bandula) Square, opposite City Hall near the Sulé Pagoda. The events were joyful moments etched into my memory.

But why 4:20 a.m.? Why was that early hour chosen as the precise moment for Burma to proclaim its independence? That was the moment astrologers had foretold as being the most auspicious. Burmese are in fact deadly earnest about such superstitions. A telegram Governor Sir Hubert Rance sent to the Earl of Listowel, Secretary of State for Burma, on 2 August 1947, drives home the point:

> At about 5 pm yesterday evening, as the sun was shining for the first time in many days, I determined to get a little exercise in an attempt to reduce my figure to within the limits ordained by my tailor when he built my clothes. I accordingly took some golf balls and clubs on the front lawn and was enjoying myself immensely when, at a few minutes to 6, McGuire informed that Kyaw Nyein wanted to see me on a matter of great importance and would arrive at G.H. [Government House] in about ten minutes time with some other Ministers.
>
> My heart sank, and I was left wondering what further catastrophe had occurred. I was awaiting the Delegation in my study when at about 18.18 hours my ADC reported that the whole Cabinet had arrived and were awaiting me at my office.
>
> I proceeded as quickly as possible to the office, assured now that something frightful must have happened and there I met Thakin Nu dressed in his best clothes with a gaungbaung on his head. Nu then told me that it had been discovered that Sunday 20th July when the majority of the new Cabinet were sworn in was a most inauspicious day.

The Cabinet therefore tendered me their resignations individually and in writing. I was then asked to re-swear the Cabinet in immediately as Friday 1st August between 18.00 and 18.25 hours was most auspicious. The time was then about 18.21 hours and the chap that held the key of the office containing the form of oaths and the regalia could not be found. Tin Tut reminded me that the oaths were in Government of Burma Act 1935 and that book luckily I had with me. The Cabinet stood up and with their right hands lifted repeated after me the oath of allegiance.

I then discovered that the oath of secrecy was not included in the Act so while the remainder of the Cabinet stood strictly to attention with right hands lifted, Tin Tut hastily scribbled out an oath of secrecy which was duly repeated after me. The ceremony was over by about 18.27 hours and I then called for drinks which were enjoyed by all so much so that at 19.00 hours I had to remind them that the curfew was now on and it was almost dark.

There was an immediate scurry. It is incidents like these that make us love the country and the people so much.

Rangoon had been heavily bombed and emerged badly scarred from three years of Japanese occupation. The occupation, which began when I was eight years old, had traumatized me. All my life I've suffered from the effects of malnutrition during the war. Burmese society as a whole suffered in a similar way. During the occupation, I saw people being slapped on the face and beaten by Japanese soldiers for little or no reason at all. To the Burmese, as with other Asians, the head is the most sacred part of the human anatomy. To be slapped on the face is the ultimate humiliation. When the war ended, the country was badly bruised, its people's spirits at an all time low. Then we were dealt another blow when General Aung San and his cabinet were assassinated six months before independence. So 4 January 1948 was looked forward to with great anticipation. At the Secretariat the Union Jack was lowered and the new six-starred flag of the Union of Burma ceremoniously hoisted. Afterwards there was a march-past of Gurkha soldiers. Sir Hubert Rance returned them his final salute in farewell.

Finally, the crowds congregated at Brooking Street jetty to watch Sir Hubert, dressed in tails and wearing a top hat, inspect the honor guard and proceed up the gangway. The boatswain's mate sounded the little high-pitched whistle. In naval tradition, when the captain or a high ranking officer comes aboard, the boatswain's (bosun's) mate blows a little whistle that goes "Whe-ee!"

His Majesty's Ship *Birmingham* then saluted the new Union of Burma with a burst of twenty-five volleys from its four-inch guns. The explosions were so loud that crows cawed and scattered helter skelter. People around me put their hands over their ears, but I took it all in. After a pause, the return salute came from the *Mayu*. The *Mayu* was formerly the frigate HMS *Fal,* which was gifted to Burma. Captained by Lieutenant Commander Khin Maung Bo, it became Burma Navy's flagship. It was anchored upstream, at the mouth of the Twante Canal. As the *Birmingham* sailed away, the band struck up *Auld Lang Syne* from its aft deck. It was a day full of fanfare; the pomp and ceremony, which the British excel in, was seamless—very dignified indeed.

A bevy of Burma Navy officers, including Lieutenant Kin Oung, who became a friend many years later in America, watched from the terrace of the Mayo Marine Club, one block east of the jetty. They joined in singing *Auld Lang Syne*. How proudly their hearts must have throbbed! It was a moving moment.

Then Burma's first president, Sao Shwe Thaike, spoke in a heavy Shan accent from the City Hall balcony that faced Fytche Square. Afterward he and his family rode away in a Rolls-Royce to Government House, which had become the President's official residence. Prime Minister U Nu and members of his cabinet paraded from City Hall around Sulé Pagoda. U Nu was forty at the time. A biplane flew near Sulé Pagoda—not directly above it, which would have been disrespectful, but over City Hall nearby, quite low.

I had never witnessed anything like that. The plane was allegedly piloted by the dashing Squadron Leader Samuel Shi Sho, whose mother and younger brother stayed with us for a while before the war, when their home was in Lédaungkan. On the ground I saw a mounted army officer, saluting. He was Major Tun Sein Gyi, smartly dressed in uniform, complete with a sword dangling from his left hip. Tun Sein Gyi was a Twante boy known there as "Kah-Kaah." His father *Saya* U Pya Gyi and family were our neighbors. They lived just down the rise from the Methodist Mission. Shi Sho and Tun Sein Gyi were both Karens.

It was a glorious day for this thirteen-year-old river boy from Thongwa. I took in all the pomp and ceremony with eyes wide open.

INDEPENDENCE UNRAVELS

From the very beginning, the Union of Burma began to unravel. The Karen ethnic minority felt that they had been short-shrifted when the British turned over the government to the nationalists dominated by Burmans.

"How about us?" they challenged, and went into open rebellion. The uprising peaked in 1949, when the government came close to collapsing. The
Karens operated a radio station upcountry in Toungoo, from which they
blared news of their victories across the rest of the land, in an attempt to
boost the morale of their warriors and sway public opinion. They occupied
much of the Irrawaddy Delta. People joked that the Government of Burma
was merely the Government of Rangoon. The Communists also rose up.
Prime Minister U Nu's government had its hands full.

The next ominous event was the assassination, just offstage so to speak,
of Mahatma Gandhi in New Delhi on 30 January 1948. My other memory of
that time was of Karen refugees fleeing the crossfire between Karen National
Defence Organization (KNDO) forces and government troops in Insein.
The refugees were housed in the old chapel at St. Paul's.

A camp on an island on the Royal Lakes was established into which
Karen servicemen were herded. It was euphemistically called the Armed
Forces Rest Camp. A leaked classified document titled *Operation Aung San*
circulated secretly among the internees. It was a government directive, the
gist of which was to eliminate Karens from the armed forces and civil service because they were allegedly becoming a threat to the country's stability.
Did *Operation Aung San* reflect genocidal intentions? Nevertheless it was
true that the Karens were not just asking for autonomy; they wanted to secede from the Union.

Burma was not a nation-state before the British colonized it. It was
a land of many ethnic peoples engaged in perpetual rivalry for territory.
The rulers of parts of what we now call Burma would pay tribute to each
other, or they would bestow their daughters in marriage, or present albino
elephants or claimed sacred relics of the Buddha, to keep each other's army
at bay. During the colonial period, the British did in Burma what they did
everywhere else; they divided and ruled, with results that were effective for
them in the short term, but disastrous for their subjects in the long term.

Every group in Burma held its notion of its own importance and relationship with the other clans. If you asked the Karen, they would say one
thing. If you asked the Shan, they would say something else. The Karenni
maintained, and with some justification, that their ancestral homeland had
never actually been part of the British annexation of Burma. And if you
asked the Wa, they would say, "We are wild people; we don't need roads,
homes, or schools." Many Wa were cannibals, and the British left them
alone in their wilderness. The majority Burmans felt that it was their destiny
to rule the rest. Many condescended to the other groups and considered
themselves to be the big brothers. On the newly independent country's
flag, common lore had the large white star representing the Burmans while

the five smaller ones surrounding it stood for the largest minority groups: Arakanese, Kachin, Karen, Mon, and Shan. Even though this was not written in the Constitution of 1947, it was given credence by many Burmans, who maintain that there are 135 ethnic peoples in the land, as recorded by colonial authorities.

It is telling to contrast the Burma of those early post-independence days with Indonesia, which was called Dutch East Indies during the colonial era. In Burma in the late 1940s, strife between the KNDO and the Burma Army was the order of the day. Indonesia is at least as diverse as Burma, and its predominant group, the Javanese, is afflicted with the same sense of entitlement as the Burmans hold in Burma. But Indonesia's anti-colonialists, led by Sukarno and Mohammad Hatta, succeeded in instilling a unifying nationalism directed against the Dutch as early as the Kongres Perempuan Indonesia, the Indonesian Women's Congress of 1928. The slogan was "One nation—Indonesia; one language—Indonesian." Jakarta's airport today is named after Sukarno and Hatta, the co-founding fathers of the Republic. It is significant that while Sukarno was Javanese, his mother was Balinese, and Hatta was a Sumatran.

The poignancy and confusion of Burma's ethnic divisions is expressed movingly in *Life's Journey in Faith: Burma, from Riches to Rags*, the autobiography of a Karen of my generation named Saw Spencer Zan, who wrote:

> I wondered why Dad was so worried about my safety because I knew I was among people I considered my friends. I could take care of myself. But I became very worried for my family in Insein. I trusted the K.N.D.O.s to be capable defenders of the town but I still worried because I did not want anything to happen between our two peoples. We didn't deserve it. We were only pawns in this political drama. I did not hate the Burman then, nor do I today. I grew up with Burman kids, played with them, fought with them, I was cursed by them and I cursed back in turn. I did not consider myself their enemy, nor do I regard them mine, just because we spoke different languages. *I always believe that we should and can live together in harmony as we are all Burmese.* [Italics mine]

The Zans were my neighbors in Twante during the war. In the same spirit Colonel (now Major General) Na Deh Mya, son of the late Karen leader General Bo Mya, said on another occasion, "We don't hate Burmans. We are Burmese and we want to live in peace and unity." However, the attitude of all too many Burmans was expressed in 1992 by Major General Khet Sein of the Burma Army, who said, "In the next decade, the only Karen you see will be in the museum."

While at St. Paul's every chance I got, I would spend the night with my parents in their tiny room at the Methodist school on Creek Street. My buddy Robert Anthony and I would jog around the Royal Lakes before dawn. At one point on our counter-clockwise route, behind the zoo down a slope to our right, was a British cemetery. Whenever we approached it, we would pick up our pace because it was spooky. It was also dark and, in the winter, cold. On several runs, Robert and I saw a bright comet over Rangoon's skies. I enquired of the Harvard-Smithsonian Center for Astrophysics what they could tell me about that comet. Christine Pulliam and her scientist colleagues confirmed our sighting as being Comet C/1948 V1 (Eclipse Comet; O. S. 1948 XI) which appeared over the southern hemisphere and lower northern latitudes between 1 November and 20 December 1948. At its brightest it had a magnitude of 3.5 with a tail as long as 30 degrees and was clearly visible to the unaided eye above Rangoon. It was so thrilling to see that long bridal-trained spectacle. And I am happy to be vindicated.

The Karen uprising climaxed the following year, but was a comet necessary to warn us of the impending insurrection? On 1 January 1949, the Karens captured Twante. Our home on the canal was looted bare. Among the possessions looted were photographs I had taken of the independence celebrations and the departure of Governor Hubert Rance on board the HMS *Birmingham*. But it was not because of the astrologers' calculations that Burma went so badly off the rails so soon after independence. It was because of our own national disunity. The Burmese obsession with astrology has always put me in mind of the line from Shakespeare's *Julius Caesar*, "The fault, dear Brutus, is not in our stars but in ourselves."

THE BROTHERS GO TO AMERICA

Early in 1949, my brother Irwin returned from India after graduating from Woodstock School in Mussoorie. He was home for a couple of months, while he applied for a Fulbright-Smith Mundt travel grant to study in the United States. Irwin was full of yarns of the three years he had spent at Woodstock. So many things that happen in life are serendipitous. Irwin's own attendance at Woodstock was an accidental result of his hitching a ride on an empty Allied Forces plane that was returning to Calcutta after delivering supplies to Burma after the Japanese retreated. He happened to be at Lee Memorial Mission on Dharamtala Street in Calcutta when Methodist

Bishop Clement D. Rockey was also there. It was through that encounter that Irwin was given the opportunity to attend Woodstock School.

Woodstock is a boarding school founded in 1854 for the education of Western missionary children whose parents were stationed in India. It welcomes children of all races and religions. A few Indian children attended Woodstock, but Irwin was the first Burmese. He arrived there in 1946, and became part of the student body that had to hunker down through the violent upheaval attending the Indian partition of 1947. While he was at Woodstock, Irwin and two friends had hiked to the source of the Ganges River. He talked a lot about the Himalayas and their snow-capped peaks. I was so impressed that I wanted to enroll at Woodstock as well.

Woodstock School campus, 1950s. Top left, Parker Hall/classrooms; foreground, high school boys' hostel; top right, high school girls' dormitory.

Irwin's travel grant came through and he left for America on 1 April 1949. My sister, May May Kyi, and I went with our parents to the airport to see him off. The first leg of his flight on China National Aviation Corporation (CNAC), a Hong Kong-based British flag carrier, took him to Kunming. Petite Chinese stewardesses in tight silk *cheomsans* invited us on board. They assured Mother that they would take good care of Irwin during the flight. He was never to see Burma again.

Our two older brothers were already in America. In China, the Communists were advancing toward the capital Peking. Mao Zedong proclaimed the People's Republic in Tiananmen Square on 1 October 1949. From

Kunming, Irwin flew to Shanghai and then to Midway Island, and on to San Francisco.

On the way to the airport, we saw a procession bearing the body of the first Burmese army officer to be killed in a plane by small-arms fire from KNDO soldiers on the ground. He was Bo Sein Hman, who was given a hero's funeral. My generation remembers that incident as a pivotal harbinger of the civil war that has been going on almost unabated, ever since.

Had it not been for Irwin's example, I probably would have remained at St. Paul's. I had a desire to go to America, though, and Woodstock was a stepping-stone toward that goal. My parents were eager for us all to get a good education abroad, so that we could come back and serve our country. On that score, all but our eldest brother, U Kyaw Nyein, failed them—not through our fault, but through the cruel vicissitudes of history. But at that time we didn't yet know how things would turn out, and my parents were happy to support my aspiration to study at Woodstock.

The four brothers in 1980. Left to right: Kyaw Nyein, Simon, Irwin, and Win. Photo by Zali Win.

I sailed on the *Jalagopal* on 25 February 1950. The ship's first port of call was Akyab, where some Rangoon University co-eds disembarked. They were going home at the end of the term. I witnessed a burial at sea one night. A stillborn baby was committed to the deep somewhere in the Bay of Bengal. The ship's master ordered the engines stopped and the tiny baby, wrapped and weighted was gently lowered from the ship's fantail. When the ship reached Calcutta, it docked seaward of the Howrah Bridge which spanned the Hooghly River. I arrived in Calcutta on 2 March 1950.

The Chatterjees, a gentle Bengali family, met me at the pier and took me to their home in the Alipore section of Calcutta. Mr. A.C. Chatterjee was a tall man who had worked many years for the United Industrial Bank of India. The eldest of the three brothers, Pratap, had graduated from Woodstock two years before with Irwin. The middle brother, Ashoke, was to be my classmate at Woodstock.

Romir, the youngest, would climb all over me. He was tickled by my name and called me "Windjammer." It was at the Chatterjees' home that I saw my first dial telephone. High tea was served at 5:30. I gobbled up the *samosas* and delicacies with gusto, and was surprised when dinner was served around 10 o'clock. I thought high tea *was* dinner!

I had to register at the police station. At first I was a little intimidated. In Burma, you distanced yourself from policemen and police stations. I didn't know what to expect at the Indian station. A Burmese pilgrim monk was also there to register. The clerk who took my passport was dressed in a Bengali *dhoti*. "*Di-hma-let-hmat-htoe*" [sign here], he said, in perfect unaccented Burmese as he handed me a document. He probably was born and bred in Burma; Indians traveled back and forth to Burma in those days. I felt so relieved that someone there spoke my language. I did speak a smattering of bread-and- butter Hindustani, but it was inadequate.

Next I went to the bank to pick up a draft that my father had sent ahead for me. Mrs. Romola Chatterjee took me shopping at New Market for toiletries, including a toothbrush, Kolynos toothpaste, and Brylcreem. I had never owned a toothbrush until I left Burma. We cleaned our teeth using the forefinger with salt, ash, or a piece of charcoal as "toothpaste." Sometimes a twig was used. Calcutta, the former capital, was a grand city. It was exciting. Every time I saw something new, I thought of my family and friends in Burma and wished they could enjoy it with me. Ashoke introduced me to Kwality and Firpos, popular eateries. I liked the Indian foods and smells.

I met the Reverend Charles Woolever, who was in charge of organizing the "going-up party." Woodstock School chartered two coaches on the Doon Express—one for the girls and the other for the boys. The ride was most enjoyable. There were white kids from all over India, and a few from East Pakistan, the Middle East, and Thailand. It was the first time in my life that I came into contact with American contemporaries.

They were children of missionaries, diplomats, or petroleum engineers whose family names were Griffiths, Hostetler, Parker, Schiller, Weaver, and the like. They spoke English in an accent that was strange to my ears.

It was a two-night journey to Dehra Dun, the northern terminus for the Doon Express. From there we had to take a bus to Mussoorie, and then hike up a steep mountain to Landour, where Woodstock School is located. I had never seen mountains before, much less hiked up one. Coolies carried our belongings on their backs, secured by a strap attached to their foreheads. The loads were heavier than the coolies themselves; I have seen coolies transport refrigerators in this manner.

Woodstock was named after the birthplace of Winston Churchill, and it had been established by the East India Company as a school for children of that huge British mercantile conglomerate before the Christian missions acquired it in 1854. It educated children from kindergarten through the tenth standard (American equivalent of twelfth grade). The high school boys lived in the Boys' Hostel, while the high school girls resided in the College, which was situated on another hill above the Boys' Hostel. The sports we played were American ones, such as baseball and basketball. The school sprawled up and down the hillside. We spent a good deal of time negotiating the slope to go to class. That was conducive to creating lifelong friendships because students walked together.

Woodstock opened my eyes to the world beyond Burma. The atmosphere was informal and enjoyable. The teacher-student relationships were relaxed and highly conducive to learning. The classes were small and an active exchange of ideas was encouraged. We didn't stand up when the teacher walked into the classroom, as was done in Burma. Among my buddies at Woodstock was Ho-Kang Liu, whose family were refugees from China when the Communists took over the country. Liu's father was now a businessman in Calcutta. Liu and I enjoyed hiking in the Himalayas. We attempted but failed to reach Gangotri, source of the Ganges River; exhaustion and inexperience forced us to return by bus when we reached Rishikesh. I visited Ho-Kang before he died on 20 October 2015.

On our first night out, villagers discouraged us from proceeding farther. So we camped at the edge of their village and built a fire. At the fireside chat, the villagers asked me, "Is it true that in your country, the rivers alternately flow in both directions?" I said "Yes," and explained to them how the two events are caused by the tides—rivers in the delta flow inland at high tide and seaward at low, and that farmers and fishermen in the Irrawaddy Delta know how to calculate these two events using the waxing and waning phases of the moon. They were fascinated, but I was more intrigued. How did these villagers, living high up in the Himalayas, know to ask such a question? They taught us that tigers are afraid of fire and a good way to keep them at bay at night is to build a campfire.

At Woodstock I took part in extracurricular activities. I did not understand baseball, even though it was similar to rounders I had played in Burma. I continued in scouting, earning enough merit badges to become a King's Scout, equivalent of the American Eagle Scout. Dr. Robert Leland Fleming was the scoutmaster. India had recently become independent of Britain but not all the infrastructure had yet been Indianized. I was a long-distance runner and a high jumper, and I dabbled in leading cheers at athletic events. It was a novel experience for me. Every chance I got, when we had a few days off, I would go to Dehra Dun, New Delhi, and Agra with my buddies. I would rent a bicycle at Rajpur, below Mussoorie, and ride down to Dehra Dun. I also traveled quite a bit around north India. In fact, one night Kenneth Bonham and I slept beneath the front right minaret as you face the Taj Mahal from the main gate.

During the long winter break of 1950, I took a trip around India and Ceylon with Boyd Murdoch, the math and science teacher. By train we went to Simla, where my second eldest brother Ko Tun Nyein was buried at the Christian cemetery in Sanjauli. Then we went to Ludhiana, Amritsar, New Delhi, Agra, Ajmer, Shahjahanpur, Lucknow, Kanpur, and Gwalior. In Bombay I experienced racial discrimination for the first time at a swimming club called Breach Candy. The guard at the gate prevented my entry. "Non- Europeans not allowed," he said. Had he not been of larger build, my impetuosity might have made me alter his facial anatomy. I was humiliated, but he was only doing his job, obeying his residual colonial masters' legacy. I was outraged, nevertheless. This was still happening in India—after the British raj had departed?

From Bombay we went further south to Sholapur, Bangalore, Cochin, and Mysore. We crisscrossed the subcontinent. We had to carry our own bedding. At Dhanushkodi we crossed the Gulf of Manar to Ceylon (now Sri Lanka) and landed at Talamanar Pier. We toured the ruins of Anuradhapura. We went to Kandy, which had been the headquarters of Admiral Lord Louis Mountbatten when he was chief of the South East Asia Command (SEAC) during World War II, and where the movie *The Bridge on the River Kwai* was filmed. The man who built the set for that film, Eddie Fowlie, later also built the set for the 1994 John Boorman film *Beyond Rangoon*. Back in India, Mr. Murdoch and I made a beeline for Mussoorie back to Woodstock for the start of the next term.

What I remember best of my senior year at Woodstock was the sociology class taught by Dr. Fleming, whose physician-wife, Bethel, was the school medical officer. During the time they were at Woodstock, the Flemings pioneered in opening up Nepal to the Western world. He was a biologist who went there to collect ferns and birds. Dr. Fleming's sociology class was the high point of my senior year. We took field trips to Dehra Dun to the Ayurvedic Medical School, the Forest Research Institute, and the Ramakrishna Ashram, where a Dutch *swami* (religious teacher), gave us a lecture about the Ramakrishna sect. The renowned Doon School, Woodstock's competitor, and the Indian Military Academy were also located in Dehra Dun. We learned about Guru Nanak and the Sikh religion, Jainism, Parsis and the Persian influence in India, and the Moghul Empire. We learned about Indian music and dance and went to the places where they were taught in Mussoorie. We went to Hardwar on the Ganges, where we saw many *sadhus* (holy men) and pilgrims everywhere. Dr. Fleming was also caring and most helpful, and he filled in many of the gaps in the hit-or-miss education I had received in Burma during the Japanese occupation.

I graduated from Woodstock on 24 November 1951. There were ten girls and twenty boys in my class. I then joined the "going-down" party to Calcutta to return home to Burma. On my final night in India, I dined alone across the table with Bishop Clement D. Rockey, who happened to be at Lee Memorial Mission. It was he who got Irwin enrolled at Woodstock in 1946.

The next day, 1 December, I flew to Rangoon. It was the first time I had ever flown in an airplane. It felt very good to be back in Rangoon after a two-hour flight from Calcutta's Dum Dum airport. I was so happy to see my parents and eldest brother and sister. But I was back for only a month, because I had been admitted to Phoenix College in Arizona. While my visa was being processed at the American embassy, I spotted Dr. Gordon Seagrave, the famous Burma surgeon, who was in another part of the same room. He was chatting with Sam Rickard, Jr., an attaché, another Woodstock alumnus. Sam's father was principal of Judson College in Rangoon before the war.

During the month I was home, I visited friends and relatives in Twante and Thongwa. My classmate Warren Crain, whose parents were Baptist missionaries in Burma, and I went to Pegu by train where we were escorted by the Rev. U Ba Saing, the Methodist pastor, to see the Reclining Buddha. The shrine was surrounded by thick vegetation and we were the only three there. I left Rangoon on 3 January 1952. Warren Crain and Margaret Winfield, another Woodstock classmate, joined my sister and parents, to see me off at Mingaladon Airport. Margaret's father was with the Special Technical and Economic Mission (STEM), predecessor of the U.S. Agency for International Development (USAID), at the embassy in Rangoon.

My first stop was Bangkok, where I had to spend the night for a continuing flight to Hong Kong. Bangkok was rustic in those days, a backwater compared to Rangoon. Arriving in Hong Kong the next day I stayed several days in style as the guest of the Christian Brothers. Brother Patrick, Father's friend who had been the director of De La Salle Institute during the war, was now director of La Salle College in Kowloon. I was lodged in his expansive suite while he was on home leave in Ireland. Food was brought to me on a tray.

I tasted a California Sunkist orange for the first time in Hong Kong. From Hong Kong I sailed on the *President Cleveland* to San Francisco. The ship called at Kobé, Yokohama, and Honolulu. It docked in Honolulu early in the morning, beneath the Aloha Tower. I was picked up by a Jacob Pung, his wife, and their young son Clayton, and taken to their home and shown the sights of Honolulu including the "Pink Lady" (Royal Hawaiian Hotel), and Pali Pass and the National War Cemetery. Mother had befriended Mrs. Pung when they were passengers on board the *President Wilson* from San Francisco to Honolulu after she had attended the Women's Christian Temperance Union Conference held in London in the spring of 1950; she had extended her itinerary home via America so that she could visit Simon and Irwin. Simon was then in medical school in Chicago and Irwin was attending Ohio Wesleyan University.

In San Francisco, Marjorie Merrill of the Methodist Church's Board of Foreign Missions' reception office gave me a ticket for a Gray Line tour of the city. The tour included Mission Dolores, Telegraph Hill, Presidio of San Francisco, Golden Gate Park, Golden Gate Bridge, Fisherman's Wharf, Cliff House, and the Opera House. It was all very exciting.

After the tour, I took a Greyhound bus to Phoenix. The Reverend Dr. Charles Kendall, pastor of the Central Methodist Church in Phoenix, met me at the bus station the next evening and took me to dinner at a restaurant called Golden Drumstick, on North Central Avenue, where his family and friends waited. I lived the next three years with Mrs. Ada Campbell Travis, his mother-in-law, next door at 131 West Coronado Road.

I worked part-time in the church office folding envelopes, picking up the mail, and locking up the buildings at night. Fees for the semester at Phoenix College came to $235, and Dr. Kendall wrote out a check. But I didn't want to be dependent on anybody for my school fees, so I attended summer school at Arizona State College at Tempe, (now Arizona State University.) ASC waived my fees because it was welcoming a diversity of students from abroad. I carried heavier loads, attended summer sessions at the University of Colorado, and completed the requirements for the bachelor's degree (psychology) in January 1955. I was in a hurry to return home to Burma. I was in Boulder when the movie, *The Glenn Miller Story*, in which James Stewart and June Allyson starred, was filmed on the university campus in the summer of 1953.

In January 1955, I enrolled at The American University in Washington to work for a master's degree. I roomed with Irwin in his studio apartment at 2136 O Street NW. On the second floor lived an Indonesian gal who had recently graduated from Swarthmore College. Her name was Supadmirin Martadirdja but we called her Wies. She was a Javanese Catholic who hailed from Jogjakarta. She was the assistant to Mr. Suryotjondro, minister counselor (deputy chief of mission) of the Indonesian embassy which was two blocks away in the former Walsh Mansion at 2020 Massachusetts Avenue NW. When Irwin's studio apartment became too crowded, we moved to the third floor into a larger apartment. A few days later, a young couple from the embassy moved into another apartment on the same floor while they were looking for a larger place.

Djoko Sanjoto, head of the family, was the cultural attaché at the embassy. He and his wife Suherni had a baby boy named Kukuh Widiatmoko Afro-Asianto Sanjoto who was born at the time the Asian African Conference was being held in Bandung in April 1955. Suherni had a younger sister named Tati Haryati Marsosudiro.

I knew nothing about Indonesia. In Burma Dr. Sukarno's name was heard on the radio practically every night in the late 1940s, but I didn't really understand his importance. Burma's government under Prime Minister U Nu had sent a planeload of weapons to aid Indonesia in its revolution against the Dutch. Burma was the first country to recognize Indonesia's independence.

The Sanjotos became family to me. I would do errands and drive them to places and take them to the airport whenever they traveled. Tati would knock on our door and say, "Win, come. Let's we eat."

In the summer of 1955, the Sanjotos moved into a duplex, at 4431 Fessenden Street NW, but we remained close. I drove Tati to Boulder when she enrolled at the University of Colorado in the fall of 1956. After she graduated, she worked for the Voice of America in Washington, broadcasting in Indonesian until she retired.

One day in late September 1956, while I was playing with Kukuh in the Sanjoto's living room, a pretty girl came down the stairs. She was Gandasari Abdullah, but she went by Riri. "Oh, you're new here," I said. She had recently moved from Seattle but the Sanjotos had not yet told me she was the new occupant of Tati's room. "I'll show you around," I offered. I don't remember what she answered, but in the next several weeks, I showed her Mount Vernon, the Washington Monument, the White House, and Arlington National Cemetery. I even took her in my Volkswagen Beetle to Gettysburg, Valley Forge, and Monticello (Thomas Jeffrerson's home in Charlottesville), and the Luray Caverns.

Riri's and my relationship heated up and on a snowy day in the winter of 1957, I slipped on the ice and fell on the Indonesian embassy's circular driveway. She let out a guffaw. After my embarrassment stabilized and I regained composure, I asked her, "Will you marry me?" She said, "Yes!" It was very quick. I was walking on cloud nine.

Riri went to the Islamic Center on Massachusetts Avenue and asked the imam to marry us. It is not permissible under Islamic law, he told her. A Muslim man can marry a non-Muslim woman, but a Muslim woman is not allowed under Islamic law to marry a non-Muslim man. Riri felt that this prohibition was not true to the spirit of Islam. We went together to the pastor of Foundry Methodist Church, the Reverend Dr. Theodore Henry Palmquist. He told us, "Either you, Win, become a Muslim, or you, Riri, become a Christian." I asked him, "How do we know our love is secure?" He said, "You don't. You can never be sure. You have to go with your heart." I never asked Riri to change her religion nor did she ask me to change mine.

Still, we were grist for the embassy's gossip mill. In 1950, Riri's father, Baginda Dahlan Abdullah, was Indonesia's first ambassador to Iraq and Trans-Jordania. Moekarto Notowidigdo, his friend, was now the Indonesian ambassador in Washington. At her mother's behest, he summoned Riri to his office, and said, "I don't want you to marry that *orang birma*" [Burmese man] and made her surrender her passport. She waited outside his office and said, "I will not leave until you return my passport." She was adamant. Brenda, his secretary, finally returned it to her at closing time.

Riri and I were married on 5 September 1958 in Hollywood, after we drove across the continent in my Volkswagen Beetle. We wanted our wedding to be small, private, and as far away as possible from the embassy's eyes. We stopped in Hillsboro, Indiana, at Dr. George W. Crane's family farm, where we picked up my Woodstock classmate Gordon Hostetler. We stopped at Enid, Oklahoma, to see Ken Bonham, another Woodstock classmate. Dr. Charles Kendall, who had welcomed me to Phoenix in 1952, was by that time the pastor of the First Methodist Church in Hollywood, and he officiated. No family member could be present. There were about twenty friends at the wedding, several of my Woodstock connection. We were dirt poor. The Kendalls gave a reception of punch and cake. My father sent two gold bands from Burma. We felt blessed and were very happy. Dr. Frank Williams, another family friend and Methodist minister, gave away the bride, and Judie Schiller Landry, another Woodstock classmate, and her husband, Bob, acted as bridesmaid and best man. Bob died on 15 September 2015. Carol Doyle, Riri's schoolmate at the University of Washington, was her only friend who could attend.

We drove up the coast to Seattle. Riri had spent a year there at the University of Washington in 1955–1956 and her friends there gave us a shower. Then we made our way east through Idaho, Yellowstone National Park, Minnesota, Michigan via the new Mackinac Bridge, and Ohio, stopping to visit friends along the way.

When we moved to Burma in July 1959, and she met my parents for the first time, my father told her, "It doesn't matter what religion you follow. It's like a rainbow in the sky. All the colors are beautiful." But a year later Riri decided to become a Christian, and asked my father to baptize her.

In the early 1950s, parts of the District of Columbia, Virginia, and Maryland were still segregated. Some of the darker-complexioned Indonesian embassy staff were refused service at Hot Shoppes in Arlington and Fairfax counties. There were still signs on the Capitol Transit trams and buses that designated seats at the rear for "colored" people. I paid no heed and sat in the front. Nobody asked me to move.

It was a simpler time, and Washington in those days was an easier place. Construction of the beltway had just begun. Streetcars clanked up and down Wisconsin and Connecticut Avenues and along F Street downtown. You could walk into the White House grounds during certain hours; no permit was necessary. I remember being there once and seeing Dr. Paul Dudley White, President Dwight D. Eisenhower's cardiologist. In 1959, Riri and I showed up at Arlington National Cemetery during the funeral for Secretary of State John Foster Dulles. President and Mrs. Eisenhower were sitting in their limousine only a few feet from where we stood. I can't remember how many times I took Indonesian visitors to Skyline Drive and Luray Caverns, and showed them the changing of the guards at the Tomb of the Unknown Soldier at Arlington.

I was invited to the home of the Burmese ambassador at 2223 R Street NW (former home of Chief Justice Charles Evans Hughes) for a reception for Prime Minister U Nu in July 1955, after he had attended the Bandung Conference in Indonesia. The ambassador's name was James Barrington. He was an Anglo-Burman who was initiated into the ranks of the distinguished Indian Civil Service under the colonial administration.

After U Nu fell from power, the Ne Win regime gradually but systematically got rid of non-Burmans from such positions. Richard Nixon was President Eisenhower's vice president, and I remember that he was at the Burmese ambassador's residence that afternoon. I met U Nu on that occasion. I told him who my father and uncle were, and that they were from Thongwa. "*Thi dar paw*[I know them]," he said, and he gave me some parental counsel, "Don't drink. Don't gamble. Live right." He was put up at

Blair House, the government guest house. When he departed, he left a small Buddha icon there as his way of gaining merit.

Another small incident that drew attention in the press was when Secretary of Agriculture Ezra Taft Benson presented him with a tie clasp as a memento to make amends for a diplomatic faux pas. U Nu had been kept waiting before Secretary Benson could see him. U Nu had another appointment, so he left without seeing Mr. Benson. U Nu never wore a tie, but he politely wore the tie clasp on his Burmese jacket.

In 1957 Riri was awarded a scholarship at Howard University, where she pursued a master's degree in government. One of her professors was Bernard B. Fall, the Frenchman who became famous for his prophetic writings on Vietnam. (This was still the 1950s, when the average American could not point to Vietnam on the map.) Professor Fall guided Riri through the academic process and would drop her off at the bus stop after class. Riri and I became friends with him and his wife, Dorothy, and we were invited to their home a number of times.

In 1965, when Riri applied for a scholarship to pursue a doctoral degree at Claremont Graduate School, she listed him as a reference. The other referee, her former boss at the U.S. Information Service in Jakarta long ago, advised her that it was unwise to mention Bernard B. Fall because of his books such as *Street Without Joy* and *Hell in a Very Small Place*, which described vividly the French and American military assaults on the innocent people of Vietnam. In 1966, Professor Fall was invited to Vietnam to be shown how the U.S. military had pacified Vietnamese hamlets. His jeep drove over a land mine, and he and the Marine driver were killed instantly.

I was attending The American University when the first coup in Burma took place in 1958. I didn't think much of it. U Nu said he had asked General Ne Win to assume the reins of government and to hold elections within six months.

Riri and I worked on our theses during the spring of 1959. We rented two manual typewriters and pounded on them constantly, typing our theses. The apartment floor was uncarpeted. The downstairs occupants thought we were partying and complained to the landlord. But at last we both got our theses written and received our degrees. We left Washington in June 1959 and went to Burma.

We flew out of New York's Idlewild Airport on a Pan Am DC-6 that landed at Prestwick in Scotland. We took in the sights in Scotland which included a ride across Loch Lomond on the *Maid of the Loch*. In London we met my first cousin Pearl (Purcell) Oliver.

We stayed at Bermondsey Settlement, where my pen friend Marion Davies and her fiancé Kenneth Freeman, were resident social workers. Marion had been a Girl Guide who volunteered at a Women's Christian Temperance Union conference that Mother had attended in London in 1950. Marion had wanted a pen pal, so Mother gave her my name and address (I was at Woodstock School) at the time. In 1959, Marion and I met for the first time in person.

With Marion we went to Oxford, where she had never been before. I wanted to see two in particular of Oxford's colleges: Balliol, because a Burmese graduate had gone on to become Burma's first ambassador to the United States; and Christ Church, because John Wesley, the founder of Methodism, had been a don there. Our friendship with Marion and Ken continued to blossom over the years. When our son, Zali, attended King's School in Worcester, doing the A Levels, from 1978 to 1980, Ken and Marion looked after him as their American son. Marion passed away in 2013.

We had wanted to go to The Netherlands, but its embassy in Washington denied Riri a visa because Indonesia was at war with The Netherlands over the issue of West Irian.

Her family history also worked against her. In November 1917, at a conference of student revolutionaries from the then Dutch East Indies held at Leiden, Dahlan Abdullah, Riri's father, exhorted his school mates to re-claim their homeland from the Dutch and call it Indonesia.[1] It was the first time the new name *Indonesia* was heard uttered. Among the tight group who helped launch the revolution against the Dutch included Mohammad Hatta, Tan Malaka, Ali Sastroamidjojo, Raden Soerjomihardjo, S. H. Teng, Hubertus Van Mook, and Sutan Mohammad Zain. Riri's father had lived in the Netherlands for more than a dozen years as a student.

At Düsseldorf airport we were fetched by Mr. Dasaad, an Indonesian businessman, and taken to the residence of the Indonesian ambassador to the Federal Republic of Germany. The ambassador was a relative of Riri's and still a bachelor. We enjoyed after-dinner chats with him and his father, Professor Sutan Mohammad Zain. He assigned an embassy employee to show us the sights of Bonn. A few hundred feet below the ambassadorial residence in Koenigswinter, up a hill overlooking the Rhine, was the home of the West German chancellor. I could see Chancellor Konrad Adenauer walking up to his home from the car, toting a briefcase.

From Germany we went to Paris, Rome, Athens, and on to New Delhi. In Rome, we enjoyed our first opera. It was *Lohengrin*, performed at the Baths of Caracalla. In India we visited Woodstock School. The much loved teacher and librarian, Miss Vera Marley, was still there, and her memory of long-past students and events was as sharp as ever. From New Delhi we flew

1. Indolegenblad, 9th year, Thursday, 20 December 1917, pp 95–99.

to Calcutta, where we stayed with my Woodstock classmate Ashoke Chatterjee, and from there to Rangoon. My parents welcomed us at Rangoon's Mingaladon Airport. After being away for nearly eight years, I was happy to be home. The rain came crashing down in sheets. It is liquid gold to Burma's farmers. The monsoons had arrived.

I am home again.

2

The Burmese Way to
Socialism and Father

My desire was to make my life and career in my own country. But I ended up leaving Burma again after less than two years, because I couldn't find a job that would fulfill me. I had been all hyped up to do something for my country. I wanted to work for the Foreign Office because I believed I could make a significant contribution. In undergraduate college and graduate school, I had taken courses in American history, anthropology, classics (Greece), diplomatic history of the United States, economics, French, German, political science, Spanish, and western civilization outside my major, which was psychology. I had attended law school and taken courses in civil procedure, criminal law, and legal research. I had also gained some experience in the inner workings of an embassy in Washington. I am also adept at picking up spoken foreign languages. In addition to my native Burmese, I am fluent in English and can "manage" in Hindustani, Indonesian, and Karen.

The Foreign Office official who handled my employment application was abrupt; he said, "You're married to a foreigner, why would you even think of working for the Foreign Office?" The interview was cut short and the door to the Foreign Office slammed shut on me. Forty years later I visited him as he lay terminally ill at his suburban Washington home. He was asleep, unaware of my presence at his bedside. In the early 1970s, he had left his senior position at the embassy in Washington and remained in the United States to turn over a new leaf in his life. A large, iconic monogram of Arahan, an early disciple of the Buddha, was affixed to the ceiling directly above his head.

Arahan monogram

In July 1959, I took a job at Kingswood School in the town of Kalaw in Southern Shan State. I taught English and mathematics. But I stayed at Kingswood for only one school year; Riri's health suffered, as did mine, and medical care in Kalaw was inadequate. Kalaw was home to the Burma Army Staff College. Whenever top brass came to inspect the college, students and staff of the town's schools would be required to assemble at the football field to lend them audience. The students loved these times out of the classroom, but the disruptions happened too frequently. The principal of the Staff College was Colonel Ko Ko, who later became secretary of the Revolutionary Council that overthrew the civilian government on 2 March 1962. Also, Riri and I were newlyweds, and men in army greens milling about the small town intimidated us. It was reminiscent of my World War II days in Twante, when menacing Japanese soldiers roamed around town and families had to hide their womenfolk. We did not feel safe.

We lived above the railway station on Circular Road and up the road at No. 46, in a house called *Daffynant*, lived retired General Smith Dun, who was ousted in 1949 as commander in chief of the Burma Army and replaced by his deputy, Lieutenant General Ne Win. The house's original owner must have had a connection with the village by that name in Wales because Kalaw in colonial times was a hill station, a respite from the heat on the plains for the raj. Smith Dun's daughter, Mercy, was a student in my class at Kingswood. Although I had known her father's legendary name, I met him for the first time in 1959. Only four feet tall and sporting a handlebar moustache, he looked the ferocious warrior he truly was. He was putting the finishing touches on his *Memoirs of the Four-foot Colonel*. The walls of his living room were plastered with pictures of his army adventures. His military career had started with the Indian Army, because Burma in earlier colonial times was a part of British India. He was Burma's first graduate of the Indian Military Academy at Dehra Dun, where he earned the Sword of Honour, awarded to the most outstanding cadet of the graduating class. A proud Pwo Karen like my mother—which was the main reason he was ousted as army chief—he would say to me, "You should call yourself *Mahn* Kyaw Win, instead of *U* Kyaw Win." *Mahn* is a Pwo Karen male honorific. (I made U [pron. Oo] my legal "first" name by order of the United States District Court of San Francisco in 1966.)

I would stroll over to Smith Dun's house and listen to tales of his military exploits. Celebrating Karen New Year was a big event for the Karen community. On that day, Smith Dun served monkey curry in a silver bowl. He hunted the monkeys himself, using a rifle he kept in his home. I asked him why the army hadn't confiscated it. "I warned those buggers to stay away from my house," he said. "If they come here, I'll shoot them!" He maintained a pack of guard dogs and had a bow that shot pellets instead of arrows. He liked to demonstrate his prowess with it. Each time he took aim at a target on his front yard, he never missed. "Here, you try it," he said, handing me the weapon. I declined, for fear of shattering my thumb. "Will it kill your target?" I asked him. "If you hit him on the right spot, like the temple, it would," he said, "otherwise, it would disable him."

Feeling unsafe in Kalaw, I began applying for jobs in Rangoon. I applied at the Methodist English High School, where Aung San Suu Kyi was a student, but I did not have any luck there. The principal, a Eurasian woman named Doreen Logie, was of the colonial mold and I was a freshly minted American graduate from the village. Those attributes did not sit well with her. (In December 1984, Riri and I visited Doreen and her husband, George, at their retirement home in Stourport-on-Severn in England. She fixed lunch and we had an amicable visit.)

I also answered a newspaper advertisement for some faculty openings at the University of Rangoon. S. D. Verma, owner of Central Enterprises, offered me a job as his son's private tutor. That didn't appeal to me, although the remuneration was attractive.

Before returning to Burma in 1959, I had given some Burmese-language lessons to a Major Richard Cross, who was attending the U.S. Army Strategic Intelligence School in Washington preparatory to a posting in Rangoon. Dick was now the assistant army attaché at the U.S. embassy. He told me about an opening for a Burmese instructor at the U.S. Army Language School at the Presidio of Monterey in California. So I filled out the application form and recorded a voice audition, and Dick submitted them for me through U.S. military channels.

While I waited to hear from the U.S. Army, I inquired whether there might be an opening at the embassy. Konrad Bekker, chief of the economic section, asked to see a sample of my writing. I showed him my master's thesis. He offered me a job on the spot, and I started on 3 May 1960 as an assistant in the economic section. United States embassies of the time had four sections—consular, economic, general services, and political. I was put in the economic section's library, which held materials on American companies that wanted to do business in Burma. These included Campbell's Soup. I also served Burmese companies that wanted to export products to America (a wide range, including bat guano); I checked their credit rating with banks, and compiled economic and commercial statistics from Burmese government sources for transmittal to Washington.

Sometime in the fall of 1960, in the course of an errand, I spotted a gentleman who was waiting in the lobby of the Burma Broadcasting Service. His eyes exuded warmth and tenderness. Benevolence was written all over his face. I approached him and engaged in chitchat. I had no idea who he was, but I had a visceral feeling that I might learn something from him. I later discovered that he was *Dhammika* U Ba Than, a Burmese army colonel who had become disillusioned with the military, resigned his commission, and gone upcountry as a Buddhist missionary. I think he foresaw a coup on the horizon. "If I were a young man like you," he told me, "I would get out of this country. The future looks grim."

Riri and I were in a quandary. We had been in Burma less than two years. I had been unable to find a job for which my education had prepared me, and we couldn't find an affordable place to live. My elder brother Simon was a surgeon, and he partitioned part of his apartment's dining area at Ramakrishna Hospital for our "bedroom." Riri had found a temporary job at the Indonesian embassy while I was actively pursuing work. She was a graduate of the Academy for the Foreign Service in Jakarta and was working at the United Nations Section at the Foreign Ministry when she was sent abroad for further study, first at the University of Washington in Seattle and later at Johns Hopkins University School of Advanced International Studies in Washington, DC. She had resigned from the Foreign Ministry when we got married. Now, in Rangoon, she worked as an assistant to the information officer, who had been her classmate at the Academy.

Teaching at Methodist English High School was also closed to me but, irony of ironies, U San Shain, chairman of the governing board, asked me to serve as its secretary. I accepted the non-paying job hoping it might open other doors. It was during this period, in 1960, that I had a glimpse of the teen-aged Aung San Suu Kyi at MEHS. I had seen the young Suu romping about her lakeside family home many years before when I was camping out with my Boy Scout troop.

U.S. ARMY LANGUAGE SCHOOL

Finally, an offer from the U.S. Army Language School came, several months after I had started working at the embassy. I struck a deal with the Language School: If Riri were also offered a job teaching Indonesian, we would both consider it. The U.S. Army was in need of a Burmese language teacher, so it bent the rule and offered her a job as well. But I was in a dilemma. How could I leave my parents again, after having been abroad almost eight years? It was an extremely difficult decision to make, but eventually the die was cast. Even so, I wrestled with an uneasy feeling. I did not have the heart to break the news to my parents, so Riri took the delicate task. She spoke to my father, who took it philosophically, muttering only, "Your mum will be very sad." But he did not try to dissuade us from going. He believed passionately in freedom and that each of us makes his own choices. When Father took the news to Mother, she was indeed very sad. "We will return in two years, *Ah May*," I promised her.

In late February 1961, the day before I cleared my desk, there was a demonstration in front of the building. Protesters pelted tomatoes and yelled anti-American slogans. The Kuomintang, the Chinese nationalist army of Chiang Kai-shek, was hiding out in Burma's Shan State in those days, and a KMT base had been captured by the Chinese People's Liberation Army with the help of the Burmese army. The protesters were angry because American arms were found at the base. The CIA and the U.S. military really were dreaming about invading China, or at least of getting their proxies to do so, just like they did later in South Vietnam and at the Bay of Pigs in Cuba. I was inside the embassy when the protest took place. My office was on the second floor, and we were ordered to remain inside and not to look out the windows. To add muscle to the order, a side-armed Marine stood guard in the hallway at the entrance to the chancery (the ambassador's suite). When the hubbub died down and the protesters had dispersed, the embassy's general services officer and his crew went outside to clean up the mess.

I felt uneasy and unsettled leaving Burma, feeling that I had let my parents down. At the airport on 8 March 1961, Mother held me tight until I broke away from her. I was never to see my parents again in Burma. Riri and I took six weeks getting to California by way of Malaya, Singapore,

Indonesia, Hong Kong, Japan, and Hawaii. In Singapore we were invited, along with Bishop Hobart Amstutz and his wife Celeste, our hosts, to the home of David Marshall, the Jewish businessman who had lost the 1959 election to Lee Kuan Yew, who went on to become Singapore's longtime strongman. Marshall showed us home movies of the Forbidden City in Peking. At that time China was a closed country, and those in the "free world" craned their necks to learn whatever they could of what was going on there.

We went on to Jakarta, where Riri's family lived, but I was apprehensive about the reception we could expect there. We did our duty by first going to her family home, but we went only once, and only for thirty minutes. Riri's elder sister in particular got hysterical that Riri had married a non-Muslim, a foreigner, and someone who was not of their Minangkabau tribe. Her mother also was angry and made her feelings known to the relatives. She did not want to see us and we were offered nothing to eat or drink. This was uncharacteristically un-Indonesian, where no visitor to a home departs without at least being offered a drink of water.

The message came across loud and clear: we were unwelcome. Riri's elder brother Djamal shouted: "Kill him," to Taufik, another brother, and came after me. Adrenaline rushed and I was ready to defend myself when Riri shielded me with her body and admonished, "Don't! You are a Christian!" Hearing her speak that way infuriated them all the more, and we made a quick exit from an acrimonious situation. But time, that great healer of ruptured relationships, had done its work. When we returned to Indonesia nine years later, in 1970, Djamal could not have been a more loving uncle to Zali and Dewi. The relationship between his children and ours warmed considerably. When cousin Sisi, his daughter, visited Zali in New York City many years later, Zali went all-out to make her visit memorable. He hired a special limousine to take her to JFK Airport when she left.

My parents never met any of Riri's relatives, even though my mother sent gifts to her mother. Father counseled Riri never to forsake her family, and her mother had relented by the time we took our children to see her in 1970. The feelings of love were mutual. Zali presented a golden pendant to his grandmother. In April 1997, Dewi took Brad, her newly-wed husband, to meet her grandmother. This cheered her. Riri and I were at her bedside at the time. She passed away a fortnight later.

In April 1961, Riri and I began our jobs at the U.S. Army Language School. First, we had to undergo training, playing the role of students ourselves for two weeks. We were assigned to learn Korean under the U.S. Army's total-immersion, intensive drilling and recitation method for eight hours a day. I took the U.S. Army job as a temporary one, because I did not want to shut the door on Burma, but when I received a letter from the University of Rangoon inviting me for an interview, I was already in California.

So, we got on with our lives and work. After China and India had fought a brief war in 1962, a group of Indian Army officers came to the U.S. Army Language School to learn Chinese. They were billeted at the Presidio. We frequently invited some of them to our home for dinner. I remember that one of them, Captain B. Vishnoi, had purchased a Lionel train set for his son and brought it to our home to try it out on the living room floor.

Even though I was a civilian employee of the U.S. Army, I found the military protocol and regulations on the base onerous. But I made the most of the situation. I was allowed to bring only $75.00 out of Burma, but the U.S. embassy was cooperative by agreeing to pay my final month's wages in U.S. dollars, although it had to be sent to America. When the check arrived, it was unsigned! I had to return the check, printed on a green IBM card, to the embassy to have it signed and returned to me.

We needed money to make a deposit to rent an apartment before the valid check got back. It was then that I learned about credit unions, when I went to borrow from the USALS Credit Union. I learned as much as I could about the operations, procedures, and policies of the credit union. Two years later, I got elected to its board of directors. Seven years after that, in 1970, while on a visit to Indonesia, I was asked by the management of Hotel Indonesia in Jakarta to give a talk about the management and operations of credit unions to its managers. I have been a credit union member for fifty-five years.

I was in Monterey when General Ne Win seized power in a military coup on 2 March 1962. I was jubilant at first for the country's sake, because after the first coup the army had cleaned up the streets, made people work, and got the trains to run on time. I received a letter from Father, written five days after the coup when he was away in India on church business:

> Though away from Burma, I am well informed of the situation. . . . The country is better in the hands of the Army at the present moment, though I do not approve of it but it is the case of lesser evil of the two.

On 1 August 1962, he wrote:

> Now I have completed my 68th year. . .I can vitally preach, write and operate my "Peasants' Economic Society". . . . Your mum has been elected as a delegate to represent Burma at the World Women's Temperance Convention to be held in Delhi. So your mum asked me to accompany her as a registered visitor.

The Peasants' Economic Society that Father founded was a cooperative that made small loans to farmers for the purchase of seeds and farming implements, to improve their lot as well as overall economic conditions. On return home after attending the Methodist General Conference held in San Francisco in 1948, he had visited Denmark to study farmers' cooperatives there and learned how they formed mutual aid societies. He was enthusiastic about this method of self-help and wished to introduce it to Burma. He was always pursuing village-level development. Some farmers who were unable to repay their loans had them written off. "Yes, we think and pray for Riri's delivery of our grandchild," Father added in the same letter.

Our son, Zali, was born on 21 August 1962. Mother wanted so earnestly to be present when he was born, but she was robbed of the joy of being with her youngest son's wife when her grandchild was born. The sadness of being deprived of the opportunity to bless the newborn and our home never left her.

Father wrote again on 30 September 1962:

> How happy we are to welcome our precious grand baby boy! We all are very, very pleased to learn that both mother and baby are well. Now you both must have realized that your parents had a great momentous moment when both of you were born. . . . How we wish we could come over there and watch our grandchild, Zali Win.

On 23 June 1963, after the military regime had taken full control of the schools, he wrote:

> Your Mum is still at the helm of the school . . . we have reduced the school to the status of middle school with strength of 250. I have now stopped my Peasants' Economic Society since the revolutionary Govt is making a splendid effort to help improve the condition of the farmers. . . . It is a great credit on the Govt.

On Friday, 22 November 1963, I walked into a classroom and told the students that President Kennedy had been shot. They thought I was pulling their leg, because I was noted for kidding. But this time I was serious, and they got it. The following Thursday was Thanksgiving, and we drove down to Hollywood to spend it with Dr. Charles Kendall and his wife, Mary Lou. Dr. Kendall had helped me through college in Arizona and married us. Americans' eyes were glued to their televisions that long weekend.

We were watching television with the Kendalls when Jack Ruby stepped forward and shot Lee Harvey Oswald in the stomach—live homicide on national TV. In the aftermath, when an appeal went out to aid Oswald's

Russian widow, Marina, and her two young children, who were unjustly tarnished by their father's action, I sent her a small donation. I have saved the canceled check all these years.

LONG TIME GETTING PASSPORTS

My parents had wanted to be present when our first child was born and, of course, see my brothers Simon and Irwin as well. Father had been to America five times, as a ministerial delegate to the quadrennial General Conference of the Methodist Church at eight-year intervals, between 1932 and 1960. He was again elected to attend in 1964, but the military regime would not issue him a passport. Mother had visited America in 1950 and 1953. The junta would not let citizens out of the country, except those who were leaving the country "for good." Burmese citizens who wished to emigrate were issued Certificates of Identity. Some of the embassies in Rangoon knew what these documents stood for and they honored them and issued visas.

Father had seen a good deal of America on his previous visits, even though his main purpose was to attend the General Conferences. In 1932, in Atlantic City, he and Bishop Jashwant Rao Chitambar, the first native elected bishop of the Methodist Church in India, were denied seating in a restaurant. Bishop Chitambar was proud of his Indian identity and always dressed in Indian attire, topped with a dignified turban. His granddaughter Charlene was my classmate at Woodstock. Father had ridden a train from Seattle to Niagara Falls. On his way home in 1940, he sailed through the Panama Canal, en route to Rio de Janeiro to attend the World Sunday School Convention.

The experience of his ship being towed through the locks by a steam-driven locomotive thrilled him immensely. He took many photographs with a Kodak Rainbow Hawkeye camera someone in America had gifted him. It had bellows and used size 116 roll films. It might have been on that same voyage that his ship embarked from San Diego, where he picked up the snatch of lyric that he sang when he returned home, "*South of the border. . . Down Mex-i-co way . . .*" He talked about the theaters on Broadway, how the stages moved up and down and sideways. I think he also saw the Grand Canyon. People in Burma would ask him, "How can the people in America live where it's so cold?" He would tell them that the homes were heated in the winter. America was the first place where Father saw African Americans, who were then called Negroes. People in Burma first saw Africans when the British, returning after World War II, brought in a corps of

East Africans to rebuild bridges and roads. The Ugandan dictator Idi Amin claimed to have done duty in Burma then.

I was a graduate student at The American University in Washington in 1956 when Father was a delegate to the Methodist General Conference held in Minneapolis. The Church's Crusade for Christ scholarship program had been adopted at the 1948 General Conference to help young people from countries that had suffered in World War II. I was invited to come to Minneapolis to stand on the stage with other Crusade Scholars, dressed colorfully in native garb, and bring greetings to the Conference. Burmese garb didn't do well in the Minnesota April; I was shivering the whole time. However, on that occasion I was able to spend some time with Father. The last time he attended the General Conference was in 1960 in Denver, but I was back in Burma.

Father had faith that he and Mother would be issued passports to come to America to be with us when their grandchildren were born. Even though the passports were not issued, he held no bitterness, but remained loyal to the authorities. He was a nationalist to the core. His attitude was that you don't rebel against your country's government. You must be loyal to the rulers, and he associated the rulers with the country, which was just what they wanted him to do. He had summed up his attitude explicitly in *Cruising Down the Irrawaddy*:

> As I am a nationalist, it is my deepest concern that we as Christians defend our political independence, our view of life and our security by seriously committing ourselves to the welfare state as enacted by our political leaders. We pledge our lives—all that we are and all that we do—to our Union. In the home, the school, the assembly room, the neighbourhood, we accept its Constitution as the standard by which we try to live. We work for the stability of our Union, no other. We vigorously and with zeal and endeavour support those projects under the Welfare State.

Father was optimistic about the junta, just as before the coup he had been optimistic about U Nu's administration. He was against colonialism, but he could not see that Ne Win and his regime had taken the place of the British colonialists. When you oppress your own people, as Ne Win did, you do it with a vengeance. It would be easy, with hindsight, to rue my father's attitude, but naïve would be too strong a word to describe him. He really believed in his heart that the country was going to make progress. I would say that he was generous toward the junta. He was very upbeat, "The government is doing great things for the country," he would say. He genuinely believed it—until, many years later, he wrote me cryptically, "*Our great power* [italics mine] is clearly out of control." But for many years he was wrong, just as the astrologers had been wrong. So I wondered: Who are the good guys? Well, the good guys were the ones who courageously spoke the truth. But they got shot down.

I had left Burma in 1961, not with the intention of staying away permanently, but because I was denied the chance to put to best use the education and experiences I had acquired abroad to benefit my fledgling country. In the first few years after I came to California, I made active plans to return. When the military regime revoked my citizenship, I was made a man without a country. The unmistakable allegation was, "You deserted your country, you must not return." Father counseled, "Keep calm and get yourself organized. Don't let things or circumstances disintegrate you. God will keep you intact morally and spiritually as our God is great and wonderful." So I was compelled to file a petition for naturalization in 1966.

On 2 January 1965, our daughter, Dewi Sita, was born. My friend George Kyaw Than had a falling out with his brother-in-law, the dictator General Ne Win, and returned to America in 1965. George was issued a green Certificate of Identity. In effect, a "C-of-I" was a one-way travel document to exile. He first went to Minnesota, his wife Nancy's home state, where he had trained in urology at the University of Minnesota Hospital in the mid-1950s, but things failed to work out for him when he returned there this time. So he brought his family to Monterey, where he got a temporary job as a Burmese language instructor at the U.S. Army Language School while he prepared for licensure in California.

George and his family lived with us for a few weeks until I could make a down payment on a small house for them. But shortly after the family moved into that house, the entire Burmese language faculty received notice that the department was to be eliminated. It was 1965—the year Defense Secretary Robert McNamara made huge spending cuts. Suddenly I was out of a job, four years after I had begun. I looked for a job in the Monterey public schools, in vain. So I decided to go back to school to pursue a PhD. Those were good old days in America when financial aid was available for education.

I was admitted to the Graduate School at the University of Southern California in the summer of 1965. I commuted between Monterey and Los Angeles, going to Los Angeles on Sunday afternoon and arriving back in Monterey every Friday morning. Leaving Riri at home with two infants took a heavy toll on us. She needed to hold her job to put food on the table. I always brought back a box of donuts for the family, bought from a specialty shop on Seventh Street near the Los Angeles Greyhound bus terminal.

One night in August, after I got off the city bus and started walking to the campus, I was stopped at a roadblock. "The campus is closed," a National Guardsman told me. "You can't go in there." I told him that my room was at the University Methodist Church on the campus and I had no place else to go. He was understanding and let me through. "Be careful," he said. The next morning when I walked around the campus, which was almost devoid of students, I saw a big tank parked in front of the Student Union. Guardsmen were posing for photographs beneath Tommy Trojan, the university's iconic bronze statue of the mascot. It turned out the Watts riots were going on.

Meanwhile, Indonesia was in the throes of its own turmoil, and that was affecting Riri and me, both personally and in terms of our political commitments. President Sukarno had been a pillar of the Non-Aligned Movement of Third World countries trying to keep the Cold War at arm's length. Prime Ministers U Nu of Burma, Sir John Kotelawala of Ceylon, Jawaharlal Nehru of India, Mohammed Ali of Pakistan, and Ali Sastroamidjojo of Indonesia saw the Cold War as a tug of war between America and the Soviet Union, and they saw the compulsion to align with one or the other as the thin end of a wedge opening the door to what was branded neo-colonialism.

To maintain a non-aligned stance at the height of the Cold War was problematic, to put it mildly. Beginning as early as 1960, both the domestic and the international situation for Indonesia became increasingly tense. Sukarno went so far as to declare war on Malaya in 1963, as a way of diverting attention from his domestic problems. Later, he moved to the left and the Communist Party of Indonesia became an increasingly important factor in the country's stability.

Sukarno declared a national policy called NASAKOM, an acronym standing for coexistence between nationalism and communism. Some generals in the army opposed this policy shift and attempted a coup in which seven generals who supported Sukarno were kidnapped and murdered. Some Indonesian-language students at the U.S. Army Language School were invited to San Francisco by the Indonesian Consul General to meet General Ahmad Yani, who, upon return to Indonesia, ended up being one of the seven murdered.

The failure of the coup left a power vacuum. Suharto, who was a senior general, had sat on the sidelines but now took charge and went so far as to arrest the coup leaders. Sukarno escaped, but the head of the Communist Party, Dipa Nusantara Aidit, was killed.

For a whole year during 1965 and 1966, there were mass killings under the pretext of fighting Communism. Hundreds of thousands of citizens were slaughtered. The conventional figure given was 500,000, but some independent sources claim that as many as a million people might have been killed. (The celebrated documentary *The Act of Killing*, by Joshua Oppenheimer, released in 2012, is a grim reminder of the long shadow those events have cast over Indonesian society.) An atmosphere of confusion and intimidation pervaded Indonesian society. Most of the killings took place in central and east Java and on Bali. There were also some killings in Alor and Sumatra.

Some believed that Bali was targeted because Sukarno's mother was Balinese. Australia, Britain, and the United States all supported Suharto's anti-Communist purge, and the U.S. embassy in Jakarta even gave the Suharto regime a list it had compiled of the names of 5,000 Indonesians suspected of being Communists.

Joshua Oppenheimer, maker of *The Act of Killing*, has completed filming a sequel, called *The Look of Silence*, which was released in 2014. Surviving next-of-kin of those massacred were interviewed and their stories told in the documentary. Its impetus is to force the United States government to make public its involvement in the Indonesian military's genocide of its own people, in the name of defeating Communism in that island nation.

The brutality and callousness of the Indonesian military's actions during this period reinforced Riri's and my conviction that military rule anywhere is dangerous, regardless of the pretext, and strengthened our resolve to stand against it. Still, even though Indonesia was under a dictatorship, its citizens were not restricted from traveling abroad. Because I could not go to Burma and my parents couldn't leave the country, I would ask friends from America, England, India, and Malaya to go there and look in on them.

My parents missed us very much. Needless to say, the feeling was mutual. In those days, to make a telephone call to Rangoon was a challenge. Land lines did not always work. Satellites were not yet in use. The only way we could really stay in touch was by letter and word of mouth. Letters sometimes didn't get delivered. Mailing letters in Burma was also a challenge: You had to push and shove to reach the counter at the post office, and the clerk was often not at work.

Father was a prolific letter writer. I have saved most of his letters, and I cherish them as reminders of his personality and of his love. "We think of you all in our thoughts—life and prayers, particularly of Zali and the other one yet unborn," he wrote on 19 August 1964. "Riri, you have our prayers and best wishes. Wherever you are, stick to God and of His Christ and of the presence of the Holy Ghost. . . . Teach Zali about his God and let him have the knowledge of God from his youth so that he may grow from strength to strength to stem the tide of this world and come out victorious."

We always spoke in Burmese at home, but he always wrote his letters in English. He also spoke Hindustani. He wrote using a fountain pen; the brand name of the ink popular at the time was Quink. Mother was also a prolific letter writer, and she also wrote in English, but she would save postage by writing between the lines and in the margins of Father's letters, like this one on 28 August 1961:

> I left Twante to see Bishop Francis Ah Mya consecrated as the first national [Anglican] Bishop of Burma. The Cathedral was packed, the service lasted two hours. It was indeed very impressive and solemn. Last Sunday we three paid a visit to the Djokos [the Indonesian family of Djoko Sanjoto, whom I had befriended in Washington in 1955]. He is now the acting Ambassador of Indonesia.

"We were at Thongwa District Conference," she told us on 22 October 1962. "We went to visit the grave of Charles before we came back. All the memories of the past came back." Charles was my parents' fourth child, who was born in 1926 but lived only a year and ten months. Then, on 5 May 1964, my mother wrote, "You all are very near to me in my dreams, but when I woke up you are far away. Let us hope that the regulation is relaxed. Then we can visit with Zali & all."

There came a time when you could buy only one air letter (aerogramme) at a time at the post office in Rangoon—and if you wrote a letter and mailed it in an envelope, it would probably be censored. Father wrote his letters to reassure us that the family was fine, and to keep us abreast of events among family and friends in Burma. He and Mother both wrote affectionately in every letter about Zali and Dewi for years before they actually met them.

He never wrote about particular official policies—those were taboo—but he often praised the Ne Win regime in general terms, nearly to the point of almost being an apologist for it. For example, on 14 September 1967, he wrote, "Our Govt. is not to blame as we have two great powers—China on one side and U.S. on the other." If he was concerned about the political upheaval in Burma, he would not allow it to bother us. He continued:

> Some of our people went to both sides—Maoism—and so-called capitalist power. The one from China in collaboration played havoc with us recently and the other in cahoots with CIA is like a lion crouching to jump on us in case the other starts the showdown. So we find ourselves between the two. Such is the fate of a small country like ours. So we have to be very cautious of people who come and go—that is the reason we have to be very alert and vigilant.

I am convinced that Father truly believed the things that he wrote about the regime. As a preacher of the Word of God, he respected words in general and would not abuse them. But it is also true that, even if he had wanted to write critically about the regime, he could not. He knew that the censors would read what he wrote, and this intimidated him. He had not been afraid of the British, but during the war he had been afraid of the Japanese, and with good reason. His sermons were powerfully piercing, and the possibility was all too real that the Japanese might arrest or even behead him. He composed and delivered his sermons with care, always couching his words thoughtfully and reverting to Scripture, and he also was adept at drawing parallels from Buddhist teachings and vocabulary.

Similarly, he now had reason to fear the Ne Win regime. He knew that crossing the regime would be risky. He had not feared the British because he knew they would not imprison him for his anti-colonial sermons and activities, and he probably also sensed, correctly, that the British colonialists' days were numbered. The Ne Win regime, on the other hand, was in its ascendancy . . . and it was of our own. This meant that, unlike the British and the Japanese, it had no other homeland to go back to.

As a Burmese regime, it also complicated the emotional dimension of Father's patriotic loyalties. He did not see the military as a new colonial power. My own views were and remained completely the opposite of his, but I rarely confronted him. It hurts me to reflect on how a dictator can cause so much physical and emotional pain within a family. But regardless of the political situation, my parents always thought of us first.

I don't think, though, that Father was afraid of the regime. He was defiant, but he did not want to lock horns with it. He preached stridently against power, injustice, and corruption. He was a student of the Roman and British Empires. "He's off preaching his colonial business again," Mother would say ruefully. But there is another important thing to understand about Father's sermons and letters: He always looked for the positive side of any situation. He did not talk about the dark sides. I learned the meanings of the words *vice* and *virtue* from him. He said that every nation has its vices and its virtues, and he would rather dwell on the virtues.

"So far things move quite passably and are looking up in the direction of the peasants and farmers who constitute the bulk of the population." And again, on 26 September 1963, "It is very likely that [the] majority of the members of the Conference desire me to represent Burma at the General Conference. But we cannot predict the outcome. Your Mum is very lonely having all of her [loved] ones away from home. She is always yearning after you." But on 14 April 1964 he wrote, "No national is allowed to attend the

General Conference, but Doctor Manton, who is a foreigner, might be allowed to come away." Eight days later, on 22 April, he remained upbeat:

> Our Revolutionary Council is forging ahead in the right direction. In order to eliminate the semblances of colonial aftermath effects and to outbid Communism, this is the only course to fall back on. Some people feel hurt as they can't exploit the country as they please.

Throughout everything, he remained unstintingly optimistic about the likelihood that our family would be allowed to visit each other. In an undated letter in 1964, he told us:

> We are planning to come out next year—say after the school term, i.e., April or May 1965. By that time things will relax. . . . I am interested in animal husbandry on co-operative basis. So my next move is in that direction and Govt. is quite pleased with that scheme of my idea.

And, as in his letter of 5 May 1964, he always reiterated his belief that infernal external powers were thwarting the regime's nationalistic agenda:

> Burma is not isolating herself, but very unfortunately, foreigners have come to exploit her through their conquest. At the present moment we cannot afford to entertain foreigners who are out here to bleach us from time immemorial.

By the time of my father's next letter, two momentous events had occurred: Jawaharlal Nehru, the founding Prime Minister of independent India and a colossus of postcolonial world leadership, had died, and Riri had conceived our second child. "Thank you very, very much for the picture booklet entitled *The Torch is Passed*," he wrote on 28 May 1964. (The booklet was about the succession to the presidency of Lyndon Johnson after the assassination of John Kennedy.) Three days later he followed with:

> We closed all the village schools. Our so-called Christians are using the institutes as stepping stones to feather their nests. Now in the affairs of the Church, after we get our autonomy, we will weed out all misguided help to safeguard against pauperization.

SCHOOLS NATIONALIZED

Nationalization of schools portended a momentous harbinger of Burma's self-inflicted long-term isolation as a matter of national policy. Various

Christian denominations—the Anglicans, Baptists, Catholics, Methodists, Salvation Army, and Seventh-Day Adventists—operated schools, hospitals, and other social institutions all over Burma. I myself am a product of Catholic and Methodist schools. The Anglicans operated leprosaria in Mandalay and Moulmein, the only two in the country. The Little Sisters of the Poor, an Italian Catholic Order, operated an old people's home in Rangoon. My alma mater, St. Paul's High School, was the premier school run by the Brothers of Christian Schools. Although the Brothers no longer do it today, in 2014 alumni celebrated the 150th anniversary of its founding.

The best of the church-run schools, including St. Paul's, used English as their medium of instruction. There was one high school in Rangoon that taught in Burmese: the Myoma National Boys' High School on Godwin (now Lanmadaw) Road. Its headmaster, U Ba Lwin, was a friend of Father's who wrote the foreword to his book, *China as a Burman Saw It*. Its founders felt the need to preserve the traditional Burmese way of life and wanted to inculcate it in future generations of young men. They resented the fact that students taught in English at the church-run schools enjoyed special privileges and advantages in the colonial administration. There also were Muslim *madrasas* and other Indian schools like the Gujerati High School. The Chinese community had its own schools.

Buddhist monasteries taught boys—only boys—to read and write Burmese, so they could recite the Buddhist scriptures. Also, the colonial government ran municipal schools, whose medium of instruction was Burmese. In short, education in Burma was a multifaceted mixture.

Ne Win changed all that. After coming to power in the 1962 coup, he declared that all private schools, including foreign-run institutions, were to be nationalized. All foreign missionaries, including teachers, were required to leave the country. The change addressed the feelings of Burmese nationalists, including Father, who felt that foreign influence in Burma was excessive and that some of the schools were exploitative because their graduates enjoyed preferential consideration for jobs and in business, as well as higher social status. But the bottom line was that Ne Win wanted to control every aspect of national life. The intelligentsia also threatened him. If people were too smart or well informed, he wouldn't be able to boss them around.

Ne Win's obsession with control explains why he did not stop at schools, but also nationalized foreign-run hospitals and all businesses, including retail shops. In theory, even the little betel-nut stand around the corner did not escape his megalomania. He could not really control everything completely, but officially he did. The regime retained some of the teachers of the private schools it had nationalized, but overall it staffed the schools with teachers of its own choosing. The inevitable consequence was that the quality of education suffered. And as if that weren't bad enough, Ne Win actually banned the teaching of English.

Nationalization of the faith-based schools also meant that they lost financial support from abroad. "Now we are about to attain our autonomy and we assume the entire financial responsibility," Father wrote on 23 September 1964. "With $ from U.S. base make our people the spoiled children of the bountiful missionary enterprise." St. Gabriel's, an Anglican school in Rangoon, was commandeered by the army and turned into the War Office (Defense Ministry). When the regime abruptly moved the national capital to Naypyidaw in 2005, they no longer needed the buildings for the War Office, but they have not given them back to the church.

Kingswood School in Kalaw, where Riri and I taught, suffered a similar fate. The army turned it first into a hospital, then into quarters for officers at the Staff College. When I visited Kalaw in 2003 and walked onto the school grounds, a man came out and challenged me, "What is your business?" I disarmed him by saying, "I have no business here; I come from far away." A lieutenant colonel who overheard our exchange came out. I told him I had been a teacher at Kingswood in 1959. "Oh, Uncle!" he exclaimed. "I wasn't even born then!"

It was on that trip, when I worshiped at Rangoon's Anglican Cathedral of the Holy Trinity with Archbishop Andrew Mya Han, that I suggested suing the junta for return of St. Gabriel's and other Anglican schools. His response was quick, "We don't need to sue them. They told us sarcastically, 'tear down your schools; haul the bricks away one by one, but the land is ours.'"

After the regime nationalized the private schools, Father wrote to say:

> All of our schools with the exception of some primary ones have been nationalized. To me, it is all to the good. Our Govt assumes the responsibility of employing all qualified teachers. There are 887 private schools in Burma. All the high schools, middle schools run by the different denominations, namely R.C. [Roman Catholic], Anglican, Baptist throughout Burma have been taken over by the Govt. I feel that our Govt is doing the right thing for reasons best known to me.

The military regime's xenophobia was directed not only at Westerners, but against all groups whose presence had made Burma a cosmopolitan society. "After we got the Indians and Chinese out of the country, then they will ease up the regulations," Father assured me on 24 July 1964:

> Our R.C. [Revolutionary Council] Govt hated the foreigners. We will not blame the Indians & Chinese as they are the victims

of colonial regime. They have had their heydays . . . under their colonial scheme. Ours is socialism and there is a world of difference between Socialism and Communism as there is that of so-called Capitalism and Socialism of the present day. U Thant is coming tomorrow . . . will stay 3 days only. Thakin Kodaw Hmaing the writer and politician is dead. The R.C. Govt is doing as best it could cutting down the prices of all commodities, launching industrialization and giving aid to the peasants to boost up their earning. RC is giving us back the demonetized value of our money. 200,000 foreigners—mostly Indians & Chinese are getting away from the shores of Burma everyday. Even then it will take a year to clear them out of Burma, all to the good.

BURMESE WAY TO SOCIALISM

The regime dubbed its ideology the Burmese Way to Socialism. "Since our Govt is busy repatriating the foreigners, it will not be possible to get passports this year," Father wrote on 23 September 1964. "When things relax, we will seize the opportunity. You may have read the 'Burmese Way to Socialism' in The Guardian, slightly different from both right and left wings." If he was beginning to perceive the injustices of the military regime, he denied or suppressed it. To him, it was inconceivable that a Burmese regime would oppress its own people. On 6 November 1964, he wrote: "Congratulations to the American people on having Johnson as their President. Our Government under the caption of Burmese Way to Socialism is improving the lot of the peasants and affecting the wealthiest group very much. In a way I deeply appreciate it."

Still optimistic of the national course, on 12 May 1965 he wrote:

> The Govt reappointed your mum to head the school and entire staff as a No.1 State Middle School in Twante. Amidst changes so meteoric and dynamic we live with our risen Christ to survive and outlive. . . . Above all, there is a place eternal where we shall be free from the dust of this mundane world.

Around this point his intense desire to be with us in the United States became more urgent. Sometime in 1965, after Dewi Sita's birth, he wrote:

> Well, we miss our dear grandchildren who are blood of our blood and bone of our bones. The other day we had a grand time with your student friend [USAF Col. Fred Haupt, defense

attaché at the US embassy, along with his wife, Alice] who are very good to us. They have our message to you on tape recorder which you will get in due time. Our Govt is too benign, and the people in its administration are incompetent and most corrupt. Well, this will pass away soon. Let the compulsion of circumstances toughen your caliber.

When my parents began applying for passports, the military regime began investigating them. Apparently the regime saw a connection to my work in America. "Somebody from Foreign Office made enquiry of your time of departure from Burma," Father informed me in a letter of 18 August 1965. He continued:

As you know I love the Church in the name of Christ, my country and the people in it, particularly the farmers. . . . By the way we have heard of the riots in the suburb of Los Angeles—toll of death—26—over 200 injured. It is bad that such a crisis should have occurred in U.S.A. Keep yourself out of it.

He became increasingly involved in working within Burma's Christian community, which was now completely in the hands of Burmese nationals. On 1 April 1966 he told us:

Tomorrow your Mum, your sister and I are sailing up country as far as the town on the shore of the Irrawaddy and then we will strike across to another town called Thayetmyo where your mum taught school after she graduated from the teacher training school. We are going to treasure the place—i.e., 50 years ago (1916). By the way, all foreign missionaries numbering 500 of all denominations, namely, Roman Catholic, Baptist, Methodist, Anglican, Seventh Day Adventist, are asked to leave the country by the end of May. To us it is a blessing in disguise. Now is the time to get rid of opportunists and rice Christians. Yes we are able to carry on the work of the Church even without the financial aid from the Board. Our Govt will eventually cut out the aid from foreign sources as it pauperizes and demoralizes the people.

On 8 August 1966 he wrote:

As time passes on, the sense of separation between you folk there and us grows tenser and tenser and our faith in immortality as exhibited by our Lord Jesus becomes a reality. Congratulations to you all on your acquisition of U.S. citizenship. It is a great country and a land of varieties surcharged with issues of problems of

all kinds. I would urge you all to be loyal to the country to which
you belong and to acquit like man. Our country where you were
born and brought up is still in the shape of things to come. The
era of Western rule over the Near and Far East that had begun
under Alexander the Great is drawing to its end. As of today, the
peoples of Africa and Asia regard Christianity as the religion of
the West and its mission as forces—but however our Lord is not
a dead God but He rose and lives eternally. So we live with Him.
With Him in our front line, background, sides right and left,
up in the outer space and down to earth—we can be more than
conquerors, I assure you.

He tried to separate political upheaval from Christian love, as in his
letter of 10 August 1966: "Recently I was up in Kalaw and Mandalay for two
weeks and while in Kalaw I had a visit with Smith Dun who asked me to
remember them to you and met some teachers who made enquiries of you
and your home. As far as we are free from politics, we are OK."

Although he was a devout Christian, and despite the ostracism he had
suffered following his conversion, Father always remained close to his Buddhist family. On 31 August 1966, he wrote to tell us of the death of his eldest
brother:

Your *Bagyi* U Nyunt passed away [*Bagyi*, literally "Big Father,"
the eldest brother of one's father]. I am the only one surviving
the family tree. God blessed him and take him in His Heavenly
abode not to suffer and not to have physical attachment. . . . I
was up in Mandalay en route to Rgn [Rangoon]. I received the
telegram, but I could not get down to attend the funeral. Your
Mum and Akyi-lone attended. . . . Just the other day fed some
phongyis [monks] in memory of their father. I do appreciate
your way of sympathy and condolence in that direction. [I had
funded the feeding of the monks and guests.]

Not to be outdone, Mother followed all the letters between my father
and us. To make use of all the space on the pages of my father's letters, and to
save postage, she wrote in tiny script. "When I saw Djoko's mother & aunt,
I got an idea that your mother will be like them—not so big and bulky," she
told Riri on 28 August 1966.

Mrs. Djoko asked me if I would like to go to Indonesia free
of charge—by rice freighter.. . . I will visit my loved ones first.
ACho's pupil [Col. Fred Haupt] served us sausage buns, beans,
hot dogs.—My, how it reminded me of my foreign trips. Please

tell Zali that we want to see all of them before we die. I dreamt of the children many times. Well Riri, take care of your health.

Mother often complained about my father's activities and worried about his whereabouts. She would have preferred that he stay home and relax. She felt that his preaching was sometimes unhelpfully excessive, and she expressed that sentiment on 2 September 1966:

> Your Pa returned from Rgn yesterday P.M. though he said that he would return on Wednesday night after the usual midweek prayer meeting, due to the reappearance of his cherished gout. When that happened or attacked, he could scarcely walk even to the toilet in our hideout (hermitage) at Creek Street, only after 8 doses of Simon's medicine relieved him of the pain etc. He went to Konewetchaung, inviting the Christian people, then *lei-pan* [written in Burmese, meaning 'hot air']. Bible class, more of Colonialism business, gave a meat lunch saying that he does *hpa-yah a-loke* [God's work].

All throughout the 1960s, Ne Win was riding high. In truth, he had been riding high ever since 1 April 1949, when he ousted General Smith Dun and appointed himself commander in chief of the army. In the 1950s, until the first coup that was not a coup in 1958, Ne Win worked to make the army unaccountable to civilians. And because of the sheer firepower that he commanded, civilians became subservient to the army. The country was an instrumentality of the army, rather than vice versa. This was made official in August 1958, when U Nu "invited" Ne Win to take over the administration of the government. And the point was brought home with full force on 2 March 1962, by the coup that really was a coup.

Much of the problem, as in other military-ruled countries, was the sheer brute supremacy of the army as an institution. But in Burma this was made worse by the malevolent personal character of General Ne Win himself. At the same time, the divisiveness and unrealistic ambitions of the ethnic minorities gave him an excuse to enforce the unity of the army and to crack down on everyone else. Meanwhile, Burman civil society in the country's heartland was feckless and demoralized. There were too many chiefs and not enough Indians: no unity of purpose and no credible, authoritative leadership among civilians.

Burma's first and last credible leader, who might have been able to pull the country together, was Aung San, and he was only 32 years old when he was assassinated. The only unity in Burma was found in the military, and that unity was enforced at both ends of a loaded gun. Military discipline was harshly enforced from above, and the soldiers themselves were unhappy.

The only people in Burma who were happy were the senior officer corps and their ilk.

Ne Win was a ruthless ruler, a womanizing tyrant. He was a walking illustration of the truth of Lord Acton's maxim that "absolute power corrupts absolutely"—and he exercised his absolute power to satiate his own whims and appetites. His extracurricular activities made Henry VIII's look like a Sunday school picnic. In 1955, he had invited a secretary at the British embassy to play tennis. He asked her to stay over at his house, and his wife, Katy, asked the young guest to leave her room door slightly ajar, to allow the mighty general to pay her a nocturnal call. While the record does not show what actually happened, opprobrium and British rectitude hushed up the incident and, discretion being the better part of valor, the embassy probably shipped the mighty general's would-be sweet morsel of the night out of the country soon after.

The general once fancied a Union of Burma Airways stewardess of pulchritude. He ordered a staff officer to procure her. A senior officer had to beg off, pleading that she was one with family.

Once in Maymyo he believed that a young member of the wealthy family that made Tiger Balm was involved with Katy. One version of that story claims that Ne Win himself attacked the man with a golf club; another says he only punched him once and then ordered his bodyguards to finish the job. Writing under a pseudonym in *The Burma Bulletin*, the late Edward Law-Yone quipped that "it would take many jars of Tiger Balm to heal Ne Win's hapless golf-course victim." Ne Win also punched a hole in the drum of a band that was annoying him by playing too loudly at a 1976 New Year's party. I happened to be in Bangkok when the incident was reported in big bold headline of the *Bangkok Post*. Another time, he even kicked a cocky young American diplomat in the derriere because he was blocking Ne Win's car at Inya Lake Hotel.

Then there was the Italian call girl who taught Ne Win a lesson about foreigners that he never forgot. Actually, the story began in 1948, as Law-Yone, writing under the pseudonym Ngway Yoe, told it in the January 1975 issue of *The Burma Bulletin*:

> The Italians offered a secret arms factory at short notice. Ne Win, a political general, knew nothing about guns, but he was a connoisseur of the female form divine, and when a beauteous female called Corice de Sevigny was put out as bait on a yacht in the Mediterranean, Ne Win took it, hook, line and sinker. In due course a covey of Italians arrived in Rangoon. . .and a heap of war surplus materiel was shipped to Burma. For years the

factory produced nothing. New machinery had to be ordered because the parts imported were worn with use in World War II. But no matter, General Ne Win was awaiting his consort, the raving beauty Corice de Sevigny. Corice was of the blue blood of France, no doubt a cousin of the Count of Paris. She was at least a Countess; more probably—although she herself did not claim it—a Princess!

A thousand years ago, King Anawrahta of Pagan fell for a beautiful princess called Thambula. The King was busy with affairs of state, so he deputed a trusted aide, Kyansittha, to fetch his affianced bride. Kyansittha deputed for the King in more ways than was proper, which so enraged the King that he hurled a lance at the special envoy.

This vignette of history repeated itself when Ne Win deputed Bo Set Kya to bring "Mademoiselle" to Burma. In the beginning Bo Set Kya covered his tracks well. His friendship with General Ne Win did not break up for several months, but truth, like murder, will out. When the falling out did take place, it was bitter and final. Bo Set Kya lost all his perquisites and was driven into exile, to die in penury in Bangkok. But of course the Princess did arrive and was put up in a special suite at the Strand Hotel. The manager of this excellent establishment was an Armenian, Pete Aratoon. Pete, a pugnacious businessman, was a deacon of the Armenian Church. He would have no prostitution, even high-class prostitution, in his hotel.

Another foreigner-owned estate, named after Sir John Darwood, was quickly acquired for the Princess' stay. Ne Win strung out barbed wire and posted sentries against intruders. Then he settled back for the long-awaited honeymoon. The idyll, sad to relate, did not last for any length of time. U Nu, the bead-counting Buddhist premier, must have got wind of the affair because, suddenly, the Princess was wending her way back to Rome. The army assured her with large sums of money that the separation from her precious general would be temporary. Just a few details needing tidying up before she would return in triumph, this time as wife rather than mistress.

Ne Win was inconsolable. He did not cancel any appointments because he never has any appointments to keep, but he threw tantrums and books and files at subordinates. He was eaten with longing for the departed Princess and the deepest resentment for the hypocritical politicians who had caused the estrangement. Let those confounded politicians fight the rebels with their levees and *sitwundans* (volunteers)!

It must have been a frustrating time for the colonels who were under constant pressure to get the ban against the Princess' return lifted. Then, on a dank and dismal day, a colonel appeared unbidden at Ne Win's side. He produced a copy of an Italian newspaper, which he left for Ne Win to read, saluted, turned on his heel and left.

Ne Win did not have to know Italian. Under bold headings was the lead story of a banker who had "flogged" some funds and, after a glorious weekend at the beach, blown his brains out. The "babe" he had taken for his last fling was named Maria Minelli, but the blown-up picture accompanying the article showed her to be unmistakably Corice de Sevigny!

Thenceforth, in General Ne Win's simple hurt mind, all foreigners were cheats, deceivers, and liars, their women unspeakably vile. How wrong, how misguided (off with Set Kya's ugly head!) he had been. He would take unto himself a Burmese woman of pulchritude (that he already had a wife of many years' standing seemed to have bothered him not at all); he would show the world. And that was how Katy Ne Win (that was to be) got him on the rebound. But that, as Kipling would have said, is another story.

Ne Win was an angry, violent man with a short fuse. Because he could not exorcise the demons within, he externalized his anger at those he could. He traveled to Vienna frequently to consult a psychiatrist. A trusted Indian cook was taken along on his travels to prepare his meals. He was paranoid about being poisoned in the food he ate.

A friend of mine who was in the Burmese diplomatic service once told me of an incident that would have resulted in disastrous consequences had it been executed. A Pan American World Airways plane made a routine stop at Rangoon's Mingaladon Airport on its round the world route. The Boeing 707 made such a deafening roar at take off, audible from Ne Win's home, that he wanted it shot down. Fortunately, thinking heads at the Foreign Office prevailed and averted a catastrophe.

An entire battalion of the Burma Army was at General Ne Win's disposal to keep him secure. He was deathly afraid of perceived attempts on his life. Once, to quash such an eventuality, rumored or forecast by astrologers, he looked in a mirror and shot the image he saw there. *Yadaya chay* is a belief held by many superstitious Burmans that a foretold calamity can be quashed if the act is executed symbolically, like shooting at an image or representation of one's self.

He followed his soothsayers' advice to steer the ship of state to the right to avoid peril by decreeing all vehicular traffic in the land to move from the left to the right lane. He also demonetized the currency to denominations divisible by 9, his lucky number. Thus, those holding 50 and 100 *kyat* notes lost fortunes when 45 and 90 *kyat* notes replaced them, without compensation, even though this was allegedly done to bankrupt the "insurgents."

In 1966, at the invitation of President Lyndon Johnson, Ne Win visited America. Burma hands at the State Department and Pentagon were courting him. The Vietnam War was heating up, and the United States was looking for allies in Southeast Asia—or at least it wanted to quash any ambitions that Ne Win might have had to go to the "Red" side. "Our Revolutionary Council Chairman *Bogyoke* [General] Ne Win made a great impression on the U.S.," Father informed me on 15 September 1966.

Simon, my surgeon brother, was married to a woman named Ann, and they had a daughter named Mary Jane. The two women stayed in Burma for a year and returned to America in 1960. Simon himself followed them in 1963. My parents doted on Mary Jane and were delighted when she and Ann came to visit on a 24-hour visa. Mary Jane was so cute. She gathered biscuits, soap, and toothpaste on the plane to give to her grandparents. "Mary Jane played her role like a girl in wonderland," Father wrote. "After we met them in the rough and tumble we find life worth living and dying. The scene at the airport just on the eve of their departure was a heart rending spectacle which drew tears from all those at the aerodrome."

Through it all, Mother's longing for us intensified, as she felt her remaining days getting shorter. On 23 January 1967 she wrote, "We are thinking of you folks over there very often—Praying for you and longing to see you before we die."

In 1968, I was offered a tenure-track job as a counselor and psychology instructor at Orange Coast College in Costa Mesa, California. Orange Coast College did not have a foreign student advisor at the time, so I was asked if I would take on that role as part of my load, and I agreed. For a short period I was also asked to coach the soccer team. I had completed the course work for the PhD in counselor education at USC, but I still had to pass the qualifying exams and write a dissertation. With lots of pushing from Riri, I finally got the dissertation done in time to graduate in June 1971.

I had many opportunities at Orange Coast College to get to know students from many countries. Like many campuses around the country, OCC was in turmoil in those days because of protests against the war in Vietnam. One morning, some antiwar students tried to take down the American flag from the quad flagpole. The dean of students, Joe Kroll, came out of his office and stood his ground. "You can't do that," he told them. There was a shouting match. I had to give Joe credit for his courage, as I went and stood by him near the flagpole. Joe was not going to let troublemakers mess around with him. There were goofy fashions among the students, like girls wearing bikini bottoms over their black leotards. And streaking! One time a young man disrobed himself right outside my office window before he sprinted off across the quad in the rain.

Riri earned a second master's degree, as well as a PhD in Government, in 1968, from Claremont Graduate School (now University) and began applying to teach at various community colleges. Most told her she lacked experience. She eventually was hired at Golden West College in Huntington Beach. Even though her specialty was International Affairs, her main assignment was to teach American Government and American History. As a foreign-born person, her strength was in providing an international perspective on those subjects.

Orange County, where we lived, was well known as a bastion of conservative views, and there were rumblings on the Golden West campus about Riri's political leanings. One student even wrote a letter to the *Orange County Register* calling her a "pinko liberal." The college president called her into her office and urged her not to engage with the newspaper, because he said she wouldn't win. Riri was an active member of the American Federation of Teachers, though, and enjoyed the union's protection.

Some students became close to us and remained friends, including Martin Yan, who became known for the syndicated *Yan Can Cook* series on TV. Riri received several awards from the Student Government and was awarded a Fulbright Scholarship to India in 1987.

There was no telephone communication into Burma, and letters from home touched us deeply. On 20 July 1968, Father wrote to us longingly after receiving photographs we had sent:

> Dewi is such a cute girl whom I like to hug and kiss to my heart's desire. Zali is also very lovely and cute and also intelligent. One day we will be with you all and play together, sing together and talk, talk, kiss, kiss and carry on my back. Riri—congratulations! How we wish we could be with you all and share the joy on that day together [her graduation from Claremont Graduate School]. We never forget you all and pray for you all in our nightly family group. I am in Rgn most of the time looking after the Church. We are tackling with our Govt to get across to your sector.

In the 1960s, the Vietnam War was raging. Every day the newspapers were full of accounts of violence, and casualties were heavy on both sides.

Most Asian nations were glad that they were not involved in the Vietnam War. This sentiment was widespread in Burma, even as Burma's military regime was wreaking havoc with the economy and with domestic politics.

On 4 April 1969 Father wrote:

> Regarding our passports, our chances are very slim this year, as the directive from the R.C. [Revolutionary Council] is rather adamant. Your Akogyi [eldest brother] called on the highest one [at the passport office] and he advises us to put in an appeal because of our age and of our fundamental desire to see our grandchildren before we pass out from this scene of mundane world of ours. [The] RC might consider it favorably.

Acquiring passports required not only paperwork but also interrogation by the military regime. On 1 May he updated us:

> We are still tackling the [passport] problem with our might and main. As time is on our side let us be patient for a while. In the meantime, don't you be confused and get excited. Just finish your dissertation and get your PhD. We do remember you all in our prayers. Under separate mail, we will send you our pictures taken on the 50th anniversary of our wedding.

On 20 July 1969, Apollo 11 landed on the moon. After it splashed down four days later, President Richard Nixon enthused that this was the greatest week in the history of the world since Creation. Father was also impressed, but less so. "Yes, moon-landing is perhaps the greatest among man's feats as man did an erstwhile impossible thing," he wrote to us on 23 July:

> He strives to become a superman, but hardly realizes that he is fast becoming a robot. With his computerized knowledge he has the key to the mysteries of the universe, but his knowledge of his self is poor. However no one can deny this human feat of moon-landing as the greatest achievement. Far greater would be the human achievement of leaving the moon to itself and making peace and understanding prevail on the planet earth if only man had the heart for it.

His outlook on technological progress had not changed in the thirty years since he wrote in *China as a Burman Saw It*:

> The trouble with our rapidly developing civilization has been that while scientific discoveries and mechanical inventions and the fast progress of communications have made the world into a neighbourhood and produced a surface unity in external and material things, the mental, moral and spiritual discords are

hampering the building up of a world consciousness and community of spirit.

U NU COMES TO CALIFORNIA

On 27 August 1969 U Nu, the elected Prime Minister of Burma who was ousted in the 1962 coup, gave a press conference in London, announcing that he was launching a movement against Ne Win. That boosted the morale of the expatriates a bit. U Nu had come out of Burma under the pretense of going on a religious pilgrimage to India. Once outside the country, he changed his stance. He chose to give his press conference in London because, subconsciously, he had hoped that the British would help him, or at least withhold aid from the military regime while he raised an army to overthrow the military junta. The treaty that granted Burma independence was called the Nu-Attlee Treaty of 1947. It had started as the Aung San-Attlee Treaty, but after Aung San's assassination, U Nu had seen it through.

Although his time in office from independence in 1948 until the 1962 coup had been undistinguished and ultimately a failure, some expatriates held out hope that his effort now would make a difference, or at least that his return to power might prove the lesser of two evils. Others were skeptical, pointing out that it had been because of his failure that the military had taken over in the first place. For my part, I thought that he might offer an alternative, but only if a large number of people joined him. I would have gone with anybody who stood against the military, but few did.

U Nu used a radio station from the Thailand-Burma border for a while, and he even minted his own currency. I inquired for him about how to issue postage stamps by writing to the Universal Postal Union asking for recognition. They answered me in French. U Nu's Elected Government of the Union of Burma, whose capital was at Taung-Gyi-Ko-Lone on Burmese soil in the jungle across the border from Thailand, issued tiny 22-carat gold coins to use as legal tender once its troops entered Burma. I was appointed the elected government's honorary consul at-large and was issued an impressive but unusable diplomatic passport.

Gold tokens issued by U Nu's government.

In the fall of 1969, U Nu came to California. He was accompanied by his aide, Captain Moe Gyaw, a former Burma Army officer, and Edward Law-Yone, the exiled former editor of the independent newspaper *The Nation*. They were put up at the posh Balboa Bay Club in Newport Beach by a woman named Nadine Henley, who had a business relationship with Hughes Tool Company. Supposedly, the billionaire Howard Hughes was interested in helping U Nu's movement overthrow Burma's military regime, with an eye to some mining and oil ventures. There was some private chatter about a $2 million contribution to U Nu's movement from Howard Hughes. While in Orange County, U Nu was received by a gathering of Burmese expatriates in a warehouse in Long Beach arranged by Dr. Ohn Tin, a Burmese businessman of Chinese descent. "Hold your donations for the moment," U Nu told the group. "I will ask when the time comes."

During the few days U Nu was in Orange County, some expatriates took him sightseeing. I brought him to Orange Coast College and showed him the campus. He particularly liked the bookstore, where he selected a couple of books, including a science fiction by Françoise Sagan. I drove him and Edward Law-Yone to a home in Santa Monica where they were received by the actor Sam Jaffe and his nephew by the same name. The junior Sam Jaffe had recently returned from Cambodia, where he was reporting for the ABC television network. The senior Sam Jaffe prepared tea for the guests. "I make one heck of a tea," he said. I had no idea who he was. He told me, "In the movie *Gunga Din*, I was the skinny one who blew the bugle from atop a hill." U Nu had come to see the junior Sam Jaffe to facilitate his movement in Cambodia, and probably to get some publicity.

On their final day at the Balboa Bay Club, Edward Law-Yone pulled me aside and whispered into my ear, "Can you take the old man home and put him up tonight? Lou Walinsky is arriving from Washington this evening to see him. They leave for Los Angeles airport in the morning." Walinsky was an economist the U Nu government had hired as a consultant in the 1950s. I sensed that U Law Yone was looking for a way to shield Lou Walinsky and U Nu from Nadine Henley and a mysterious man named Ahmad Kamal.

"Sure," I said. How could I refuse? I called Riri immediately. "The old man and his aide are coming home with me," I told her.

"Wow, how did you pull that one?" She snapped back.

"Never mind," I said, "just fix dinner."

Our home at 1661 Labrador Drive in Costa Mesa was a modest one. It had a master bedroom plus three smaller bedrooms and a second bathroom. Riri and I used one of the bedrooms as our shared study. We had only recently purchased the house, and when the guests arrived we had just settled in. While U Nu and Walinsky were engaged in deep conversation in the living room, Moe Gyaw and I prepared three rooms for the guests. The children moved in with Riri and me. Our joint study was turned into Moe Gyaw's bedroom, while U Nu and Lou Walinsky were each given one of the children's rooms.

Riri was busy in the kitchen, cooking an impromptu dinner. After dinner, Moe Gyaw meditated in his room before retiring for the night, while U Nu and Lou Walinsky continued their private conversation in the living room while I tidied up the kitchen and dining room.

In the morning, after the guests had finished breakfast, a black limousine pulled up in front of our house, followed by two cars. Out came Edward Law-Yone and another Burmese gentleman. Ahmad Kamal and Nadine Henley were in the third car. After an exchange of pleasantries at the front door, U Nu, Edward Law-Yone, and Lou Walinsky piled into the limousine and left for the airport, followed by Nadine Henley and Ahmad Kamal in a second car.

We had decided that in the summer of 1970, when Zali was seven and Dewi five, we would take a round-the-world trip and present them to both their paternal grandparents in Burma and the maternal grandmother in Indonesia. Life takes many twists and turns, and politics can separate a family for a lifetime. So it was with my brother Irwin. "It kept me awake to hear that you are coming to see us," Mother wrote on 17 February 1970. "Irwin would like to come too."

Her letter was full of anguish, which she did not adequately express. "I know the 24 hrs [transit visa] is too short for a visit after all these years. Haven't seen Irwin since 1953—17 yrs!!" she continued. "I don't want anything for my birthday but I want to be with my children. You never know how much I miss you all. I need Simon these days for health reasons."

Five days later, this letter followed:

> I dreamt of Acho [me] and a small child etc. before we heard of Zali's tonsils. Repeatedly in my dreams Acho approached me with the child, etc. So it is all over; thank God, I am praying constantly for my loved ones. Last nite, I dreamt that Irwin came home—slept in Twante house and I had to wake him up for he overslept. Previously, I dreamt of Simon too. So I sensed that something was amiss. Then he wrote that he was down with flu. . . . I am counting the days for your visit. I want to see all of you, especially Zali—Dewi.

Meanwhile, Father kept busy with church work, taking time on 2 March 1970 to tell us:

> Last week I was up in Mandalay, Maymyo and Kyaukme visiting our members and . . . taking charge of the Thanksgiving Service on the 12th anniversary of Lieut. Colonel Maung Maung Aye and his better half. . . . at Kyaukme in Northern Shan State. I preached 4 times last Sunday. . . . I am holding a memorial service for Rev. Boyles on 5th April. [Reverend Boyles was a missionary who, with Father, had co-founded the Methodist school in Twante in 1919. He died in California in 1970.]

On 27 November 1970, Father wrote, "Your friends, Dr. & Mrs. Frederic Young came and went and enjoyed us and vice versa.. . .[We are] building a new church near the paper mill just on the edge of the Sittang River over which there is the span of bridge."

On 5 December he followed with this:

> We were up in Kayah State visiting Lawpita Hydro-Electric Plant and [the] big reservoir underway, meeting two Kayah girls whom we sponsored their education at Twante for a year. Now your Mum desires to visit her brother at Pa-An and thence to a place a distance of 20 miles within the State to attend the 125th year of [the] Pwo Karen Church celebration.

Riri and I and the children left Los Angeles on 2 June 1970 and stopped first in Jonesboro, Arkansas, to visit Bonnie Hallett, who had been the children's babysitter in Pacific Grove, California; her husband, Eugene; and their extended family. From there we went to Washington, where my brother Irwin was still living. We left the U.S. from the new Dulles International Airport and flew to London. Our English friends Marion and Ken had two children by then, and the four children got along very well. "I'm so tickled," said Marion. "It's so nice to hear your children speaking in American accents!"

From Amsterdam we flew to Athens and on from there to Baghdad, where Soetan Bahroemsyah was the Indonesian ambassador. We landed at night. The lights in the terminal were dimmed, for "security." It was dark and scary. Riri's father, Haji Baginda Dahlan Abdullah, died there suddenly on 12 May 1950, shortly after he presented his ambassadorial credentials to the regent for King Faisal II, who was only fifteen at the time. He was accorded a state funeral and laid to rest at Baghdad's holy Abdul Kadir Gailani Mosque. The sanctity of the tidily manicured cemetery for pilgrims within the mosque evoked a meditative mood as we gazed upon his tombstone, which was inscribed with the names of all the immediate family members. It was truly a moment of remembrance. (Riri had accompanied her father to Baghdad in 1950 and acted as his consort at diplomatic receptions. Her mother, Siti Akmar Abdullah, and the rest of the family were to follow. Riri was fifteen when her father died of cardiac arrest before the rest of the family arrived.)

The imam was a Pakistani, and he and I hit it off because I greeted him in Urdu. While we were in Baghdad, we also saw the ancient Hanging Gardens of Babylon. At departure, Ambassador Bahroemsyah took us to the airport in the official limousine with the Indonesian flag fluttering on the fender. He saw to it that we boarded the plane without a hitch. We flew on to India. Of course, we visited Woodstock School, and we had the special treat of being received in private audience by His Holiness the Dalai Lama in Dharamsala on 3 July 1970. (It was to be forty-four years later, in September 2014, when His Holiness again received Riri and me in the same reception hall.)

Overlooking the Kangra Valley, Dharamsala is beautiful and serene, high up in the Himalayas. The air was clean, prayer flags fluttered from every building against the blue sky, and birds chirped. It was the monsoon season, and the vegetation was lush and green but it rained very little while we were there. I had arranged the meeting well in advance through three Tibetan students at Orange Coast College.

The Dalai Lama's staff fetched us in a World War II jeep at the Pathankot railway station and drove us to Dharamsala. The jeep was put at our disposal while we were there. Zali remained outside and tinkered with the vehicle while we were with the Dalai Lama. At age seven, he was more interested in the jeep than in the Dalai Lama.

Security for the Dalai Lama, provided by the Indian government, was tight. We had to first check in with them. I had never visited a personage who was so securely protected by armed guards. "Sir," said the chief of the detail, "being security officers, it is our duty to inspect every guest's bags." Next we checked in with The Dalai Lama's own Tibetan staff, which loaned us the white ceremonial scarves and briefed us on protocol.

The protocol is for the visitor to present the scarf with both hands to His Holiness, who accepts it in blessing and then hands it back. The audience hall was well appointed, with lit candles, and a large Buddha statue at the altar. His Holiness was on his feet when we came in. His secretary, Tenzing Geyche, introduced us to him. Dewi played on the carpeted floor all the while.

The Dalai Lama with Win, Dewi, and Riri, 3 Jul 1970. Photo by Tenzin Geyche.

Our conversation covered a range of subjects. The first thing His Holiness said was, "Welcome. Thank you for helping our students at Orange Coast College." I asked him about his health and about the future of the Tibetan people. "We have to live with the situation," he said. "We have to co-exist. We have to love the Chinese." I invited him to our home in California. "That will not be possible at the present," he said. He was not free to leave India. The impression we got of the Dalai Lama was that he was stoic of the situation in the world; there was no rancor or worry in him.

His voice was deep and relaxed. He displayed no pretense of authority; his laughter was spontaneous and came straight from the heart. He had a sense of humor and spoke with a frequent chuckle. When I asked him what counsel he had for the elderly, he smiled and, with a chuckle, said, "I don't know! I'm not old!" We were with him three days before his thirty-fifth birthday. Riri asked him to tell us something about the Tibetan Book of the Dead. It was a little beyond me to comprehend its depth.

"I'm an alumnus of Woodstock School," I told him. "Good, good!" he enthused, as his eyes glistened. Mussoorie, where Woodstock School is located, was one of the first places he had gone when he was smuggled out of Tibet. He visits the Tibetan refugees and Woodstock School in Mussoorie occasionally. After a short while I realized that our time must be nearly up; his staff had advised us that we had only fifteen minutes, and many others were waiting for their turn. "Thank you, Your Holiness," I said. "May we take leave of you?"

"No, no, please sit down," he said, patting my knee, and began preaching his message, "We have to be compassionate. We have to be kind. We have to forgive." He ended up keeping us for nearly an hour. I asked him to bless us as we took his leave. "I pray for you," he said, and as he escorted us to the door, I said to him, "The next time we meet, I would like it to be in Lhasa." He smiled. It was not to be. The entire audience was conducted with his secretary acting as interpreter. I had recorded it on a tape recorder but over the years, the tape has been misplaced.

From Dharamsala we returned to New Delhi, from there we flew to Calcutta, where we stayed with my Woodstock classmate Ashoke Chatterjee. Then we flew to Katmandu to visit Dr. Robert Fleming, my former Woodstock School teacher, and his family. At Dr. Fleming's home I was happy to meet U Hla, the Burmese chargé d'affaires and his wife, whom the Flemings had invited for dinner. Our conversation was purely social. I had just begun my anti-military activities, but U Hla did not know who I was or where my sympathies lay. He knew Dr. Fleming through the Rotary Club. (I was for fifteen years a Rotarian and had served the Costa Mesa club as its president in 1979–1980 when it was my privilege to attend Rotary International's Annual Conference held in Rome where we were received by Pope John Paul II.)

The chargé's wife said to us, "You must come visit our home."

"What are you going to cook?" I asked in jest. I don't know whether she had meant the invitation seriously, but now she was committed. The next evening U Hla drove his official Mercedes to the Flemings' home to pick us up. He did not want the driver or other embassy staff to know that he was entertaining a Burmese exile.

The next day, Riri took the children on a Union of Burma Airways flight to Rangoon. They had visas to stay for 48 hours. Bruce and Nan Amstutz, Woodstock alumni, were also on board. They were returning to Rangoon where Bruce was on the U.S. embassy staff. There was also another American couple on board—a total of seven passengers on the Lockheed Electra. The navigator was a Karen named Saw Arthur, and he radioed Rangoon tower while the plane was still on the tarmac, to telephone my parents to let them know Riri and the children were on board.

In Rangoon my eldest brother, U Kyaw Nyein, picked up the trio at the airport. They took a lot of canned goods for my parents, as well as about a dozen pairs of underwear for my father. Many essentials were in short supply in Burma. The next day, Father visited his friends and gave away all of the underwear. That was the kind of man he was. My mother shrieked in delight at the special soap, lipstick, and perfume that Riri gave her. Their joy at meeting the grandchildren for the first time was tinged with sadness that their three sons could not come along.

They were consoled somewhat to see the pictures that Riri had brought. Zali and Dewi had been brought up without the benefit of coddling grand-parents, so they were excited to meet them. It must have been on this visit that they learned from their relatives how to properly perform the *shikoe* [prostration] before their elders.

Mother said to Dewi, "I knew you before you were born." Dewi didn't understand what she meant. "You should become a lawyer," Mother added. (Dewi didn't become one.) And she asked Zali, "In what month were you born?" "August," he told her. "Then your middle name is Augustus," she said. Zali was not given a middle name.

They rode around Rangoon in my brother's car, which was so old and poorly maintained that the floorboards had rusted through and you could see the ground below. Riri and the children stayed at the Strand Hotel but visited my parents at the parsonage on Creek Street. The parsonage was a wooden structure and the Burmese habit is to coat it with creosote, to pro-tect it. The creosote blackens the wood, which was disturbing to Dewi when she had to use the bathroom, until Riri comforted her.

One subject that never came up during the visit was the military re-gime or the situation in the country. After forty-eight hours, when Riri and the children had to leave, the whole family saw them off at the airport. It was a heart rending farewell.

I met their arrival at Bangkok Airport, and Fred and Alice Haupt took us to their apartment on Soi Ruam Rudee. Colonel Haupt, my former stu-dent at the U.S. Army Language School who was the defense attaché at the embassy in Rangoon, was now posted to the Joint U.S. Military Assistance Group (JUSMAG) in Bangkok. From Bangkok we went to Singapore and on to Jakarta.

Relations with Riri's family had thawed since our last visit in 1961, so this time we stayed with them. The children did not speak Indonesian, and Riri's mother did not speak English. "I feel like a mother hen nursing duck-lings," she said. Riri's eldest half-brother took us around the city; afterwards we went to Bali and stayed at Tanjung Sari cottages on Sanur beach. Bali then was still pristine and uncrowded.

Then we flew to Saigon, where an old friend, U Thaung Tin, was work-ing for World Vision. (U Thaung Tin was the elder brother of Dora Than É.) The terminal at Tan Son Nhat airport was surrounded by sandbags, and se-curity was very tight. On the afternoon we arrived, a Buddhist monk immo-lated himself near the opera house. We went for a picnic on the outskirts of Saigon and saw American paratroopers descending from military aircraft.

We then continued on to Hong Kong, Tokyo, and Honolulu. In Honolulu our hosts, Bob and Dottie Williams Bobilin, gave Zali a cake for his eighth birthday.

On the flight home to Los Angeles, a grandfatherly gentleman traveling solo asked where our home was. "Costa Mesa," I told him.

"I live in Garden Grove," he said. "How are you getting home?" he asked.

"We will take a shuttle or a taxi," I told him.

"My son is picking me up. Let me give your family a ride home." We were finally home from a long around-the-world journey.

Throughout our travels the world over, we have been met with kindness everywhere. In the summer of 1977 in a very small remote place in northern Finland, I had only travelers' checks to pay for gasoline. There was no money changing facility anywhere nearby. A kindly fellow motorist stepped forward and paid for enough gasoline for us to reach the next facility. He declined my offer of a traveler's check.

"I shall never forget the scene of Dewi getting away from us at the airport to the ramp of the P.A.A. waving [to] us," Father wrote on 7 January 1971. "Such is the romance of our tiny world. Your Mum, sister and I are contemplating to come but the expenditure on our account is tremendous. The philosophy of our home up bringing is self-support and self reliance."

On the day I took the PhD oral examination, 24 March 1971, a violent earthquake shook the San Fernando Valley. It happened early in the morning, but I hadn't listened to the radio because I was tied up in knots. I did not know that the earthquake had struck until later in the morning, when I came out of the examination room on the second floor of Bovard Hall. I felt so relieved to have the examination behind me that I felt like I was walking on air. I had been working full-time throughout the period that I was also writing my dissertation. My parents had been hoping to be granted passports in time to attend the commencement exercises on 10 June 1971. Father wrote on 14 May 1971:

> Just to say that things are being procrastinated in the process from one Dept to another and on top of that most of the responsible Heads are out on tour throughout the country checking up things. So the piles and piles of applications for visas, passports and what not are waiting for their approval. On that occasion, we are with you in spirit. . .accept our congratulations.

Father had given up. He realized that he was not going to make it for my graduation. But he was grateful to everybody who had helped me. He asked if he could write to Professor Earl Carnes, chairman of my dissertation committee, to express appreciation. He did write to Dr. Carnes, who acknowledged his letter and said he'd like to meet Father when he comes. I had almost given up hope of ever seeing my parents again, but I took strength in Father's faith. His letter of 24 May 1971 expressed how he himself managed to endure:

> This is not a question of why and wherefore, just and unjust, fair and unequal. This is the kind of world in which we live— half baked and foolhardy; carnal minded and material things, centered, arrogant and aggressive. Every dog must have its day, of course. So it is not a question of fatalistic attitude. Many of us Christians will live out our lives with some problem left unsolved to our own satisfaction. St. Paul is a case in point of one who prayed three times that God would remove some annoyance in his life, but each time he was refused. Some people would say that God either did not hear or did not care, and they would become bitter. Paul discovered a spiritual secret, namely that God could supply sufficient strength and patience so that man could endure. You can discover the same truth for your life. God doesn't always remove the problem, but He gives us grace to accept it if all trust Him.

Unexpectedly, around the same time, I was nonplussed to receive a letter from General Smith Dun, dated 25 July 1971:

> Burma will change some day, but I do hope it's for the better!! Even then it must have the charms of her own. I heard from many people who had left her, wishing to return again like you do, including Indians and Pakistanis who had lived in Burma most of their lives.. . . My only complaint about you chaps who left your mother country are so easily influenced by the people and country of your adoption, you completely change in the way and habits of that country with you. I noticed that you never failed an Easter letter. For the rest of the year, you just went into hibernation like the bears and completely forgotten the rest of the world and friends which is contrary to my way of thought.

Soon I had the occasion to hope that Father was right about the grace to accept things. On 19 August 1971 he wrote:

> You will be very disappointed to hear that our applications for P.P. were rejected on the grounds of change of policy. If the French proverb is true, which says: "The more it changes, the more it is the same." Never mind, God will open the way one of these days. Your Mum is OK after she wept over the sad news.

General Smith Dun was not wrong, but he could not fathom the intense feeling of an exile who longs to return to help develop his country. He continued:

> We are still in the same place with same bodies & souls. Life is bloody of course, nothing in sufficient supply. Last month even rice only four milk tins per head. This month 8 milk tins, an improvement. God alone knows what's happening.. . . I am not surprised to hear that your parents could not get exit visa. No one could as these miscreants are so suspicious of every one but themselves. As for them with a headache or aching of the balls they will at once go to London, Moscow, Washington or Vienna for check up. Where do they get the money I wonder! In my days, even touring round the little confines of Burma, I never took with me any of my family for a free ride.

Father was beginning to sense the oppressiveness of the military regime, but he always tried to see the positive side, as for example in his letter of 5 December 1972, to my great surprise, he wrote, "We are awaiting the directions from Simon. May be we are coming next month, i.e. near the end of January. We all are just fine."

My parents had been applying for passports and exit permits at this point for more than a decade and, even amid all the fruitless effort and hope, all of us tried to live resigned to the likelihood that we would not see each other again. Mother was the best of us at accepting with grace that matters were out of our power, though I know our lifelong separation caused her no end of grief. Then on 13 December, we received this happy news from my father:

> Now you will be pleased to know that we have got our passports. But I have to appear before the US Consular Section to have them visaed. I can safely hold them for three months from the date of issue—i.e., 23 December 72. Since your Mum is just recuperating, we do not feel that she will be able to stand the rigour of the journey and intense cold at this time of the winter. So we would rather strike across the first week of February 1973—a little bit over two months in our favour.

Finally, on 6 January 1973, he added:

> Mighty glad to announce that we are coming to you all. According to our itinerary [we] leave Burma on 7th of February—direct flight to Hong Kong by BOAC stay over 48 hours in H.K. thence on to Japan, Honolulu en route to Los Angeles.

Irwin, who was in England, flew to Hong Kong to meet them. He saw them off at Hong Kong's Kai Tak Airport for their flight to Honolulu before returning to England. Simon met them in Honolulu and, after they had had a couple of nights' rest, brought them to Los Angeles, where our family met them at Los Angeles International Airport. We accompanied them to Simon's home in the San Fernando Valley. I had not seen them in twelve years. They had aged considerably since I last saw them in 1961.

We took them to the Monterey Peninsula to show them our former home, and we showed them Yosemite National Park. They really enjoyed Yosemite, Vernal Falls, the pines, redwoods, Half Dome, and El Capitan. They stayed with Simon and generally spent their time worshipping at church, visiting friends, and cooking. We brought them to our home in Costa Mesa, and my father danced a traditional Burmese puppet dance for the children. I was afraid for him, exerting himself in such a way at age 79. We introduced them to friends who came to our home, and I took them to a few Burma Association potluck lunches. During the nine months they were in America they also went to Portland, Oregon, where they visited Bishop Clement D. Rockey, who no longer recognized them. They went to Phoenix, where Simon dedicated a stained-glass window in their honor at Dr. Kendall's former Central Methodist Church. Dr. Kendall had died unexpectedly of a heart attack while they were en route to America. They also went to Lake Junaluska, North Carolina.

Sometime in the spring they stayed in our home, and it was then that my father and I had a blow-up. I felt terrible over that incident. I should not have allowed my anger at the military regime to trigger an outburst. I told him, "Ne Win is exploiting you!" He got very angry and quoted the thirteenth chapter of Paul's letter to the Romans, about the importance of being loyal to the authority in power. He went into his room and covered himself with a blanket and would not come out. My mother interceded. After that we never spoke again about such matters. I felt very guilty about the incident.

U NU: SATURDAY'S SON

After my parents had been in California for a few months, U Nu came to Southern California. He arrived in September and left in November. He had decided to give up leading the movement against the Ne Win regime from Thailand. His daughter, Than Than Nu, wrote from Bangkok, saying that he could no longer remain in Thailand and asked if I would help. Of course, I agreed. How could I not help? We were happy to give him refuge, as well as to insulate him from Burmese expatriates in America. His desire to keep a low profile put an added burden on us, because word got around and people started asking me: "Is U Nu staying with you?" I kept mum but had to confirm it to the Burma Desk Officer at the State Department, who telephoned to ask.

In our household, U Nu was a grandfatherly figure. He loved the children and called Zali "Sheik" because one time, trying to be funny, Zali had tied a *longyi* around his head to look like an Arab. When we visited U Nu two years later at his exile home in Bhopal, India, he inscribed my copy of his memoir, *Saturday's Son*, "Ko Kyaw Win and Riri, and my dear grandchildren Sheik & Dewi Sita, with sincere affection and good wishes," and signed it "Maung Nu."

It was while he was with us that U Nu put the finishing touches on *Saturday's Son: Memoirs of the Former Prime Minister of Burma*. He had already written it in Burmese, which Edward Law-Yone had translated into English. My job was to edit the English text, make telephone calls, research, and check the facts, and find a publisher. I worked in one room while he worked in another, and we would go back and forth, "Is this what you meant?" For example, the book mentions Sir Hubert Rance, the last British governor of Burma, and U Nu was curious whether he was still alive.

I inquired of the British embassy in Washington, and was given Sir Hubert's contact in England. He was not well and died in 1974. A woman in Santa Ana typed the manuscript. U Nu's son, Ko Aung, would take the day's draft over to her and the typed pages would come back reeking of tobacco. U Nu asked me, "Could you get her to stop smoking while she types?" I didn't try, because I was afraid she might drop the job. But the pages smelled terrible. We had to send Ko Aung every other day to get the typed pages photocopied at a facility near the USC campus, an hour's drive away. In those days photocopying (then universally called *xeroxing*) was not so readily available in Costa Mesa.

Yale University Press published *Saturday's Son*. Like anyone writing an autobiography, U Nu wanted to be remembered. He wanted to put on record his involvement with Burma's struggle for liberation from British colonial rule. But his other concern was to gain merit by propagating Buddhism. As he put it, he wanted to let people know the Buddhist truths. I helped arrange for him to give a few lectures on Buddhism, but his purpose and that of the institutions that invited him were not the same. They wanted to hear about Buddhism as a subject of academic inquiry; he wanted to share the joy of meditation. His lectures were as long as two hours—too long for many people, especially for senior citizens.

I walked with him in the evenings around our Costa Mesa neighborhood and on the beach at Newport Beach. He was cautious not to step on ants or other critters. During our walks we observed silence. I took him to see the movie *The Sound of Music*, which he thoroughly enjoyed. I found him very relaxed. He was particularly tickled by the *frau* who repeatedly took the stage for more applause. He enjoyed the music and the songs, especially those sung by Julie Andrews. During the two months he was with us, he was a vegetarian. Riri had a challenging time preparing the meals. The irony was that later, when we visited him in India, where vegetarianism is common and where there was a cook to prepare his meals, he was carnivorous. He was affectionate toward Riri, saying that she reminded him of his mother. Sometimes on the telephone he seemed to prefer talking to her rather than to me.

U Nu was an intensely interesting person, and yet I feel his life was a little tragic. He was an enigmatic person. He was a passionate Buddhist and meditated a lot. He was deeply preoccupied with lives to come in the cycle of *samsara*, and he aspired to Buddhahood in millennia hence. Everything he did, he did with a passion to attain that goal. To that end, he was continually doing good deeds. His speech was measured, and he spoke in a gentle, soft voice. He liked to quote Shakespeare's line from *Twelfth Night* about how some are born great, some achieve greatness, and some have greatness thrust upon them.

Some of the things he did were contradictory. For example, when he was in office in the 1950s, he brought back to Burma water from the River Jordan to share with the Christian communities, and he funded Muslims to go on pilgrimage to Mecca. But in his heart of hearts, he felt that Buddhism was the only truth. Also, he talked about federalism, but he really believed that the majority Burmans should rule over all the peoples in Burma and that Buddhism should be the state religion. He would note that Lord Listowel, the colonial Secretary of State for Burma, had advised that a special place for Buddhism be written into the Burmese constitution. That was one of the reasons U Nu parted ways with the movement. The other ethnic groups—the Arakanese, the Kachin, the Karen, the Karenni, the Mon, and the Shan, and so on—were, in his mind, appendages of the Burman hegemony. And to be Burman was to be Buddhist. Yet at the same time, he was tolerant. I am a Christian, my whole family from the maternal line is Christian, and yet, when he was expelled from Thailand, he did not feel uncomfortable turning to me.

U Nu left, but the movement against Ne Win continued. Bo Let Ya, one of the Thirty Comrades who had been Aung San's right-hand man, continued to lead it from Thailand. The movement had never been completely nonviolent, even when U Nu was leading it. He received letters from American Buddhists accusing him: "You preach non-violence, and yet you are raising an army." In 1973, when he gave up leading the movement, he declared that he was finished with politics and gave the impression that he was planning to spend the rest of his life meditating.

But U Nu was like a campfire that has not been completely extinguished. When the wind stirs, the embers flame up again. He had a heart, even when he was fighting political battles. But he could also be strangely fickle and oddly remote. One time I had driven him to San Francisco. On the way back to Costa Mesa on Interstate 5, I pulled in at a rest stop. Another car pulled in with its radiator steaming. I walked over and asked the motorist if I could help. After the steam had dissipated, I checked the upper radiator hose and discovered a gash on its underside. So I got some duct tape from my car and patched it up, and, after adding some water into the radiator, told the lady motorist to stop at the next facility and have the hose replaced. Back in my car, U Nu said to me, "You're an extraordinary fellow."

In October 1973, U Nu received an affirmative response to the request for asylum in India that he had initiated before he left Bangkok. The news was conveyed personally to him by Eric Gonsalves, a senior diplomat at the Indian embassy in Washington, while he was lecturing on Buddhism at the New Paltz campus of the State University of New York. Before he left America for exile in India, I reminded him that the last Burmese political figure the British exiled to India—King Thibaw—never returned to Burma. He took it stoically. The night before his departure from New York City, he telephoned to say good bye to Riri and me and the children. He was accompanied to India on the plane by an Indian Foreign Ministry official.

While he was in Calfiornia, U Nu had wanted to pay respects to my parents, but my parents preferred to avoid him, because once they got back to Burma they would be interrogated. They never saw each other while they were in California. I didn't tell U Nu that my father had declined to see him; I just didn't follow through on his suggestion. Father was wise, because if he had met U Nu, the military regime would have made his life miserable. Implicit in granting him a passport was the condition that he would not engage in any political activity while abroad. The regime's definition of political activity was very broad. If you spoke to or met anyone who was opposed to the regime, that was their definition of "political activity." As it was, Father must already have been hoping the regime would never have occasion to reread his booklet *Cruising Down the Irrawaddy*, in which he had written, "[T]he hour produces a man like U Nu—a people's leader—and puts him at the head of the people. He is a great man, with fine ideals and ability. He knows what his people want, and he means to get it for them."

THE FINAL FAREWELL

My parents returned to Burma sooner than I had expected or wanted them to. I had filled out the forms to adjust their status to permanent residents. This would have given them the liberty to remain in the United States as long as they wished and leave and return at will. In my role as foreign student advisor at Orange Coast College, I had come to know George Rosenberg, the Los Angeles district director of the U.S. Immigration and Naturalization Service. Mr. Rosenberg pushed the process through, and my parents were granted permanent residence quickly. But my sister back in Rangoon was putting a lot of pressure on them to return; she was dependent on them. And my father felt lost without a congregation to serve. My parents would have led a lonely life in America. In Burma, their home was always abuzz with friends and relatives calling on them regularly. They left in the winter, not long after U Nu left. During the two months that U Nu was with us, I did not see as much of my parents as I would have liked. And then suddenly, to my sorrow, they were on the verge of returning home. I felt sure that I would never see them again. I was right.

At the airport my mother wept. My father, ever the preacher, quoted from the Book of Ecclesiastes, "A time to be born, and a time to die." Those were his last words to me in person as they boarded the plane. My heart was burdened. It was in September 1973.

I never saw my parents again.

3

In Coalition with My Conscience

BY THE 1970S, BURMA's military regime was becoming increasingly oppressive. My father felt the need to caution me about the stifling political culture. In a letter, he urged:

> Now my son, just a word of advice. Never write things about Burma—weal or woes. Things are just in flux. You cannot put your finger here and there—as somebody said, "What I believe today, I may not do so tomorrow." Some cunning writers from outside write some nasty articles about Burma making a hill out of a mole hill.

I respected Father immensely, but my conscience told me otherwise. I was therefore unwilling to heed his advice. Throughout the 1970s and 1980s, I was demonstrating, writing letters to newspaper editors and members of Congress, helping organize opposition in the United States to Ne Win. I became more and more antagonistic to the regime and felt compelled to take a stand against it. There was hardly any mention in the American press of the atrocities taking place in Burma, so I used every opportunity I could find to get the word out. But it was difficult to interest news outlets in covering Burma: It was far away, little known, and poorly understood. Also, most Burmese living abroad were really intimidated by the military regime, because it was commonly known that their family members back home were at risk of being hounded and punished by its secret police, the feared and much hated Military Intelligence Service (MIS). But I was not going to be intimidated and held hostage. The little voice inside told me I had to speak out. So I went ahead and created my own outlet, an eight-paged quarterly newsletter called *The Burma Bulletin*. This was how I announced its launch, on the front page of the first issue in April 1973:

> The Burma Bulletin. . . .is an idea whose time has arrived. For the time being we shall publish quarterly, until our footing is sure. Our learned Mandalay *bay-din saya* (astrologer) has had some difficulty foretelling our reception and, "for there to be poets there must be audiences." Our pages shall be devoted to articles of interest to the Burmese community in the United States. Book reviews, undated news items, helpful hints for effective living, both culturally and economically, in a milieu that is not native to us, will make their occasional appearances.
>
> To those who are uncertain of the definition of our being, let the word be heard that in personal terms we shall be friend to all and foe to none. We will turn the other cheek and even walk that second mile but we will not shirk from our commitment to the human condition when addressing ourselves against the actions and policies of those who seek the deliberate destruction of the dignity of man. We reserve the right to dissent but resolve to love.

The reason I published *The Burma Bulletin* was to arouse the feelings of Burmese expatriates living in the United States so that they would say something about Burma. Not necessarily even to do anything—just to say something. People excused themselves, saying, "Oh, I have family in Burma." I would say to them, "Show me one Burmese who does not have relatives back home." My idea was to speak out against the military regime's injustices and violations of Burmese citizens' human rights. Sure, it was one-sided. But I was certain the side I was on was the right one.

Out of respect for Father, and aware of his high hopes for the regime, I did not confront him on the political situation in Burma. As a Burmese nationalist, and like so many other Southeast Asians, he disapproved of the American involvement in Vietnam. That also strengthened his resolve to stand by the Burmese regime, right or wrong. He felt passionately that

American involvement in Vietnam was a reflection of the colonialism that he detested.

At the time, I had no idea that the things I was writing in *The Bulletin* would someday be of historical value. Now, I see the point. I printed 250 copies of every issue, although I never had more than 100 paying subscribers. I gave many copies away. I sent the first two or three complimentary issues to people I knew. One Karen lady asked me, "Please don't send your bulletin to me anymore. We plan to return to Burma." She lived in New Jersey, but she was afraid. Someone who had been a very close family friend for many years wrote to me from Burma, "I request you most sincerely not to send me any Bulletins of any kind whatever. . . . I hope you will comply." That was how far and wide the military regime's pernicious tentacles reached. However, I also received congratulatory letters from inside Burma. One man wrote to tell me that he was walking one day near the Royal Lakes in Rangoon when a Westerner, presumably from an embassy, jogged past and thrust a copy of *The Burma Bulletin* at him, saying, "Here—read this." Several subscribers had APO addresses, meaning they likely were posted at U.S. embassies. The University of California at Santa Barbara was a subscriber.

I edited and published *The Burma Bulletin* for its nineteen-year run entirely by gut feeling, and I never took ads. That's no way to run a periodical if you expect to cover your costs, but I never did cover my costs. Initially I typed the entire issue myself. It was time-consuming; there were no computers in those days.

I tried to bring a balance to the issues I was covering. I would even publish letters critical of me. But few people would write anything, because they were afraid. When you write things like what I was writing, you get a lot of flak. I did also get encouragement, but what most of the people who encouraged me meant was: You do it, because we're afraid to. One of the reasons I'm writing this memoir is that I want people to read some of the things that people in Burma were afraid to read or say in those days. I published as many articles by others as I could. Professor James Gould of Scripps College wrote an article about standing your ground on moral principle. That fit right in with my premise that the pen is mightier than the sword. Or, as I put it in the April 1974 issue:

> We possess no network of intelligence agents or divisions of infantry, armor and artillery. Nor do we need them. Our only intelligence is a manifestation of an unattractive piece of gray matter weighing about 2½ lbs that resides in our cranium. Our only weapon is a pen.

Robert N. Weed, publisher of the *Orange Coast Daily Pilot*, who was a fellow Rotarian, gave me an article called "The First Freedom," which I published in the same issue. "About two hundred years ago, you and I were bequeathed a legacy," he wrote. "Lately we have been hearing a lot about that legacy and there is a great confrontation in Washington over whether or not the terms of the will are still valid. The legacy, of course, was—and is—the Constitution." On the same subject, in the same issue, I wrote:

> Clearly, the revelations of the past several months leave little doubt in our mind that if this nation is to live up to its commitment to a rule of law, there is no alternative but to impeach Richard Nixon. . . . Even the President of the United States must be given his day in court.

Edward Law-Yone, the exiled former editor of the Rangoon English-language daily *The Nation*, contributed several articles using a pseudonym. Edith Mirante, a young American artist (and later author of *Burmese Looking Glass*), who traveled around the ethnic areas of Burma and northern Thailand and became concerned about the ongoing war and related environmental issues, wrote about the Burma Army's use of the Agent Orange ingredient 2,4-D, provided by the United States. "The actual 2,4-D spraying has been confined to 'gray areas' where tribal people are caught between sides in the ongoing warfare waged by the Burma Army against ethnic minority insurgents," Mirante wrote in the January 1988 issue. "The people in the sprayed areas are dirt-poor subsistence farmers who traditionally grow opium. Due to war and economic collapse in the area, opium is currently their only viable trade crop."

I published a variety of articles. I was glad for other people to speak out. Why should I do all the talking? In my own articles, I would quote from literary sources, from Aleksandr Solzenitsyn to Alex Comfort to Sir Walter Scott. I also quoted public figures like Mahatma Gandhi and United States Attorney General Ramsey Clark. I reprinted an article from *Travel & Leisure* magazine by the humorist S. J. Perelman, called "Barefoot in Burma." A poem by the Goan poet Telo de Mascarenhas was another one. Its passion touched me deeply. It was sent to me by my mother:

> I will return one day
> One day sooner or later
> To my distant,
> Native land
> Where I passed my childhood
> To show the men
> Of vile sentiment

That my heart does not shelter
Hate or resentment
To make true
Our old saying
"Sandalwood is so generous
That it perfumes even the edge
Of the axe that cuts it."

COMMUNITY OUTREACH

As I had declared in the founding editorial, *The Burma Bulletin* was intended to be more than just a vehicle for political coverage and advocacy. It was also a community newsletter. Thus, for example, in the first issue in April 1973, I ran this item about an event that was held at the University of California at Los Angeles:

BURMA'S 25TH INDEPENDENCE ANNIVERSARY CELE-
BRATION IN LOS ANGELES DRAWS TURNOUT OF OVER
200

By Pat Thaung Win

The highlight of the evening came with the performance of Burmese dancing and music, made more enjoyable by the announcing of the able Master of Ceremonies, Mr. Usman Madha, a young college student in Los Angeles. He first introduced a special guest from Fresno, Calif., Mrs. Mabelle Selland, who had served six years as chairman of the Fresno-Moulmein Sister City Committee. A slender blonde woman wearing her *hta-mein* and *ain-gyi*, she was charming as she brought greetings to the gathering from Fresno.

And this about the Burmese lunar New Year —the festive holiday when, every April throughout Southeast Asia, people express their high spirits by drenching each other with water:

THE BURMESE COMMUNITY IN SOUTHERN CALIFOR-
NIA will celebrate the advent of *Thin-gyan* (Burmese New Year) by getting together over a pot luck picnic at Elysian Park, Los Angeles, on 15 April 1973 (Sunday), from 12:00 Noon until 3:00 P.M. The Bulletin understands that there will be a lot of water at Elysian Park. The Editor will be fully prepared and advises celebrants to be sure to bring extra sets of clothes and towels.

However, we do feel that truce should be declared until after the eating is done.

Also in 1973, four others and I founded The Burma Association, an expressly non-political group that met once a month for a potluck meal in a park, helped new arrivals, and put on cultural programs. Another organization I helped incorporate was a church, the Burmese Christian Fellowship, which continues to thrive. But it was inevitable that tension would arise between my purposes of serving the community and separately engaging in social and political activism.

The first demonstration I led took place on 25 March 1975, in front of the Hilton Hotel in San Francisco, where the Association for Asian Studies was holding its annual conference. Professor Josef Silverstein of Rutgers University, an activist named Yé Kyaw Thu, and I carried placards protesting against the Ne Win's regime and calling on the United States government to withhold military aid to Burma. Edith Piness, a PhD candidate at Claremont Graduate School, also joined us, as did Professor James Gould. A Burmese couple attending the AAS conference sneered at us.

It was four months after that, on 18 July 1975, when I demonstrated outside the White House, that The Burma Association split up. I am sorry to say that, in general, Burmese are very individualistic and resist being asked to unite. Whenever three Burmese congregate to address a specific issue, the outcome is that they will invariably emerge with at least four new organizations, each with two head honchos. Even though that remark is obviously tongue in cheek, it is not far from the truth. There was not a single meeting where someone did not challenge me. Eventually no one wanted to take charge and the Association fizzled into nothingness.

On my study wall is a picture of Mahatma Gandhi hobbling on a stick, campaigning for Indian independence. His motto was, "One would walk alone to pursue a high ideal." I was happy, on my 80th birthday to receive an e-mail from Maureen Aung-Thwin, director of the Burma Project of the Open Society Foundations, saying, "U Kyaw Win, you are my hero since you demonstrated *alone* against the military regime in the early 60's when all of us were too scared to."

It might also have been the case that the other founders of The Burma Association felt uncomfortable with my forthright editorials in *The Burma Bulletin*, which was not an organ of The Burma Association, such as this one in the January 1974 issue:

> Born on 4 January 1948, democracy as a form of government in Burma, died on 2 March 1962 when it had barely reached puberty. Those who delivered the death blow by superiority

of their weaponry rationalized that it was not democracy they murdered but a deteriorating chaos in the quality of political and economic life.

Certainly, wanting conditions were present, but democracy is not a station on a chart one arrives at because the Constitution ordained so, but a mode of travelling, a process. We assign the responsibility for democracy's death in Burma to those who were entrusted with its nurturance—the governed and the governors.

The governed, because they failed to exercise their obligation to speak out when the cancer of deterioration began eating into the body politic of national life. In a letter to William Smith on 9 January 1795, Edmund Burke wrote, "The only thing necessary for the triumph of evil is for good men to do nothing." And, the governors because they abused the mandate granted by the people in whom sovereignty resides, by being insensitive and unresponsive to the welfare of the people. The government treated its citizens as if they were its subjects and not as partners in the commonweal.

Or this one from January 1975:

General Ne Win Should Resign

Acting alone but in coalition with our conscience, we call upon General Ne Win to resign before the dawning of his thirteenth anniversary in power, which may well become his violent epilogue. A Council of Citizens from a representative spectrum, including those now in exile, selected for their administrative ability and genuine desire to reconstruct the land of their forefathers from the ashes should be appointed.

Father did not want me to be critical of Burma because, to him, that would be disloyal. He urged me to mind my duty and obligations in my adopted country. In the mid-1970s, I took that to mean that I had both an obligation and a right to express a view on the political scandal that had engulfed the Nixon administration. I was a United States citizen, after all, with a constitutionally guaranteed right to free speech—and as a publisher, to boot, I exercised freedom of the press. In an October 1974 editorial, I drew from Nixon's downfall lessons pertinent to Burma:

Regardless of what position one takes in the Watergate scandal, it's a political process wherein all forces are activated to reconstruct a more viable society. A prerequisite for reconstruction is the social concern shared by all. From the outset we spoke out in favor of impeachment.

To us the real issue was never whether Richard Nixon remained in or out of the White House but of the supremacy of the law and its equal application to all citizens, including the President of the United States. Some governments, tyrannies and democracies alike, have come and gone in the past decade while Ne Win's oppressive regime today survives its adolescence. Why? Because Burmese leaders, including those of an earlier parliamentary democratic era, do not really appreciate the intricacies of the democratic process.

The Ne Win government's oppression and its disregard for the civil rights of its citizens have brought the nation to the brink of disaster. The people in Burma are too intimidated to challenge the political status quo.

Like the Vietnam War, the Watergate scandal tested even warm and long-standing friendships among Americans. Fortunately, my friendship with one of my American families was tested only mildly, thanks to their tact and graciousness. Driving east in 1974, Riri and I stopped in Hillsboro, Indiana, at the farm of the Dr. George W. Crane family, who had been friends with my family since 1949 when my brother Simon was attending Northwestern University Medical School in Chicago. The Cranes were a prominent political family, staunch Republicans, including Congressman Philip Crane of Illinois, who died on 8 November 2014, at 84. Their sister, Judy Crane Ross, is a homemaker who was elected a DuPage County Commissioner in Illinois. David Crane is a lawyer-psychiatrist in Indiana, while Daniel Crane, is a retired dentist. All the Crane brothers served in the armed forces. When Dan's service in Vietnam ended, he smuggled Sweet Pea home in a duffel bag where she gave much joy to the extended family at their farm for several years. Sweet Pea was a gibbon.

Their grandparents, George Washington Crane Jr. and Jenny Bever, were longtime friends with Ada Campbell Travis, mother-in-law of the Reverend Dr. Charles Schilling Kendall, who helped my brother Simon and me through college in Arizona and married me and Riri in Hollywood in 1958. This was how Simon got to know them in the first place. The Cranes were so kind to our entire family. They were most hospitable to my mother when she visited Chicago in 1950. Their eldest son, George W. Crane IV, who drove her around Chicago and looked after her, was her favorite. He died on 7 July 1956 in a Marine Corps plane crash while practicing for an air show at Glenview Naval Air Station.

Riri and I had stopped at the Cranes' farm in 1958 on our way to get married and we stopped again now. There was no way we would drive through Indiana without visiting the Cranes. When Mrs. Cora Crane saw the IMPEACH NIXON bumper sticker on our car, she graciously declared herself annoyed. She was sweet about it, chuckling and saying only, "That bumper sticker—I'm not sure about it." Dr. Crane said nothing.

In the July 1974 issue of *The Burma Bulletin*, I wrote, "Yes indeed we have received several letters. To readers in Burma we ask that you not risk arrest and torture by the secret police writing us directly. Please use third parties and be cautious." In the same issue, I published this letter:

> About three years ago I managed to get out of Burma. I was bare handed because the military allowed me to take abroad only $23.00. I faced joblessness for three months. The language barrier was also there. Without the help of the Burmese monastery in Bangkok I could have turned myself into a beggar. After three months I got a job on a meager salary. My visa expired. Thai immigration came to arrest me. I evaded victoriously. Out of the bargain a Burmese lawyer turned into a fugitive in Thailand. Nevertheless, the life of a fugitive here is better than the life of a lawyer in Burma. Six months ago the haunting thing came true. Thai CID [Criminal Investigation Department] got wind of me and I was escorted to the CID headquarters.
>
> But fortunately enough through trickery, I slipped out of their hands. Then life became more stringent than before. I dared not go to work. I even have to wear a wig and sunglasses to disguise my identity.

In the April 1976 issue, I published a letter from a reader named Than Tin. "News of the execution of Ko Nyunt Tin at Insein Jail strikes us hard and close to home as one of us had lived and grown up in the shadows of the jail. Linked to a piece of our past, the memory of the man and the sacrifice will remain with us." I also printed this from Sao Ying of Shan State: "Congratulations on your excellent January 1976 issue. Please keep them coming for the sake of all of us who love our homeland." But surely the most powerful letter I published in *The Burma Bulletin* was this one in the July 1977 issue:

> This is a political and economic picture of beautiful Burma: The Constitution and Socialist State are all sham. [It is] just a guise for military dictatorship. Only a few opportunists make hay while the sun shines. People just don't care about the system and have no confidence or trust in it. Nor do they support it. Black

marketeering is the order of the day everywhere. In places like Mon and Karen states hardly anyone is farming.

They are in the black market business one way or the other. Disunity is everywhere. Tension everywhere. Hatred everywhere. Corruption everywhere. People in government offices and state controlled corporations and plants are not working conscientiously—just floating with the tide. They look for or ask for bribes. There is injustice everywhere. This is killing. The government does not know what leadership, reform, etc. are. Very depressing. Corporations are meant for the privileged class—mostly army brass (majors and up).

They are the ones who are building new buildings and buying new cars—like the ones in Cambodia before the Communists took over. Schools are crowded and children find difficulty getting into them in the bigger cities. Pitiable to see parents looking for schools for their children. There are more beggars and destitutes in Rangoon. They have to sleep in the open by the roadside and many a time whole families are there.

Rangoon is not a good place to live. It is not safe to walk alone in downtown after 9 or 10 P.M. Even your eyeglasses can be robbed. Riff-raffs, vagabonds, bad hats, thugs, dacoits are taking refuge in big cities like Rangoon. . . . Recently the Communists have been gaining momentum and increasing in strength especially in Shan State.

There is no peace in the country. It is a pity to see army recruits so young (15, 16, 17-year-olds) because they have nowhere else to go—gun fodder, most of them. Pitiable sight. Life is hard to live in this most corrupt so-called socialist, but actually, military dictatorship system.

Through it all I continued to receive personal letters from my parents. "Got in safely late at night, on Sept. 27th," Mother informed us in her first letter after returning to Burma, dated 18 October 1973.

Now, we are here in person but our hearts are over there with you in Costa Mesa, Newhall, Sylmar & U.K. . . . We parted with you at L.A. airport, with Simon at Honolulu and with Irwin at HK airport. It was all heart rending . . . . Irwin was broken hearted as we were. He said, 'Apa please give me your blessing,' then he curtsied [performed the traditional prostration to elders called *shikoe*] down on the cement floor. Paid his homage. It touched us to the quick."

Another note from her caused us concern:

You all are very blessed to see this letter. I couldn't write to anyone for a long time. I was almost on the other side of life these
two months. I do pray for all my loved ones. In case something
happens to me—Breathe a prayer. Be kind to Kyi Lone [my sis-
ter] and one another.

In a 1974 letter, my father reminisced about their time in California:

The picture card of Yosemite reminds us of our visit together
there and of the wonderful episode in the annals of our lives. I
recall the time in the big hall [Ahwanee Hotel] where Dewi, Zali
and I sat observing the scene of people there. I also could hear
the streak of water fall from the hilltop lulling us to sleep—never
to be forgotten of the excursion of those days. I still have the
bow tie made of the rocks of the hill which Zali bought for me
and which I treasure, as presented by our grandchildren. Now,
my life begins at 80, as I concentrate on the classical music of
our culture—especially in prose as I have a poetical strain in
my nature. I have the time table with difference of time between
Los Angeles and Rangoon, I know where you all are when I refer myself to it. I usually get up about 12 in the night and read,
write, pray, meditate till 3. When I return to bed your mum
wakes up and asks me what time it is. Then she will call the roll
of the names of her sons & daughter.

I wrote to him proposing to donate to Leonard Theological College,
his alma mater in India. "Thank you very much for your interest and concern and honour due to the parents," he wrote on 12 April 1974:

Yes, that kind of venture in this wise is very appropriate and
profitable and never to be forgotten. Good that your friend [U
Nu] is devoting to religious affairs [in India]. It really is a nice
place for meditation and religious exercises. . . . I find my mind
wandering back in the direction of your two colleges—also our
being together at Yosemite.
     Now our Burma is about to drench each other during Water
Festival—then monsoon will soon usher in from the middle of
May to October—rain, rain nothing but rain. I am pleased that
you have organized the Burmese group in that kind of association, apart from politics and religion. Our Burma is full of cars
now amidst energy crisis.

In the same envelope, as was her habit, Mother wrote:

Last nite Ko Kin Sein [another name for my eldest brother Kyaw
Nyein], his wife and three children were here, our fifty-fifth

wedding anniversary. My! How I remember the time we were in the states last year. . . . Your Pa appreciates your willingness in establishing an endowment fund as well as making us members of the Association.

On 28 August 1974, Father wrote, "The flood this year is unprecedented, playing havoc with the villages on both sides of rivers—namely Irrawaddy, Salween, Sittang, and Chindwin. *Our great power* [italics mine] is clearly out of control." What he meant was obvious, but still startling to read.

U Thant died of lung cancer in New York on 25 November 1974. He was well known and respected worldwide throughout his tenure as the United Nations Secretary General, a post in which he succeeded Dag Hammarskjold, who died in a plane crash in 1961. Prior to that, U Thant was Burma's ambassador to the United Nations, appointed by Prime Minister U Nu. He succeeded in consolidating the prestige of his still-new office and was widely credited with having played a crucial role in helping President John Kennedy and Soviet Premier Nikita Khrushchev avert a nuclear catastrophe in the Cuban missile crisis of October 1962. The eventful decade during which he served with great distinction also featured the Vietnam War as well as the 1967 Six-Day War in the Middle East, the Soviet invasion of Czechoslovakia in 1968, and the war between India and Pakistan in 1971 that led to the creation of Bangladesh. He was universally admired, although his public statements on Vietnam had displeased Washington. When U Thant retired, *The New York Times* recalled his "wise counsel" and called him a "dedicated man of peace."

In short, U Thant had made Burma look good. But he had been close to U Nu, serving as director of broadcasting for the new government in 1948 and later as the prime minister's own secretary, speechwriter, and closest advisor through most of the 1950s. So, a dozen years into the deep freeze of the Ne Win era, perhaps it was inevitable that U Thant's burial would become politicized. Ne Win envied U Thant's international stature and the respect he commanded among ordinary Burmese, but he resented U Thant's connection to U Nu's democratic administration.

U Thant's body lay in state at the United Nations in New York before being flown home to Rangoon, but the regime sent no honor guard or any high-ranking official to receive it. The deputy minister of education U Than Aung (Archie Rivers), my former teacher at St. Paul's, went to the airport on his own. This ruffled Ne Win's feathers. The deputy minister of education lost his job. Tens of thousands of people lined the streets the day of U Thant's funeral on 5 December. His casket was displayed at Kyaikasan racecourse for several hours, but just before it was to have left there for burial in an obscure cemetery, a group of students snatched it and buried it themselves on the former site of the Rangoon University Students Union.

The incident ignited a weeklong crisis that brought into the open the gaping maw of disaffection between the public and the Ne Win regime and culminated in soldiers storming the Rangoon University campus on 11 December, killing the students guarding the makeshift mausoleum they had erected, and re-interring the great man at Cantonment Park at the foot of the Shwedagon Pagoda.

Less than three weeks after what came to be known as the U Thant Crisis, on 11 February 1975, Mother wrote:

> Thank God that you still have a father. He was almost finished. His blood pressure was 80/40—pale, lifeless like very weak. Dr. Sisi was greatly alarmed and rushed him to R.G.H. [Rangoon General Hospital] after giving him two shots. Aung Than [my boyhood friend] took him to R.G.H. Emergency Ward. [He] was there 8–9 days. The Drs. advised him to take "complete" rest for a while—no preaching, strenuous work—e.g., talking, moving about, climbing 2nd 3rd floors. So write to him." Then, in Burmese script, she wrote: "*Chaw pyaw; yoo nay th'lo beh; pyaw z'gah nah m'htaung boo.*" [Speak to him gently; he looks insane and does not listen]. I too not quite 100% good either. Simon sent him medicine, food stuff, etc. . . . *Di hma ngat teh* [Starving here].

MY PARENTS' DECLINING HEALTH

I became increasingly concerned about my parents' declining health. I wanted so badly to be close to them and care for them, and I was disconsolate with longing and a feeling of helplessness. On 23 March 1975, Father wrote:

> I came out of the crisis quite OK and am feeling better and better. It was really a hard hit, as my doctor in General Hospital did his best to save my life. I was there in the hospital for 14 days. I was admitted unconscious and all doctors and nurses whirled over me to get me out of it. While there I often remembered you all—Zali and Dewi in particular, both in unconscious & sober moments. . . . Now, I can sit upright for two hours at a stretch. So my life begins at 81 and plus. I admire my countrymen and women how they confront the situation nonviolently.

On 18 July 1975, Riri and I, along with U Nu's son Ko Aung, demonstrated in front of the White House and the United States Capitol. Congresswoman Bella Abzug was demonstrating with a group of her own on the same sidewalk on Pennsylvania Avenue, so I walked over and told her about our demonstration. Before the demonstration, I had written several letters to ask for appointments and made the rounds on Capitol Hill.

Selig S. Harrison, a senior associate at the Carnegie Endowment for International Peace, received me in his office when it was situated on M Street NW. He gave thirty minutes listening to my views on the deteriorating situation in Burma. My purpose was to persuade Congress and the executive branch to withhold aid to the Burmese military. Aid to Burma then was minimal, but still it brought some Burmese military officers to the United States for training. I was mainly interested in the Congress, because it is the branch of the government that does the funding. He scribbled the name of a person on a slip of paper and handed it across the desk and asked what I thought of that person. I gave him my assessment of that wannabe "Burma expert" in confidence.

Congressional staffers listened politely, but nothing of substance came out of any of the meetings. The lone member of Congress who seemed mildly interested was a junior senator from Delaware named Joseph Biden. I never met Senator Biden, but his staff paid closer attention to my presentation than the others. Senator Hubert Humphrey's staff was also attentive; they wrote me a nice letter. But Burma was not strategically important to the United States then. Now, the United States and several other countries want to do business there, all the while closely watching China's intrusion into Burma's economic and political affairs.

I also went to the Washington bureau of *The New York Times*. The journalist at the desk showed me a stack of clippings the paper had written about Burma. "That's all we have," he said. "We would like to do more, but our reporters simply haven't been able to get visas to enter the country," he continued. "Do you look over your shoulder to see if somebody is following you?" He was being serious.

"I am careful," I told him. I wanted so earnestly for *The New York Times* to write about the situation in Burma, so Americans might learn about it and write to their congressmen to ask, "What's going on there?" It was an uphill battle, because Vietnam was occupying much of the nation's attention. I went to the Burmese service of the Voice of America, hoping it would cover our demonstrations at the Capitol and the White House. We held them deliberately on 18 July because in Burma it was already 19 July, Heroes' Day, when General Aung San's assassination is commemorated, and I thought the VOA would at least mention our demonstration. It did not.

I still have the placards that we carried that day. It was a hot and muggy summer. In front of the White House it was me, Riri, Ko Aung, and retired U.S. Navy Commander James Irwin Moore, a friend. We gathered at the Methodist Building at 100 Maryland Avenue NE, where Bishop James Mathews led us in prayer, then accompanied us to the Capitol steps. There was one Burmese gentleman from the World Bank who came by and spoke to us. The Burmese embassy had informed the State Department that there was going to be a demonstration. In 1993, under the Freedom of Information Act, I obtained a copy of the telegram the State Department had sent to the embassy in Rangoon:

SUBJECT: ABORTIVE ANTI NE WIN DEMONSTRATIONS

1. THE DEPARTMENT WAS INFORMED BY THE BURMESE EMBASSY JULY 18 OF PROPOSED DEMONSTRATIONS TO BE LED BY U KYAW WIN, AN ACTIVE CRITIC OF THE NE WIN GOVERNMENT AND THE PUBLISHER OF BURMA BULLETIN, AT THE EMBASSY, WHITE HOUSE, AND/OR CAPITOL HILL. INQUIRIES AT THE DC POLICE INDICATED A PERMIT FOR A DEMONSTRATION HAD BEEN GRANTED FOR JULY 18.

2. DUE TO LACK OF FOLLOWING OR INTEREST, THE INTENDED DEMONSTRATIONS APPEAR TO HAVE FIZZLED. WE HAVE RECEIVED A REPORT THAT ONLY A VERY SMALL DEMONSTRATION (5 OR 6 PERSONS) WAS HELD AT THE WHITE HOUSE. KISSINGER

Demonstration at the U.S. Capitol, 18 Jul 1975.
Left to right: Bishop James Mathews, Riri, Jim Moore, Win. Photo by U Aung.

I had been hoping that our demonstration would get some coverage. It did not get any. I wrote in the October 1975 issue of *The Burma Bulletin*:

Another item on U Kyaw Win's agenda in discussions with Capitol Hill and State Department officials was the practice of recruiting staff for the Voice of America's Burmese Service from the Burma Broadcasting Service. The Bulletin editor vehemently objected to the continuance of this practice maintaining that such recruited personnel are planted by the powerful Military Intelligence Service—Burma's secret police. He supported his argument citing that an abundant supply of highly qualified American citizens or permanent residents of Burmese origin already exists and it is highly inappropriate for the American taxpayer to be paying the wages of MIS informers in the United States. On 18 July, to honor the memory of General Aung San, Burma's founding father, and cabinet who were assassinated on 19 July 1947, U Kyaw Win and his Indonesian-born wife, Gandasari Abdullah-Win, led a demonstration on the steps of the U.S. Capitol and in front of The White House.

The demonstration against the Burmese military was the first of its kind in Washington. I have in my possession an undated letter from Father around this time:

I lost 30 lbs—now my body weight is 110. Your Mum looks very thin because of loss of her B.W. . . . She is just as beautiful as in the days of our courtship. Yes she loves you as the youngest child of hers and I too love all my sons and daughter on the basis of equality, however I keep you in the tight corner of my heart as my special. . . . I refuse to die as I have to witness the saving power of Jesus Christ.

I cried in my sleep. Riri woke me up. How can politics be so cruel? The helplessness was overwhelming. I felt like a blindfolded man, whose hands were tied behind the back, standing on a distant shore and hearing my parents' cries while they were going under, totally helpless to render aid of any sort. Father was undaunted in his support for the military regime, although I believe that in his letters he also had one eye on the censors. He was always full of hope. It was his national government, so he was sure that it would do well. In another undated letter, he wrote:

Of late our country was in the throes of the referendum and election of representatives to the Congress and Council at different levels. Now no more dictatorship as power to manage the affairs of the country is in the hands of citizens of the country.

There is rigid line drawn between religion and state. So we can carry on the work of the Church with complete freedom.

In the January 1976 issue of *The Burma Bulletin*, I reported that, "Burmese Ambassadors are finding it increasingly difficult to accept invitations from their colleagues because they are unable to reciprocate the invitations. Often the Ambassadors do not receive their salaries on time."

I was sorely disappointed with my compatriots living in America. We were living in a free country, yet most of them refused to speak out against the junta; they just went about getting and spending. I felt that one way to fight the military regime was for Burmese abroad to stand up against injustice. I gave vent to my frustration in the same issue:

> *Can Burma Count On You?* It is rather disappointing to note that many Burma experts and scholars in the West prefer to remain silent about Ne Win's atrocities in exchange for an occasional visa to Burma. One American professor openly admitted that as an academic he needs fresh knowledge about Burma and therefore could ill afford to offend the Ne Win clique by exposing its excesses and corruption. In short, no visa, no gravy (for the academic).
>
> This opportunistic and compromising character is not a rare phenomenon. Foreign officials assigned to Burma often perceive their roles as disinterested observers who must avoid embarrassing the host government at all cost. Such spineless bureaucrats are more concerned with maintaining their "stature" than in taking a stand of conscience. To these people, moral obligation, ideology, and conscience are abstract hollow words. Perhaps we should not be too harsh with these foreigners who can live with their indifference. After all, Burma is not their country. But what excuse do Burmese living comfortably abroad have for their lack of concern for those living in misery back home? In the final analysis, the Burmese mind is the biggest hindrance to Burma's progress. It is they who must put aside their selfish pettiness and unite for a common and noble cause. They should learn to respect each other regardless of ethnic origin. This is the least that one owes as children of Burma, Land of Pagodas, where once peace and prosperity reigned. This calls for a revolution, a revolution of the mind without which there can be no hope for Burma.

Sir Walter Scott's *The Lay of the Last Minstrel,* which I had to memorize at Woodstock School, speaks to these shamelessly spineless creatures:

Breathes there the man with soul so dead
Who never to himself hath said,
This is my own, my native land!
Whose heart hath ne'er within him burned,
As home his footsteps he hath turned
From wandering on a foreign strand!
If such there breathe, go, mark him well;
For him no minstrel raptures swell;
High though his titles, proud his name,
Boundless his wealth as wish can claim
Despite those titles, power, and pelf,
The wretch, concentred all in self,
Living, shall forfeit fair renown,
And, doubly dying, shall go down
To the vile dust from whence he sprung,
Unwept, unhonored, and unsung.

The Burmese epithet for such "doubly dying" creatures is *hsan kon myay lei* [rice wasters, earth's burdens].

Riri and I were on sabbatical from our respective colleges and, with Zali and Dewi, had made our way across Europe to Turkey, from there to Egypt and Tanzania, where we had gone to visit the Sanjoto family. Djoko Sanjoto was now deputy chief of mission at the Indonesian embassy in Dar-es Salaam. We then went on to India to be with U Nu in Bhopal.

IN BHOPAL WITH U NU

At the *vihara* [monastery] in the shadow of the Great Stupa and the adjoining Emperor Asoka's Pillar in Sanchi, three Sri Lankan monks shaved my head, clothed me with a saffron robe, and initiated me as a novice monk. They went into a huddle and came up with an auspicious name. "We will initiate you with the monastic name *Gawsa*," the senior monk said. When I asked what it meant, he said, in Sanskrit it means, "Voice of the Buddha." The solemn rites over, food was served. An elderly nun approached me with a gift of a Buddhist icon and wished me the peace of the Enlightened One. I was served at a table separate from the monks.

After the monks had finished eating, laypersons were fed. U Nu took charge of the entire proceedings to the minutest detail, including the feeding of the truckload of policemen armed with Enfield .303 rifles who had escorted us the 46km distance from and to Bhopal.

U Nu and I walked the immense grounds of Ahmedabad Palace where the Indian government had put up his family in a mansion that was quaintly called a bungalow. A plain clothed police officer accompanied us in the daily silent meditation walks. Food was brought to me each dawn and again before noon. No food was consumed after noon until dawn. I meditated in my room except for the walking meditations with U Nu. At the end of the week I felt light, as if all my burdens had been liberated. On more than one occasion, a mouse visited my room, but it was spared because I had taken a vow of not harming any living being.

Mr. Karr, a Burmese-speaking foreign service officer, was assigned to U Nu as a liaison officer with the Ministry of External Affairs. His family was housed in an adjoining house. He had been serving at the embassy in Washington when he received a cable transferring him to Bhopal. He told me he was puzzled and wondered if an error had been made because he could not think of any diplomatic post in the central Indian city. Mr. Karr had a daughter who was unhappy with the move and wanted to get back to Washington.

This was when Indira Gandhi was Prime Minster. Her father Prime Minister Jawarhalal Nehru was U Nu's friend. But now Nu had eschewed politics. Or had he? He was very keen on meditation, so much so that he urged me to establish a meditation center in California. He believed that meditation was salvation. Curiously, not a word about politics transpired between us. He was very careful that way, but it also seemed as though he had lost interest. His elder son Thaung Htike and daughter Than Than Nu and their spouses were living with him, together with their two sons. His Japanese daughter-in-law, Kikku, was pregnant with their second child. Riri had urged her to come to America to give birth, because health care in Bhopal was less than satisfactory. Tragically, she bled to death at delivery.

"You must take your children to see their grandparents," U Nu urged Riri at his dinner table in Bhopal one evening in November 1975. He was aware of the intimidation that a home visit might create, but insisted, "You will never feel right if you didn't try to go to Burma after being this close."

So we made plans for Riri to take the children to Burma. Under normal circumstances we could have felt confident that she would be issued a visa. But recently she had begun joining me in challenging the legitimacy of the Ne Win dictatorship, so we could not be certain.

Our original itinerary had called for a flight direct from Bombay to Bangkok, but our soft-spoken host had planted a seed. So we broke off our journey in Calcutta, where Riri went with the children to the Burmese Consulate General to apply for visas. The visas were issued the same afternoon. That night we hastily purchased canned provisions, essential medicines, powdered milk, and toilet articles, and repacked the bags. I inherited many of Riri's and the children's personal items, in favor of the added weight they would be carrying to my parents. I went through their bags and wallets and removed photographs of me and papers that bore my name.

"When you arrive in Rangoon," I had advised Riri, "go straight to the American embassy and report your arrival. Tell the embassy where you are staying. At the hotel, remain close to other tourists. When you detect the first sign of trouble, get in touch with the embassy." To thirteen-year-old Zali, I said, "Stay close to Mommy and take care of her and your sister." It was difficult to hide my apprehension, but if he was afraid, he did not show it. I gave him a detailed briefing and had him memorize a sketch of several routes to the embassy, which fortunately was near the Strand Hotel, where they would be staying. "If you sense a problem or Mommy signals you, make your way fast to the embassy and ask for help. If you can't make it to the American embassy, go to the British embassy next door. Don't worry if you don't have the passport with you. As soon as you start speaking, they'll know you're American. The British are our friends." (The children were included in Riri's passport.)

To ten-year-old Dewi I said, "Don't be afraid. Do this for Grandpa and Grandma, who long for us all. Listen to Mommy. Give Grandpa and Grandma big hugs." I reached for her shoulder. "You'll be all right," I reassured her.

We turned in for a night that seemed like an eternity, but were up at dawn. I took them to the airport but remained out of sight of Union of Burma Airways (UBA) personnel. We said hardly a word to each other at the terminal. Just before they entered the line for immigration formalities, I whispered in Riri's ear, "I'll meet your flight in Bangkok day after tomorrow." We were taking a calculated risk, but we felt that my parents' frail health made it necessary.

That morning I felt very close to Riri and the children, but was very worried. I went back into town to finalize my own travel arrangements. I had not told Riri and the children my own flight plan. I could not dismiss the possibility that the Burmese secret police might kidnap me if it learned of my movements.

I reserved a seat on the Scandinavian Airlines flight to Bangkok the next day. Then I walked over to the U.S. Consulate General to report my own flight plan. Aviation procedures designate a diversion point between any two destinations in case of an emergency. Rangoon is such a point between Calcutta and Bangkok. If the plane were diverted to Rangoon, I could be forcibly removed and silenced. Surely the U.S. government would come to my aid if that happened, I reasoned. But to my dismay, Robert O'Neill, the consular officer, said unfeelingly, "Naturalized American citizens from Eastern Europe who find themselves in a similar predicament have been apprehended by their country of origin, which claim them as their own citizens. If you're playing this political game, you should not fly over Burma." He meticulously flipped the pages of my passport and took down the names of countries and dates I had visited. He hinted that there was little the U.S. government could do. I was offended by his "playing this political game" lecture. He was abrupt. Apparently he had been assigned to the U.S. Consulate General in Chiang Mai, Thailand, because he said Burmese consulate personnel there were intelligence officers. Just as I was leaving, he summoned a stenographer. Presumably he was going to dictate a memorandum of my encounter with him after I left. In disgust, I departed the high walls of the U.S. Consulate General trembling and lonely.

Promptly at six o'clock the next morning, I boarded the airport coach in front of SAS's downtown office, heavily laden with baggage. The only other passenger on the coach, a young Canadian, was traveling light and offered to pool my baggage with his. It was a thoughtful gesture that I truly appreciated. After I checked in, I paced the floor. Suddenly, an announcement over the P.A. system delivered another blow. Poor visibility had made landing in Calcutta hazardous, so the pilot had decided to continue on to Bangkok.

Passengers were offered one of two alternatives: spend another night in Calcutta, or take a short hop to Dhaka and connect there with a Thai Airways flight to Bangkok three hours hence. Burdened with worry, I didn't want to stay another night in Calcutta. Several days earlier, some Bangladeshi army officers had fled the country via Dhaka after killing some rivals in an attempted coup. What if a bloodier counter-coup took place before the next connecting flight had taken off from there?

I was attempting to fathom the feelings of fellow passengers over the dilemma when I befriended an American gentleman. I introduced myself. "I'm Bill Jarvis," he said.

"Where are you from, Bill?" I asked.

"Valley Forge, Pennsylvania," he replied.

"What do you do there, Bill?" I asked.

"I'm treasurer of the American Baptist International Ministries," he said.

Oh, my gosh! What a happy surprise! A few years earlier I had exchanged correspondence with this very gentleman regarding disposition of some funds I had raised for a church in Burma in memory of a departed friend. Meeting Bill Jarvis at this crucial moment was a godsend. He was willing to go to Dhaka, so off we flew in a Biman Airways Fokker Friendship plane.

At Dhaka I sensed the tension at the terminal. As soon as the plane taxied to a halt at Dhaka terminal, I felt the tension. "Please don't leave the lounge," the airline's ground agent requested. Five hours later, as the sun was setting, a Thai Airways Super DC-8 landed. A large group of Russians disembarked. As we were boarding, a (West) German diplomat told me, "Don't worry, if this plane lands in Rangoon, we'll protect you." He calmed my nerves.

The plane flew over the Arakan coast of Burma and across the Irrawaddy Delta. I craned my neck. The blotch of lights below resembled a huge amoeba. I tried to identify Rangoon's landmarks in the nocturnal glow, but to my disappointment the lights of the Shwedagon and Sulé pagodas were not visible. But I could make out the outlines of Rangoon's waterfront and calculated the approximate location of the Strand Hotel. Creek Street, where the Methodist parsonage was situated, was nine short blocks to the east. A lone ocean-going vessel was anchored midstream in the once-busy harbor. An eerie atmosphere seemed to hang over the city of my youth. Several questions burdened me: Were my parents all right? Were they getting enough to eat? Were they receiving proper medical care? How about my eldest brother and sister and their families, and the other relatives and friends?

In a flashback, my mind's eye focused on my mother standing in an umbrella's shade on the other side of a wire-meshed fence at the jetty the day I left Burma for the first time in 1950. "When someone does something for you, show appreciation so that he feels good helping you," were her words to a departing son. Those words haunted me this night and choked me up. Slowly the lights of Rangoon faded in the distance. About twenty minutes later, the plane was preparing to land in Bangkok. The lights of that larger city were much brighter and more abundant, as if in festivity. And festivity it was indeed! The Thais were celebrating the birthday of their beloved king. It was midnight when Bill Jarvis and I checked in at the Bangkok Christian Guest House.

In the morning I was on my way back to the airport. From the terminal balcony I watched the passengers disembarking. My heart skipped a beat. The plane was nearly empty now, and I became alarmed. What had happened to Riri and the children? Had they missed the flight? Had they been detained? Suddenly, three figures standing by the shuttle coach came into focus. They were waving furiously. In my anxiety, I had missed seeing them descend the stairs. The ordeal of a tension-ridden week finally came to a jubilant end.

I soon learned that in Rangoon, Riri and the children had experienced a tense moment at the airport. After processing them through, the immigration officer had had second thoughts and followed them to the curb. Riri and Dewi were already seated in the taxi, a 1939 De Soto. Zali was overseeing the loading of baggage into the trunk when the officer asked, "Is your father Burmese?"

"Yes," Zali said.

"Do you have relatives in Burma?"

"Most of them are in Indonesia and the United States," he answered calmly. Before anything further developed, the taxi chugged off through the tree-lined boulevards. When they reached the American embassy, Riri rushed inside with the children in tow. The Marine guard was protective. The receptionist telephoned the secretary to Richard Howarth, the deputy chief of mission, who came down the stairs and escorted them to his office. Rick was the consular officer when I worked in the embassy fifteen years before. It was then his first posting. He was now back at the embassy as the chargé d'affaires, after Ambassador David L. Osborn had left the post. Rick was familiar with my activism against the Burmese military regime. "How did you manage to slip into the country?" he asked, somewhat surprised. "Why did you brave this?"

"Faith," answered Riri, as she sank into the sofa. "I have faith that everything will turn out all right."

When they reached the Strand Hotel, Riri called my mother.

"Mom, this is Riri," she said.

"Who?" asked Mother.

"Riri, the children are with me."

"Where is Ah Cho?" (Ah Cho is my childhood name).

"I cannot tell you where he is, but he is all right," said Riri.

Then my mother broke down and said, in a quavering voice, "*Ah Pa* is very ill. He cannot breathe at times. He has not eaten in a few days. I was about to cable you all." Then it dawned on her to ask, "Where are you?"

"I'm at the Strand Hotel, we'll be over shortly."

After gathering the items they had brought, Riri and the children went downstairs. Who would be waiting in the lobby? My mother, of course! She was sharing the happy news with the hotel employees. She had given up hope of ever seeing Riri and her grandchildren again. She was simply overjoyed.

When they reached home, Father broke down. This was very unlike him. He had always been strong and sure of himself. "Your Ah Pa cries often these days," Mother told Riri tearfully. "Often, when he wakes up in the middle of the night, he calls out your names. You live so far away."

That evening, for the first time in several days, Father ate some food. He lovingly munched on the pastries I had purchased at Calcutta airport.

The next day he was up and walked to the dining table. "Your coming is like a tonic for him," whispered Mother to Riri. That night, Riri and the children retired early to the hotel. They had to catch the plane early the next day. In taking leave, they knelt before my parents and kissed their feet.

Sometime not long after that visit, I received the following letter from Father:

> I have no doubt as to your surprise to receive this letter from one whom you must have considered as one dead and phased out. I'm leaving the shore of California [he was disoriented and confused]. I have been hospitalized five times; the last one I have had was the worst one: 20 days with day and night nurses. Your akogyi [eldest brother] took me to the hospital unconscious.

I could only weep. The emotional turmoil affected my health, even leading to a need for heart surgery. The loneliness was deep and mutual, and my parents' health declined rapidly. In a letter written on 29 May 1976, Father said:

> When Riri, Zali & Dewi came to us, how I wish I could entertain them to the best of my hospitality, but I wasn't feeling fine then. I offered them as much money as they desired, but to my disappointment, they all refused the offer. It was really a great source of delight to look at their beautiful faces. I can never forget the scene of our separation from them. I therefore live conscious of them. Many a time, I dream of them and find my mind wandering in a work a day world of theirs.

Six months later, on 22 November 1976, Mother informed us:

> The other day your Pa asked me to cable Simon for some medicine. I added milk powder, etc. It appears that we are now waiting for the ferry to cross Jordan. When he is in the mood he wants and can go anywhere. But when he's not in the mood, he wouldn't or couldn't even go to prayer meeting in the church. Today he had one tooth pulled out and was told to come again tomorrow for another tooth. I don't think that it would be good or advisable to do that, but he insisted on doing it. . . . We need milk powder, honey, peanut butter and some nice things to eat. Honey agrees with his emphysema—so small tin or bottle of peanut butter. . . . Your Pa likes/wants best of all—first choice to be with you kids. Now, good news is in the air. They will relax— allow those who are abroad to come home to visit. *Woon thar lite ta* [very happy]. Try, try, try again.

Mother passed away on 26 April 1979, fifteen days after their 60th wedding anniversary. She had woken up in the morning, gone into the garden, picked some fragrant gardenias, tucked them into her hair, and gone back to bed because she felt very tired. Quietly and peacefully, she left us, of a broken heart. She was 83. "Your Mother is gone. I will join her too." Those were the last words I heard Father say to me on the phone, two weeks after she died.

In July of that year, Riri again took Zali and Dewi to Burma. What follows is her own account of the ordeal she and our children endured, as published in the July 1979 issue of *The Burma Bulletin* under the title "Into the Lion's Den on a Humanitarian Mission." I considered rewriting it, but part of the point of the story I'm telling is precisely because for forty years I was unable to make this visit myself, for purely political reasons. The junta had denied me entry to my homeland. Riri wrote:

> Unlike the previous years, our trip to Rangoon this time was purely to see Ahpa, my father-in-law, who had just turned 85 and is on his deathbed waiting to join Mom, my mother-in-law, who suddenly passed away in April. Mom was the only person who made our stay in Burma in the past pleasant and memorable. She delighted us with some silly jokes, family gossip and memories of days gone by. She would squeal with childish delight at the little things we brought her—a cake of soap, a package of chocolate, or a bottle of perfume. Ahpa, on the other hand, had always been a prominent preacher, always serious and moralistic. He lives in a world of super nationalism and Christian love.
>
> Ahpa has been in and out of the hospital and is now recuperating from a serious physical discomfort. Before Mom passed away, she wrote that every night Ahpa called the names of his grandchildren who are far away in the United States. He pined to be with his three sons who are not allowed to re-enter Burma even for a short visit. My heart aches whenever I think of the inhumane restrictions placed politically by the present Burmese military junta on its own people. Because of the government's desire to perpetuate its power, it restricts the individual rights to basic human freedom.
>
> Our children have been taught that life is meaningful only within the context of family and community circles. They have been taught that the purpose of life is to lighten the burden of human suffering and to help those who are less fortunate to enjoy fuller lives. As such, the discomfort for a few days of going

into Burma was still a grace since we would be bringing delight and happiness to Ahpa, the declining warrior of God.

The Burma Airways plane was full of Japanese who obviously realize the potentials of Burma's natural resources. Oil has been mentioned more and more lately as a potential source of revenue, and the Japanese appreciate fully the importance of this commodity in the world market. There were also some European and American tourists on the plane, many of them dressed so comfortably that it reminded me of the hippy years of the 1960s. It is apparently true that Burma is opening up for tourists and select businessmen.

At seven o'clock that evening, the Burma Airways Boeing 727 touched down at Rangoon's Mingaladon Airport. We proceeded to go through the usual entry formalities. When we got to the immigration counter, our passports were turned over to a plain- clothed military person.

Undisturbed, we proceeded to go through the customs counter. We were forewarned of the complicated customs process in Burma, the listing of every piece of jewelry, the accounting of all foreign money, the listing of every brand of camera, electronic gadgets, etc. The officer kept on changing the customs forms on me. Over and over again my papers were switched, and I was asked to fill out different things on different forms. I was bemused by the fact that the customs officer looked more confused than I was. Finally that was finished. We now waited for our suitcases to come down from the airplane. I depended on Zali, who competently took over his father's task in taking care of travel arrangements.

Suddenly an immigration officer gently tapped my daughter's shoulder. "Are you Dewi Sita Win?" he asked softly.

"Yes," she answered.

Feeling uncomfortable, I chimed in, "I'm the mother," I said. "There are three of us. Is there a problem?"

"Please come with me to the office," he said softly, so as not to be heard by the other passengers. At that moment little did I realize that the tap on my daughter's shoulder was to be the beginning of a touch of disaster that was to last until the end of our stay, three days later. The children and I exchanged quick glances but walked calmly into the Immigration Office.

We were now isolated from the other passengers. The office was not more than twelve feet square, and a bare bulb burned dimly. The walls were filthy with betel nut spit. In the corner of the room was the familiar Burmese earthen jar with a common cup on top. Just as I was looking away, I saw a mouse crawling over the cup.

It was then that I saw "Shortie," the immigration officer in charge that evening. The expression on his face seemed to delight him with the mistaken thought that he had in custody an infamous spy—with two children.

"May I see your passport?" he asked. He leafed through it very carefully and inspected the visa forms issued by the New York consulate. His pursed thin lips made him look even shorter.

"Who is your husband?"

"U Kyaw Win," I replied.

"Where is he now?"

"In California." I immediately sensed trouble. What kind of file do they have on my husband? What are they going to do to us now?

"Is there any problem?" I asked.

"Yes," he answered curtly, "there is a problem."

Then a group of officers came into the room. They were discussing my case in Burmese. Damn it! If only I had learned Burmese and knew more of the language beyond *keit-sa ma-shi bu* ["It does not matter"].

"Do you understand Burmese?" asked Shortie.

"*Ne-ne-be na-le-de*," I said proudly. [I understand only a little]. But to brag about my very, very little knowledge of Burmese was a mistake, since that only convinced the authorities that I was a bilingual spy trying to be coy.

The room became stuffier with curious officers. The plain-clothes intelligence officer now came in with a book of photographs. Apparently my picture was there too. Somebody made a comment that it was not me in the picture. "It is she," said a stern voice, "before she became fat." The children waited calmly with me for the officers' next move.

Armed guards came in and out. A written report was handed to Shortie. He took a seat next to his desk. Sitting down, his feet barely touched the floor. (I remember that most Burmese people are uncomfortable in western outfits, and do not feel comfortable sitting on a chair with their feet down. I am sure that, had the occasion not been so serious, Shortie would have preferred to sit in his *longyi* with one foot up on the chair, chewing betel nut). In an officious voice, he read the report aloud. How I wished I understood what was written about me and about my husband. But perhaps it was a blessing that I did not fathom the seriousness of the situation as yet.

I asked Shortie innocently: "If there is a problem concerning my entry, what is to happen now?"

"You cannot go into town," he said.

"You certainly have the right to deny me entry," I said. "It is your country and it is your sovereignty. When is the next plane out?"

"Tomorrow morning at 7 o'clock," he replied. I was still calm then.

"Perhaps, you will allow the children and me to rest on the benches in the lobby outside?"

"No, wait here." I was too impertinent for a persona non grata. The children wisely remained completely silent. The airport lobby became quieter as most of the passengers began leaving. All of a sudden through the door opening, I saw my brother-in-law's face. I gave a sound of delight, but the door was immediately closed, and that was my last contact with the world. He was shoved outside and immediately interrogated. "They treated me like a criminal," he exclaimed later. "I was so mad I could not sleep the whole night."

When he left, an eerie feeling crept into me. By now, all of the passengers were gone. The telephone rang several times, and my case was mentioned over the phone. The small room became more crowded. I had to watch the immigration officers change into the more comfortable *longyi* and sandals. I could not help but see their dinky undershirts, but was spared the sight of their dirty underpants only by the adroit way they handled their *longyi*. I also noticed their socks full of holes, and they smelled like they had not been to the laundry in a long time.

Shortie came in and out of the room, accumulating information on me from the intelligence officer next door. Apparently he decided to join the act and asked for a form to write down "my confession." "Please take a seat," he said pointing to a chair in front of his desk. "Give me a statement and your marital relationship." I pretended not to hear him and refused the chair. Shortie was embarrassed by the putdown. He looked forlorn and retreated to the next room, leaving the official papers to be filled untouched. Zali was thirsty and asked for a glass of water. Some officers felt sympathetic and showed some kindness.

Shortie now decided to ask for reinforcements. He attempted to call the Director of Immigration at the airport, who was unavailable that evening. In the meantime, no word was communicated to us as to our fate. Officers, men, guards, went in and out of the room, throwing glances at us and maintaining an intimidating silence. Zali and Dewi were confident this night-mare would end soon and tried to catch some rest.

Around midnight, we heard footsteps and commotion in the hallway. Soon the door swung open, and a heavyset person in Burmese *longyi* came in, followed by an army captain, dressed in uniform complete with a holstered pistol. "Wake up, son," I said to Zali. "The boss is here."

Soon the room was full of armed guards, immigration officers, and plainclothesmen. "Mr. Fat Director" looked friendly but rather embarrassed. Where had they found him? At his mistress's house? Drinking? Anyway, soon I heard his hesitant voice. "Statement *pay-ba*," he said. "Give me your statement." I was so overwhelmed by the crowd of men surrounding me that I honestly did not follow him.

"I beg your pardon?" My voice sounded cool and collected.

"Please give me your statement," he said in English. My eyes met the harsh expression of the army captain who sat next to Mr. Fat Director. I felt a chill run through my spine, but not for long. Then a warm feeling surged up and I felt at ease almost immediately. I decided to conduct the whole thing in a formal way.

"Sir," I said, "I came to Burma with a valid passport and a tourist visa. I have been held in this room since arrival without being given any explanation."

By this time I had enough adrenaline to speak with emphasis. "My statement, Sir, is this. You have the authority to deny me entry into this country. This is your sovereignty, this is your right. However, if you detain me in here, I have the right to get in touch with my embassy. This basic human right has been denied me since seven o'clock this evening!" I chose my words very carefully and they came out clearly and emphatically.

Mr. Fat Director did not expect such oratory and for a while was nonplussed. He tried to coax me into giving information voluntarily. "Anyway," he proceeded, "we are not interrogating you. We just want some particulars."

I held my ground. "Sir, all the particulars you need to know are in the passport." I adjusted my seat so that my back was straight and my shoulders high. The captain looked at the passport and leafed through it over and over again. He was making his authoritative presence felt. I realized that he was the only person I could reason with. Judging by his rank and age, I surmised that he must have attended college and would understand the basic principles of human rights. I offered a way out.

"Sir, I will oblige and provide any information you need, but in the presence of an official of my embassy. You realize, as holder of this passport, I am under the jurisdiction of my government or its representative. I need my government's protection now, and only with the consent of my government will I give any statement."

There was silence. The overeager young intelligence officer who had been with the "case" since seven o'clock that evening could not follow the dialogue that was going on. Indeed, the Burmese officers of today are not the same as the officers of twenty years ago when I left Burma. The young Burmese leaders of today have not heard of the principles of justice, the rights of the individual, freedom of speech, and other democratic principles. Unlike their predecessors, the young officers of today have little knowledge of world history, politics, economics, and geography. These young men only know how to follow dogmas, how to annihilate public enemies, how to guard the nation from foreign influence. Nowhere have I seen such dogmatic faces, not even in the Communist nations of the Soviet Union, the People's Republic of China, or elsewhere in Southeast Asia.

It was only at that moment, when surrounded by the armed guards, military intelligence officers, and narrow-minded plainclothes men that I realized the serious predicament I was in. I could almost hear a Burmese friend telling me some time ago: "The Military Intelligence Service might interrogate any woman and harass her. They are known to electrocute the most sensitive parts of the woman." A Burmese escapee in Bangkok had once told me: "They detained my wife for three years without a trial, just to get to me. The present regime is known to torture the wives to get the husbands." Another said: "My dear, the Gestapo tactics are revived here in Rangoon. Students who were questioned by the Military Intelligence Service were tortured in front of a sun lamp. In a few hours their skin peeled off, showing the raw skin underneath." I cringed in fear. I told myself that they would not do that to me, a foreigner.

My mind raced very fast. Then I recalled an account from a foreign representative who had been held up at Mingaladon Airport. "While I was being interrogated, I heard a woman wailing and screaming next door," she said. "I had never been so petrified in my life. I suffered a mental breakdown three months after my release." I took a deep breath, and a warm feeling surfaced again. I have nothing to hide and I am not guilty of anything, I told myself. Soon that feeling of reassurance came back. I heard myself say out loud, "Since I am not allowed to go into town, I will leave Burma on the earliest flight tomorrow morning." I sounded so calm, and the authorities present were not sure whether they could let me go so easily. The crowd did not want to debate the issue in front of me. Mr. Fat Director left the room, followed by the military intelligence officer. Zali, Dewi, and I held each other close.

Apparently reason prevailed, and I was to be left alone without the usual interrogation. The door opened and Shortie came in. "Why don't you rest on the benches in the lobby," he said. "And bring all your handbags." In the corner I saw Mr. Fat Director sitting on the bench, his *longyi* covering the one uplifted foot on the bench, while his other foot dangled on the floor without the sandal. The military intelligence officer was not in sight.

The lights were turned off, and in the shadows of the hallway light I could distinguish men sleeping on the benches around us. An armed guard was in the corner, and many ears and eyes were fixed on us. There were lots of mosquitoes. When I took the mosquito spray out of my handbag and sprayed the children and myself, there was a hushed commotion. The silent armed guards were relieved to know that it was only a mosquito bomb! The squealing of rats throughout the night convinced me that there were more bodies than my eyes could see to keep us in custody.

When we were escorted to the bathroom, I noticed the police camped out on the second floor. I was kind of amused to discover the next morning that, in addition to the scores of armed guards, Mr. Fat Director, Shortie, the military captain, and others had had to sleep in the lobby that night. I could not sleep and sat straight up at 4:30 a.m. Immediately the rest of the crowd also got up. Apparently the immigration officers on duty always sleep in the lobby. In the morning, each lined up at the bathroom with a chewed-up toothbrush, no toothpaste, no soap, and a dinky hand towel over one shoulder. To me, it was a sad commentary on the Burmese economy.

We welcomed the sunrise, for at daybreak the plane that was to take us out would be ready. But the Burmese authorities were not yet ready to let us go free. The plane's departure time approached, but they did not process us out.

I became alarmed, and a feeling of desperation set in. Some foreigners proceeded to the departure lounge after completing formalities. Were we to be left alone again without the world knowing? What was to happen to us now? Were we being used by the Burmese consulate and lured into this country to be tortured and interrogated for information about my husband? I finally broke down and became almost hysterical.

I faced the departing foreigners and told them, in a loud voice: "Please let my embassy know that I have been held here since last night. I am being held incommunicado, I can't leave either."

"Why?" asked an inquisitive French girl.

"I don't know," I told her. "But I have not been able to get in touch with the representative of my government."

The foreigners were awed, and the Burmese officers became embarrassed at my outburst. They did not expect such a public scene.

Shortie approached me and said, "Please come to my office."

"Your office!" I screamed. "You held me prisoner yesterday for six hours already. I refuse to be imprisoned in your office!" He shrank a few inches and looked so small. "And let me tell you this," I said, loud enough to be heard by the foreigners, "Your government gave me the visa to enter Burma. Legally that means that I am your guest, and *you*"—leaving no doubt that I was addressing him personally—"should treat me as a guest of your government." I looked around and saw the frightened faces of the departing foreigners. Zali and Dewi realized that I was at the end of my tether. My adrenaline gave me the necessary breathing for another outburst. Now I faced the Burmese officers.

"Listen," I said to them. "I have been harassed since last night and treated like a criminal. Do I look like a criminal? Do I look like I have come to overthrow your government? Would I bring my children into Burma if my purpose were to spy on your government?"

I saw a sympathetic face amongst the crowd. It encouraged me enough to let it all hang out. "I don't understand why I have not been able to get in touch with my embassy. Even a thief is allowed to have a lawyer for his defense. I have been denied my basic human rights, and this is in violation of international law."

The whole room was watching me now. "Burma is a member of the United Nations, and your government is signatory to the Declaration of Human Rights," I said. "This detention is not in line with the Burmese Government's directive. This is obviously somebody's doing, and he is in violation of international law. Let your government know about this, and I am sure that that person will pay a high price. As a matter of fact, you should let the Foreign Office know that a foreigner is being detained at the airport. They will know what to do." The officers were embarrassed, clearly wishing they were not party to this international scene.

An immigration officer approached me and said, "Please be calm. You may want to wash your face. You are indeed our guests, and you are free to go anywhere in this airport." I did not want to give in to his coaxing.

"If you treat me like your guest, then you would feed me," I said. "But I have not been given food or drink, and this is not the Burmese way. I know of Burmese hospitality. A Burmese would share whatever he has with his guests, even if it were only rice and *ngan-pya yay* [fish sauce]." Strangely enough, the officers nodded their heads. I emphasized over and over again that this incident was not the Burmese government's wish, and that the treatment I received was incongruent with the gentle way of the Burmese. That hit the raw nerves of the people at the airport.

Immediately there was a flurry of telephone calls, and the atmosphere changed radically. Suddenly I became a guest of the airport immigration authorities, even though it was still more like being under custody. The military guards made themselves inconspicuous and seemed to be in retreat. I was confident that reason would prevail and that there would not be any further harassment. Yet the nature of the present military junta in Burma is such that any reasonable development could occur only after the military made sure of its impact on the population—in this case, on me and the children.

THE FINAL HARASSMENT

We were waiting in the lobby, and conversation was flowing freely now between us and the immigration officers. They told me of the decline of education in Burma and of their difficult living conditions. I reiterated that my detention was unnecessary, that the main reason we had come to Burma was to see Ahpa in the evening of his life. Reasonable authorities in the immigration department realized that an undue burden had been put on me, and the higher authorities wanted to correct "the small misunderstanding." At twelve o'clock that afternoon, I was told that the chief of the Burmese Immigration Department would arrive at the airport to see me. "Perhaps something could be worked out," said one immigration officer who had been assigned to be my host. However, nothing comes easy in Burma. The military made sure of that.

A few minutes after twelve, I was asked to see the Customs Department. Little did I realize that behind the calm atmosphere top brass of the Army, Military Intelligence, and Immigration Department were conferring in the next room. When I appeared before the Customs Department, a photographer took shots of me and the children. The armed guards appeared again, and some twenty Customs Officers stood ready to undertake the operation of the day. A few steps behind them were military intelligence officers taking note of the contents of every single piece of baggage I had. My blood rose again, and my temper could not be controlled. I noticed the intelligence captain who had been in charge since last night. I went straight to him and shouted out loud, "You, Sir, I told you yesterday that you have the right to restrict my movement in your country, you have the right to deny me entry, but you have no right to deny me contact with my embassy. You have violated international law, and this is not the way the Burmese government would act."

The head of the customs office came close to me and whispered, "Madam, I advise you to cool your temper." I suppose nobody had dressed down the military intelligence captain before. In despair I shouted out loud for everyone to hear.

"I have been harassed since yesterday, and this is sheer torture," I said. The crowd of officers were numb and proceeded to inspect the items I had brought in. This was the order from the Military Intelligence Service. My wallet was turned upside down, the camera case was dismantled, the umbrellas were opened and shaken so that the spokes shook and rattled. My checkbook was scrutinized, each figure was followed. The tampons I had brought along were opened and examined.

A somewhat comical episode occurred when they played a cassette I had in my tape recorder. The officer turned on the cassette as loud as possible, only to hear my students' off-key sing-a-long chorus, "Someone's in the kitchen with Dinah!" (My husband and I had visited China before I came to Burma with the children, and on our last night in China we were asked to sing some American songs, which I taped.) The whole scene was so ridiculous, with armed guards standing at attention, customs officers shaking every piece of material there was, and the silly tape sounding off "God Bless America."

I was bodily searched. When the woman kept on feeling my bra and sensitive parts, I decided to disrobe completely. "This is so much better," I declared in complete nudity. Somehow the comic atmosphere calmed me down, and I began to enjoy the stupid expressions of those around me. Zali and Dewi subjected themselves obediently to the body search. They acted so maturely.

Dewi carried a copy of *Mademoiselle* magazine to read on the plane. The customs officer who leafed through the magazine could not help but enjoy the pictures: the slim thighs, the pointed brassieres, the lipstick advertisements. He was so engrossed in the magazine until his boss had to remind him of the seriousness of the mission. Then came a friend's wedding pictures that we had taken some twenty years earlier. It was a society wedding and the ceremony was officiated by none other than Thakin Tin, the Minister of Finance under U Nu's government. The pictures went from hand to hand, and everybody pointed at the former Minister's pictures as if they had seen a ghost. It was pathetic to see how isolated Burma had become. These officers in front of me behaved as if they had come straight out of the jungle into the twentieth century. They were suspicious of everything luxurious. The wedding pictures were confiscated, the tape was confiscated, personal letters were confiscated, a blood pressure cuff was held, so was a telephone amplifier. I was filled more with pity than with disgust and did not mind the loss at all. After all, in a few minutes I would be leaving this godforsaken land into the Land of the Free, Thailand! The Burma Airways stewards were completing their departure proceedings, and Dewi and Zali helped them fill out the necessary papers.

Then I was approached by an immigration officer. "The Immigration Chief would like to see you," he said. I had forgotten all about him! And there he was, tall and handsome, sitting apart from the military. I could immediately tell that he was a university graduate of the pre-Ne Win era. He looked more educated than the rest and therefore, I suspected, more reasonable. "You were given a visa by our representative in New York," he said in a calm manner. "However, your husband is known politically to be opposed to our government."

Who isn't, I argued silently. The Chief had not come to argue with me. "You are also," he said. This was when I sat up straight and was ready to rebut. "We know about you," he added swiftly. "You translated articles into Burmese." Somehow this wrong information made me feel victorious. How disorganized and misinformed could the military intelligence be? I know only enough Burmese to exchange some pleasantries, but my pride restrained me from admitting this.

The Chief Immigration Officer must have taken my silence as acquiescence. "However," he proceeded. By now his tone was far from stern. I even detected some appreciation of my position. "I realize that you have come to Burma to see your ailing father-in-law. Therefore, I will give you permission to enter the town for 48 hours." I was bewildered at that kind offer, and he sensed it. "For humanitarian reasons," he emphasized.

I had not expected this consideration. A few minutes earlier the officers had been harassing me and proceeding to deport me, and now this Chief was telling me that he would grant me a 48-hour stay. Is this another entrapment after the harassments? The Burmese paranoia rubbed off on me. "Would I be allowed to visit my Burmese family and friends? Would I be permitted to see my foreign friends? Would I have the liberty to go into town?" He gave his personal assurance, but that was not enough for my tortured mind. "Could you put these guarantees in writing?"

He leaned back and said, "No, that I am not prepared to do. But you have my personal guarantee."

I looked at the scores of officers who surrounded us. "I want these gentlemen to be my witness," I said, "that you have guaranteed me safety and liberty to go into town for 48 hours."

"Yes," said the Chief. "You should go see your father-in-law immediately. He will be happy to see you." I shook his hand and was touched by the turn of events.

The next hour found us in the dilapidated parsonage in Creek Street. There, sitting up straight on the bed, was Ahpa. His emaciated body shook in uncontrollable sobs. He was panting, and we fanned furiously to stir some air into the stuffy room. "I refuse to die," he whispered hoarsely. "By the grace of Jesus Christ, my Lord, I will live to go to the States." Then, almost in the same breath, he said, "I lived through the days of British colonialism, and now this Socialist Republic of Burma has succeeded in freeing us from the vestiges of western imperialism." Ahpa's spirit was still alive. Why should I disturb that spirit with my woes and the maltreatment I had received at the airport? The time to depart came. The children *shikhoed* reverently. Ahpa cried, and his sobs almost choked him. I kissed his forehead. I had come and brought the love of his faraway sons. I left Ahpa with a dazed look on his face.

When I looked into the reasons for what had happened at the airport, I concluded that the Military Intelligence Service must have seen an article that Riri had published in *The Burma Bulletin*. When we visited U Nu in Bhopal in 1975, Riri became close to his daughter-in-law Kikku (the one who died in childbirth). Riri had written a tribute to her, bemoaning the tragedy. This had been translated into Burmese and published in an expatriate paper in Thailand without our knowledge, and the intelligence officer had referred to the article during her ordeal at the airport.

Father died eleven months later on Good Friday, 30 March 1980. He was 85. I think that by then he had begun to realize that what was happening in Burma was wrong. Years later Riri said to me, "I'm so glad he wasn't alive in 1988. I don't know how he would have felt about the uprising and massacre." I'm not sure that he would have said anything. He would have preached the Gospel. All along, his feelings were with the military regime. I'm sure that he would have been in tremendous pain. I was completely devastated by his death. I could only sob when I received the telegram. Father was buried beside Mother in the Christian cemetery in Rangoon.

The military regime later dug up the cemetery and removed the remains to another cemetery, to make room for a sales lot for used cars. Soon after that, the second cemetery was also emptied out.

In the summer of 1982, Riri and I took a group to China and Southeast Asia. During the trip I would rise very early every morning in each of the cities we visited and jog in the vicinity of the hotel. In Peking we were lodged at the Peking Hotel on Chang An Avenue, a short distance from Tiananmen Square. While jogging on the massive square, I felt an uncomfortable pain in my chest. I sat down on a marble bench near the white marble bridges beneath the huge portrait of Chairman Mao, and then walked back to the hotel when the pain subsided. I said nothing to Riri about the pain. I might have been sent to a hospital and kept in China. The pain subsided for the rest of the tour but it recurred again in November, after we got back home to Costa Mesa. The angiogram revealed four blocked arteries. I was operated on and discharged from the Hospital of the Good Samaritan in Los Angeles on Thanksgiving Day 1982.

THE KAREN CONNECTION

In December, still recuperating, I wanted to get out of the house. Against Riri's protests, we went on a vacation to Hawaii. Visiting Hawaii then was a small group of physicians sent by the Burmese regime. They were so afraid and intimidated to be meeting any Burmese abroad. In a private moment one of them, named Ruby, broke away from the group. She emptied her heart of all the difficulties they were having in Burma in health care and in general. She was careful not to be seen with Riri and me by others in her group. Such was the fear that the Burmese military regime had instilled in its citizens.

In the summer of 1983, while I was in Thailand, I made contact with the widow of Saw Ba U Gyi (Nita Zan), the Karen leader killed by the Burmese military in August 1950 near Kawkareik, in eastern Burma. She was living in Mae Sariang, in the Baptist hospital compound on the Thai side of the border. Her family had lived in Twante's Karen Quarter during World War II and our families knew each other. She had remarried Saw Benny Gyaw, who told me to see Soe Soe, a KIA liaison officer in Mae Sot, the Thai town across the Moei River from Burma's Myawaddy.

That night, after I had turned in, the hotel's front desk told me there was someone in the lobby who wanted to see me. This took me aback momentarily, but I went downstairs anyway. A smiling, friendly Thai gentleman who spoke English greeted me. After a few inconsequential icebreakers, he asked, "You want to see Bo Mya, why?"

"I want to cross the river to meet him," I said. "I want to see Manerplaw. Maybe I'll meet some Karen people I know. I want to know how they're doing. I am half Karen."

"Good! No *ploblem*," he said, and melted into the night.

What was that all about? He clearly was a Thai Intelligence officer who had come to check me out. Thailand's Intelligence apparatus spreads its tentacles into every nook and cranny to keep an eye and ear on Burma's many ethnic and other political dissidents in Thailand. There are so many of them that the dissidents joke among themselves that the Thai spooks themselves don't know how many of them there are.

Once I had a meeting in a restaurant on Silom Road in Bangkok with the Kachin Independence Organization (KIO) Chairman Brang Seng and his aide, James Lum Dau. Seated at the next table was a young man in blue jeans. He spoke such excellent standard Burmese that I mistook him for a Burmese. "He is Thai Intelligence," Brang Seng whispered into my ear on the sly. He might have been Burmese Intelligence as well, drawing pay from both.

Another time, after meeting with another Burmese dissident leader in a Bangkok restaurant, I needed to hail a cab. "Where you go?" asked the spook assigned to this detail.

"Bangkok Christian Guest House," I said.

"Saladaeng, Silom?" he asked.

"Yes, yes," I said.

"No *ploblem*, get on cycle. I take you there." I clung on for dear life on the back seat as he wove in and out of Bangkok's nightmarish traffic. You can't help liking these Thai spooks. Sometimes they can be so sweet.

In Mae Sot I went to a big house next to the Catholic Church on Asia Highway, which leads to the Moei River across which lies the Burmese town of Myawaddy. To the gatekeeper I offered the traditional Pwo Karen greeting, "*O su wah? Aw may wee lee yah.* [Are you okay? Have you eaten?]. *Soe Soe O wah?* [Is Soe Soe in?]"

"*Mae mae*," [yes, yes], he said, showing me to the living room. A young man appeared and said, "*Say naw, say naw.* [sit, sit]." Then Major Soe Soe of the guerrilla Karen National Liberation Army (KNLA) came down the stairs.

I related my pedigree to Soe Soe. It was not necessary. Nita Zan had already messaged him. She knew my family well. He disappeared up the stairs, reappeared momentarily. "Please come with me," he said, leading me up the stairs. Waiting in the large conference room were half a dozen senior men. They welcomed me and we talked. "Everything is arranged," they said. "Please come back after your wife and daughter link up with you. We will see you to Manerplaw."

I went back to Bangkok and waited for Riri and Dewi to fly in from Jakarta and brought them back to Mae Sot, together with Melody, a daughter of childhood friends. At Soe Soe's house one morning, we got into a pickup truck loaded with some gunnysacks full of rice. We were going to the KNLA headquarters. Riri and the two girls sat in the cab. The driver was called "Mao Zedong," probably because of his fair-complexion, the son of a Karen mother and a Chinese father. An assistant driver rode with me in the tarp-covered truck bed.

It rained sheets most of the journey north along the road through a grove of tall, massive teak trees. We stopped at a checkpoint. "Mao Zedong" showed the Thai Army guards a document. They cursorily checked the truck, then raised the bar to let us through. Hardly a word was exchanged with the guards. It took about three hours to reach Maethawaw, a landing on the Moei River. After ferrying the cargo across the river, "Mao Zedong" and his sidekick returned to Mae Sot.

The river was swollen, the current swift. We were ferried across the river. This was Kawthoolei (Land of Flowers), a KNLA guerilla army camp and an entry point for goods and people destined to be taken deep into Burma. Even though this was liberated Karen territory, beyond the reach of Rangoon's writ and the range of its artillery, it was Burma nonetheless. I was exhilarated to be stepping on Burmese soil again. A very congenial side-armed KNLA officer showed us around the camp: the toll gate, the little marketplace, and the homes of the people, soldiers' barracks, and a little shop where an Indian sold freshly fried crunchy *samosas*. They were delicious. I saw an elephant mounted with some goods exiting the tollgate destined for interior Burma.

We boarded a long-tailed boat. The KNLA officer saluted as he saw us off. The noisy boat took us up the river for an hour's ride to Manerplaw. We were lodged at the home of General Tamlabaw, vice chief of the Karen National Liberation Army general staff. (General Tamlabaw died on 26 June 2014.) At night, a bugler sounded the Last Post—very British Army. When reveille sounded early the next morning, it evoked memories of my camping with the Boy Scouts on the shores of Inya Lake, when it was my duty as bugler to awaken the scouts and call them to meals and to bed at night.

Later that morning an officer appeared to tell me that the general was ready to receive me. All three of us were escorted to another house, where the general and his staff greeted us. General Bo Mya apologized for having missed us at Maethawaw. He had gone there the day before to escort us back to Manerplaw, but we had missed a connection and showed up a day late at Soe Soe's home in Mae Sot. After pleasantries, Riri and the two ladies left me with the general and his senior staff.

The general spoke through interpreter Dr. Em Marta, a physician, who was the Karen National Union's foreign secretary. Discussions centered on the long history of how the Karens were persecuted by the Burmans, the 1942 massacre of Karens in the delta, their struggle for freedom from the Burman yoke. "We don't want to live under the Burmans," he told me in no uncertain terms. Even though he was fluent in Burmese, Bo Mya spoke to me through an interpreter on this occasion. That was the only time he did so with me.

That evening we were entertained at a sumptuous dinner. The next day a long-tailed boat crewed by two men took us down the Moei River back to Maethawaw. On the way a deer on the east bank was spotted. Quickly the crewman riding on the bow reached for a pistol concealed in a bag and took aim at the deer. Dewi screamed when the shot went off. The game provided food for the guerillas. A pick-up truck awaited us at Maethawaw and drove us back to Mae Sot.

I saw General Bo Mya many more times, almost annually, after that first meeting in August 1983. He was always welcoming and hospitable. Once, he asked me whether I could get the C.I.A. to supply him with weapons. "General," I said, "I want to concentrate on helping the refugees with their health, education, and relief." He never brought up that subject again.

There were ten camps along the Moei River on the Thai side, which were later reduced to nine after the Burmese army burned down one (Huaykalok). There were a few more in the north along the Pai River in the Mae Hong Son area and in the south in the Three Pagodas Pass area on the River Kwai. Each time I went in subsequent years, I took them food, clothing, and medical supplies, and toys for the children. Sometimes Riri went with me.

Earlier in July 1979, I visited U Thwin, who was held prisoner at a police station lock up in Bangkok. The freedom fighter, a former minister in U Nu's cabinet, was caged by the Thais at the behest of the Burmese military junta in Rangoon.

After Manerplaw fell to the Burma Army in December 1994, I visited the general at his new HQ in the jungle, south of Mae Sot but still on the Burmese side of the border. I took him some ready-to-eat food purchased from a roadside eatery on the way. "How did you find me?" he asked jovially.

"General, I have my ways," I answered in jest. When he died in December 2006, I was sorry I could not go to his funeral. Conditions in the refugee camps were pathetic: cramped, unsanitary, cold in the winter. Professor Sadako Ogata, the United Nations High Commissioner for Refugees, called them "unacceptable," and I would certainly concur with her assessment.

In 1983, I became acquainted with Floyd K. Haskell through a real estate transaction. I did not know it at the time, but he was a former Democratic United States senator from Colorado. The tall Harvard College and Harvard Law graduate opposed the war in Vietnam and championed the Korean people's struggle against the dictatorship in their country. He was in the party that escorted Kim Dae Jung back to Korea from exile in the United States in 1985. This was the kind of a stalwart I needed to know in Washington to help us in our movement against the military in Burma. When I asked Senator Haskell whether he would help, he told me to come to Washington.

In Washington he introduced me, Tin Maung Win, and Yé Kyaw Thu to Lindsey Mattison, Executive Director of the International Center for Policy Development, of which Senator Haskell was a trustee. (Serendipitously, as I paced the neighborhood, I bumped into Eric Schwartz, director of the Washington office of Human Rights, whose office was a couple of buildings down. I said to Eric, "Do something about the situation in Burma.")

Senator Haskell also made an appointment for the three of us to see Stanley Roth, Congressman Stephen Solarz's legislative aide for international aid. Mr. Solarz, chairman of the House Subcommittee on Asian and Pacific Affairs, was unavailable at the time. Our purpose was to urge the U.S. government to withhold aid from the Burmese military regime, but Stanley Roth, told us the amount being given was miniscule. On a subsequent trip, Mr. Haskell made us an appointment to see former Senator William Fulbright. Senator Fulbright, who had for years been Chairman of the Senate Foreign Relations Committee, but now maintained a consultancy in a law office. He graciously received us early in the morning. Riri went along with us. We had gone to enlist his help, but he begged off politely, saying he was getting on in years and it was thirty years too late for him. We thanked him for his time and left after a photo op.

From that point on, the Committee for Restoration of Democracy in Burma took off. Actually, CRDB was one of three committees of the Foundation for Democracy in Burma, for which the International Center's counsel drew up articles of incorporation that were filed in Washington, DC, in 1986. Bishop James K. Mathews, a family friend since my childhood when he was a Methodist missionary in India, was one of the incorporators. He was the son-in-law of the towering evangelist Dr. E. Stanley Jones, my father's one-time seminary teacher in India. (Bishop Mathews suffered a stroke on 10 June 2006 in our home while he and Mrs. Mathews were visiting us. He died on 8 September 2010.)

The Foundation's two other organs were the Committees for Refugees and Human Rights. I was the founding president of the Foundation for Democracy in Burma and, concurrently, chairman of CRDB. Bishop Mathews was really passionate about Burma, for he knew and loved the country well and had a great admiration for my father. When he was a missionary in India, and later when he was called to New York to serve on the Methodist Board of Foreign Missions, before he was elected to the Church's episcopacy, he made frequent trips to Burma on church business.

Bishop Mathews took us to see Dr. Joseph Sisco, a former Assistant Secretary of State who, given his six-foot, one-inch frame, could literally and figuratively get away with talking down his boss, Secretary of State Henry Kissinger, over some Middle East policy issues. Dr. Sisco had served as president of The American University when Bishop Mathews was chairman of its Board of Trustees. Dr. Sisco gave us some valuable tips on how to navigate the Capitol labyrinth. As we got up to take his leave, he looked Tin Maung Win, Yé Kyaw Thu, and me squarely in our eyes and said, "What's in your favor is that you fellows are so young for the battle ahead of you." (Of the five in conference that morning in Dr. Sisco's office, I am the lone survivor.)

Commuting between Washington and Laguna Hills strained my pocket book and exacted a heavy toll on my family life. So, I resigned from the executive positions in 1987. Student-led agitations against the military junta in Burma picked up momentum. The time was now ripe for CRDB to spread its wings and take flight. It landed in Australia, Canada, England, Germany, and Thailand where chapters were established. CRDB's mission intensified, necessitating that it shear off the Foundation and go it alone.

Tin Maung Win and Yé Kyaw Thu moved CRDB's base to Thailand, where they did excellent organizational work. Daw Mya Mya Thant Gyi, Dr. Kyin Ho, Dr. Aung Khin, Sunda Khin, Richard Aung Myint, Mimi Myint

Phu, Bilal Raschid, U Thaung, and U Tin Maung Thaw, carried the torch in Washington, Florida, and California. In Australia, U Kin Oung, Ida Pay, Dr. Raymond Tint Way did likewise, while U Nwe Aung, Bo Aung Din, and Bush Gulati did their part in Canada, England, and Germany. I am bound to forget the names of others who were in the thick of things. I ask for their forgiveness for any oversight. Because of its worldwide nature, the CRDB added International to its name, and I was asked to be the president of CRDB International, which I agreed to do until the demise of General Ne Win. (He died on 5 December 2002.)

I was assured that the more-or-less honorary position would not involve frequent travel, but it took David Rettie of Australia and me on a mission to a very cold Stockholm. Jan Hodann of the Olof Palme International Centre accompanied us to the foreign ministry where three senior officials, one a woman, heard us out. We had gone to seek the Swedish government's help in establishing a facility at an abandoned military base in Cairns in Australia's north east, to train Burmese refugee students for civil service work once democracy was restored in Burma. To our disappointment, the appeal got nowhere. The mission was funded by the ever-so-generous freedom fighter physician/psychiatrist Dr. A. B. Aung Khin, of California. (He died in California on 5 January 2015.)

I am grateful to Lindsey Mattison and Virginia Foote, his wife, for helping our Burma cause. Had it not been for Senator Floyd K. Haskell, husband of National Public Radio's Nina Totenberg, CRDB might not ever have come into prominence. Floyd K. Haskell, Dr. A. B. Aung Khin, Bishop James K. Mathews, Ida Pay, David Rettie, Yé Kyaw Thu, Tin Maung Win, and a few others have passed away, but the struggle for the restoration of democracy in Burma continues. Many inside the country have carried the torch. I am very happy about that. A Chinese proverb says, "The darkest hour precedes the dawn." I am hopeful.

When I made the rounds among the ethnic leaders in 1986–1987, on the Burma-Thailand borderlands, I felt that speaking to them was very important, because dislodging the military regime would require unity among all of Burma's ethnic people. This was a challenging task, because the ethnic people were suspicious and had long histories of conflict. I conferred with Nai Shwe Kyin, leader of the New Mon State Party; and Nai Nonla of the breakaway Mon group. Nai Nonla was a sincere, dedicated gentleman with lots of excellent ideas. We established rapport instantly. He died of a heart attack while speaking at a rally commemorating the first anniversary of the momentous events of 8 August 1988. His untimely death was a great loss to the movement. However, by the time of his death, the two estranged Mon factions had reconciled.

I also conferred with the Karenni leaders: Saw Mawreh, Abel Tweed, and Rimond Htoo. I found that they had big logistical challenges communicating among themselves and working together because of the physical hurdles.

In 1987 I had a meeting planned in Bangkok with KIO Chairman Brang Seng. *New York Times* correspondent Barbara Crossette had published an article saying that the hopes of Burma's ethnic minorities had been bolstered because a Burman group based in America, called the Committee for Restoration of Democracy in Burma, was sending a delegation to the border. That "delegation" was me. I had gone to the border to talk to these leaders, to tell them what the CRDB was all about, and stressed that we had to be united.

The Burmese Military Intelligence Service got wind of my planned meeting with the ethnic leaders and wanted to squelch any incipient unity; I was made aware of a threat to my life, so I had to make haste to get out of Bangkok. Staff at Bangkok Christian Guest House instructed me to cover my tracks by walking into nearby Robinson's, a department store, from its Silom Street entrance and exiting on Rama IV Road where a staffer waited for me. He dashed me off to the airport, where I checked into the Airport Hotel. "Don't leave the hotel until close to your departure time," he advised. I found a seat on a United Airlines flight to Hong Kong the next morning. The cloak-and-dagger shenanigans made me tense. To make matters worse, after my connecting flight took off from Hong Kong, the pilot announced that he had to return to the airport because there was a bomb threat. It turned out to be a hoax, but it frayed my nerves nevertheless.

Abruptly, on 5 September 1987, the military regime demonetized more than half of all the Burmese currency in circulation. They claimed to be taking aim at black marketeers and insurgents, but few were convinced, and the regime's disruptive move spurred a spate of violent outbursts. In November, students in Arakan State and in the central plains joined the protests. These were ominous harbingers of more student unrest. The timing of the move, coinciding with university exams, was ill-judged, and the discontent it unleashed mushroomed the following year and, indeed, for many years thereafter.

The fourth of January 1988 marked forty years since the stirring events that I had witnessed. They ushered in Burma's independence with the piping aboard a Royal Navy cruiser of the last British governor, Sir Hubert Rance. A lot had happened, and a lot of other things had failed to happen in the intervening years. I marked the anniversary in the January 1988 issue of *The Burma Bulletin* by writing:

As Burma marks the fortieth anniversary of independence, it would bode well for Gen. Ne Win to realize that he is not immune from the Buddhist precepts of old age, sickness, and death. He alone holds the key to the future of Burma. Ethnic secessionists have scaled down their demands. They would be willing to live in a newly reconstituted federal republic if given a measure of self-governance to the states, similarly enjoyed by the fifty American sovereign states. The U.S., by supplying aircraft, weapons, chemicals and training Burmese pilots purportedly for narcotic suppression, has become entangled in another country's civil war.

I asked several people to contribute answers to the question, "Where were you on 4 January 1948?"

"I was engaged in consolidating the independence in Karenni State pursuant to Gen. Aung San's pledge: 'Just as we do not wish the Burmans to live under British rule, we do not wish the nationalities to live under Burman rule," wrote Saw Maw Reh.

U Kin Oung remembered "feeling overjoyed at shedding the shackles of serfdom from the once arrogant imperialists, and grateful to those nationalist leaders who were in the forefront of the struggle for freedom, albeit with mixed feelings of being abandoned after the nation's devastation by war in which the British had failed to protect us, and later obliged to rebuild."

Nai Shwe Kyin, who was president of the Mon Freedom League at the time of independence, wrote: "Our organization claimed Lower Burma (old Mon Land) as Mon State from the British Government as well as from the Burmese Government of the day."

To commemorate the anniversary in the pages of *The Bulletin* was a bittersweet obligation, but within a few months the interests and concerns of January 1948 would seem quaint and distant, as events took on a new urgency. The BBC correspondent stationed in Bangkok in those years was Neil Kelly. He would come to Bangkok Christian Guest House every time I was there, to get some tidbits. (Other journalists did the same, including Yindee Lertcharoenchok, of Bangkok's *Nation,* and Swedish journalist Bertil Lintner.) When CRDB stepped up the movement, Neil Kelly asked, "Why now?"

I told him Burma had been under the military yoke far too long and it was time to move—now or never. "What would it take to get more coverage on Burma?" I asked.

"Blood, plenty of blood," he answered.

4

Blood and Loneliness

ON THE NIGHT OF 12 March 1988, two Rangoon Institute of Technology students got into a scuffle with five neighborhood young men at the *Sanda Win*, located near the RIT campus. The five outsiders, reportedly under the influence of alcohol, were already inside the tea shop. An argument over the music from the shop's speaker sparked the confrontation, which grew into a classic town-versus-gown clash. Riot police overreacted over the tempest in a tea cup and killed two RIT students: Phone Maw and Soe Naing. The unrest, and the regime's attempts to suppress it, spread to the University of Rangoon, then to the main city. On 18 March, riot police arrested seventy-one students and crammed them into a paddy wagon, in which forty-one suffocated while they were being transported to Insein Jail. This outraged the citizenry.

Retired Brigadier General Aung Gyi seized the occasion to write a series of open letters to General Ne Win, complaining about the deterioration of living conditions and public life since the military takeover in 1962. The rioting spread to other parts of the country. On 8 August, a student-led strike and mass protests erupted, involving millions of people in cities and towns all over Burma. In Rangoon the army opened fire, killing hundreds. I was at home in Laguna Hills, California, and I was hopeful. "This is the time, this is the moment," I said to myself. The expatriate community in Southern California was trying to piece together of what was happening. The uprising did not surprise me, but its intensity did.

On 26 August, Aung San Suu Kyi, who had returned to Burma from England earlier in the year to care for her terminally ill mother, addressed a rally of more than 500,000 on the open ground below the western steps to the Shwedagon Pagoda. "We are here because we want to have democracy," she told the massive throng.

> To achieve democracy, we must march forward disciplined and United. . . . People say that I don't know enough about the political situation in Burma. In truth, I know too much. The political situation is very complicated. My father suffered over this situation; our family knows it best. My father put his heart and soul into it, and he did not do it for selfish reasons. . . . This is the second struggle for independence.

Southern California's Burmese community held rallies in Los Angeles and Orange counties. We were bearing witness from outside the uprising that was taking place in our homeland. We were also consoling each other. Though far away, we stood in solidarity with our compatriots at home. The uprising brought the expatriates together. Even those who had been indifferent or quiet, and who had been afraid to get involved because "they had relatives back home," now came out. They believed that this time the regime was sure to fall. We have a term in Burmese for people like that: we brand them *hseit-l'zi*—goat testicles. That's an off-color term, but it's accurate. In English we call them chameleons, creatures that change color to match their surrounding when the road ahead looks bright.

Mysteriously, telephone lines into Burma began to open up, so I was able to get through to Rangoon. Heretofore, getting through had been a hit-or-miss affair—mostly miss. You had to call the operator, who in turn called "routing 162," then pressed 95—Burma's country code followed by 1, the Rangoon city code—plus the phone number, which for the Methodist parsonage was 18902. The operator in Burma intercepted and invariably maintained that the line was "out of order." I believe foreign calls to the parsonage were blocked, especially when the caller is a suspected "rebel." That operator was, of course, a Military Intelligence (MI) operative.

When I received the telegram informing of my mother's death, I called the parsonage. I pleaded with the operator to please allow me to speak to anyone in the home. I overheard the operator ask someone on the line, presumably his superior: "*Ah Ko: nar yay bah, hpwint pay lite par* [Older brother, it's bereavement, please open the line]." The call went through. I asked who all were assembled in the home, and how many. I had a few words with Mya Thin, a loyal friend of long years. "I am doing the best I can," he said. There are no funeral homes in Burma. Such matters are handled by the extended family, with friends and neighbors coming together without being asked; and this is one event the Burmese do well. I asked my sister-in-law to have my mother buried in Twante. The signal was weak and background noises interfered. So the operator relayed: "He said to bury his mother in Twante."

Each time I was in Bangkok, I would go to the General Post Office and try to telephone my parents. It had to be done from inside a sound-insulated booth. Sometimes, due to technical problems or whim of the Burmese operator/minder, the call would not go through, but most of the time the technical problem was real.

Now, in September 1988, with the lines to Rangoon magically opened, I talked with U Nu. I asked him whether he felt safe. He laughed and said there was nothing to worry about. He was perfectly safe. He turned around and asked how his grandchildren Zali and Dewi were. (Our children had been "grandchildren" to him ever since he was with us in Costa Mesa in 1973.) He was affectionate to them and played the grandfatherly role again when we visited him in Bhopal six years later, always calling Zali "Sheik."

I talked with Brigadier General Aung Gyi at some length. He was a member of General Ne Win's Revolutionary Council that overthrew U Nu's parliamentary government in 1962. Aung Gyi related to me the high level of excitement among the crowds and told me of the rousing reception accorded him at the public rally at the foot of the Shwedagon Pagoda. Rumors were rife that a plane stood by at Mingaladon airport to transport General Ne Win out of the country should the situation turn ugly. The rumor may well have been wishful thinking; I too was hoping that Ne Win would voluntarily take himself out of the picture, but General Aung Gyi told me emphatically that Ne Win would "never leave the country."

Aung Gyi also alleged that Aung San Suu Kyi was being influenced by communist-leaning advisors.

Before I spoke with him, I had asked Joe Silverstein what he would like me to say to Aung Gyi. Joe said, "Tell him to move to Mudon in the south and establish a provisional government there." I liked that idea as well, but Aung Gyi vetoed it outright, saying, "Our rivers will flow with blood," if that were done. When I tried to reach him the next day, he was unavailable. I spoke with a deputy, who told me the tension in Rangoon was building up.

Demonstrators by the thousands paraded the streets of Rangoon in the immediate vicinity of Bandoola Square opposite the imposing city hall adjacent to Sulé Pagoda. The American embassy at 581 Merchant Street, was on the southern perimeter of the square. Desperate students were seen demonstrating in front of the embassy bearing handcrafted American flags, chanting *"dee-mo-cracy, dee-mo-cracy."* They were asking for American help to topple the military regime. Ambassador Levin described this pathetic scene so movingly. During this tumultuous period, former prime minister U Nu quietly asked the United States to bomb the Burmese military installations. This coincided with the appearance of an American naval amphibious task force in international waters south of the Irrawaddy Delta, fueling the masses' false hopes of an impending invasion, only to be sorely disappointed.

President Mahn Win Maung, elder brother of a maternal aunt, was related to me. When I told him who I was, it refreshed his memory of my boyhood. "Are you safe, uncle?" I asked.

"Of course," he said, "General Tin Oo, my neighbor, has taken charge of our security. There is nothing to worry about." He asked whether I was happy in America. He had been "re-instated" to the presidency, which the military coup led by General Ne Win had usurped in 1962. U Nu had sent letters to all the embassies in Rangoon to say that he was still the elected prime minister. "Preposterous," said Suu of that assertion.

I next spoke with John Freidenberg, public affairs officer at the U.S. embassy. John was accommodating and told me how he reached his office without encountering the mobs by driving via World Peace Pagoda Road. He did not sound overly worried, but I could sense that he was not completely unconcerned. I had called John for confirmation as to whether the embassy was about to evacuate its staff. He got philosophical and I never did get a direct answer. However, I could sense that tension in Rangoon was rising to a heightened pitch.

When the evacuation did take place, John and his wife were among the three hundred who were evacuated. Also among the evacuees were Doug Picket and his wife, Ann, who were both my fellow Woodstock School alumni. Doug was with the U.S. Agency for International Development. He attended Woodstock School when his father, J. Wascom Picket, served as a missionary bishop of the Methodist Church in India.

I had earlier learned from a colleague at work that her son, a Marine, was on board an amphibious assault task force warship deployed to international waters off the Irrawaddy Delta coast to stand by to evacuate American citizens. The task force was comprised of five warships, which included the aircraft carrier *USS Coral Sea*. However, when it arrived, the embassy had already evacuated its staff and their families by chartered Thai Airways craft to Bangkok.

I also talked with Aung San Suu Kyi's husband, Michael Aris. Suu was in the lakeside family home at 54 University Avenue, but in conference and unavailable. Riri suggested that Michael urge Suu to listen to the demands of the ethnic people, but Michael repeated Suu's position that "the army must return to the barracks first."

Telephone calls between Nick Williams Jr., the *Los Angeles Times* Bangkok bureau chief, and me were going back and forth at a stepped-up pace. "You are working around the clock," Nick said. I was trying to keep abreast with the rapidly escalating events in Rangoon. When I asked Nick whether a leader among the students had emerged, he said, "Yes, the wire services are reporting Min Ko Naig. That's spelled N-A-I-G." I told Nick that NAIG did not sound Burmese and that it must be NAING, a *nom de guerre*, meaning one who conquered the king. "That's a good tip," he said and went with it.

In the wee hours of 18 September 1988, Joe Silverstein called from his home in Princeton, New Jersey, and said, "Kyaw Win, Denis Gray just called. He said the army has removed the roadblocks from the streets and the radio is playing martial music." I knew exactly what that meant: The army was about to begin the slaughter. Denis Gray was the Bangkok bureau chief for the Associated Press. Riri was still asleep and I did not want to disturb her, so I went into the family room and had a good cry.

The army moved in, firing into the crowds killing hundreds of unarmed people—students and bystanders alike. They fell like flies. A video clip I later viewed clearly showed a young man in a white shirt taking a direct hit on the chest, bleeding profusely as he fell to the ground. A young male voice was heard exhorting his brothers and sisters, *"ma kyauk ne, ma kyauk ne* [don't be afraid, don't be afraid]." Surviving students by the thousands fled to Burma's borders with Thailand and India. Some fled north to the Kachin highlands on the border with China. The army abrogated the Constitution and set up a new junta, which it called the State Law and Order Restoration Council (SLORC).

The student strike had begun at eight minutes past eight in the morning on 8 August 1988—8/8/88. Burmese love numerology and the four eights had a poetic ring to them. But if the students thought the numbers were auspicious, they were woefully wrong. They got gunned down anyway, by the hundreds. More than 3,000 were estimated to have been killed in Rangoon alone. The intensity of the violence horrified me. Some of the soldiers were sympathetic, but in the military orders are orders and they were obeyed.

Even so, parts of the military did join the protests—more specifically, it was some units of the navy and air force. The Burmese military is organized as single entity called *Tatmadaw*, which simply means armed forces. The army, by its sheer numbers, dominates the *Tatmadaw* over the other two branches. Other government departments joined as well, like Customs and Revenue. You can identify them in photographs by the banners they're carrying.

That was a very tense time, to put it mildly. Rangoon's Mingaladon Airport was wide open. Customs and Immigration were either not functioning or they were allowing people to slip through. It was then that Congressman Stephen Solarz of New York got into Burma. He was the chairman of the House Subcommittee on Asia and Pacific Affairs. In his brief time in Rangoon, he was able to confer with Aung San Suu Kyi at her home. He was accompanied there by Ambassador Burton Levin. I wanted to go to Rangoon myself, but my son, Zali, vetoed it, fearing for my safety.

In 1989, the regime's Military Intelligence Service, had published a tract titled *The Conspiracy of Treasonous Minions within the Myanmar Naing-Ngan and Traitorous Cohorts Abroad.* The year I first left Burma is in that book, together with the bio-data of my whole family, even though a few "facts" were incorrect. Apparently, I'm a "traitorous cohort." Those opposed to the junta are the minions, or "axe handles" in Burmese. Others mentioned in the book included U Nu's two sons, Thaung Htike and Ko Aung; as well as Professor Josef Silverstein, Senator Daniel Patrick Moynihan of New York, Congressman Dana Rohrabacher of California, and Louis Walinsky.

A "traitorous cohort" I definitely am not. I wear my inclusion in that green-covered gallery of stalwarts as a badge of honor. Strangely enough, some people who were not included in the book were envious of those who were.

FREE BURMA COALITION

In the United States, Zarni, a Burmese student and his friends, founded the Free Burma Coalition. Its motto was the Ethiopian proverb: "When spiders unite they can tie down a lion." He was an excellent organizer who was successful in pulling together students from several American universities. He also had good contacts on Capitol Hill.

In November 1988, Congressman-elect Dana Rohrabacher went to Thaybawbo, a Karen village on the Burmese side of the Thailand-Burma border, where the students who fled the regime's wrath had regrouped. He invited U Hla Shwe, Usman Madha, and me to his Orange County office and briefed us about his trip. He was very impressed with the students he had met at the camp. He was quoted telling them that they were the "Thomas Jeffersons of Burma" fighting for democracy in their homeland. The students were forming the All Burma Students Democratic Front (ABSDF), complete with an armed wing. They were training for guerrilla warfare against the

Tatmadaw. (On a personal note, I specifically remember Dana Rohrabacher telling us that he would serve in Congress only ten years and then go back surfing. Rhonda Carmony, the fellow surfer he later married, was a student at Orange Coast College.)

Senator Daniel Patrick Moynihan was another big congressional supporter, and his staff worked diligently to pass legislation imposing economic sanctions on Burma. Senator Moynihan's legislative aide who did the major work was Andrew Samet. More Republicans than Democrats supported the Burma cause. Foremost among them was Senator Mitch McConnell of Kentucky, in addition to Congressman Dana Rohrabacher. One Burmese exile told me for these reasons, he registered to vote as a Republican.

President Barack Obama sent his Secretary of State Hillary Clinton to Burma on 1 December 2011 to urge the Burmese junta to sever its ties with North Korea and also to pave the way for his own visit, which took place a year later. He made a deep impression on the audience at Rangoon University when, on 19 November 2012, in his opening salutation uttered in Burmese, he *correctly* called the country "*Myanmar Naing Ngan.*" The audience in historic Convocation Hall broke out in thunderous applause.

If "Me [is] a name I call myself," as Julie Andrews sang in *The Sound of Music,* turning a pronoun into a noun, the Burmese generals can also invoke license and, make a noun out of an adjective, by "renaming" the country *Myanmar.* But the business of statecraft is not theatre. However, the people continue to be called Burmese and not *Myanmarese* as some Indian media have done.

In his remarks, President Obama said:

> Over the last several decades, our two countries became strangers. But today, I can tell you that we always remained hopeful about the people of this country, about you. You gave us hope and we bore witness to your courage. . .I said in my inaugural address, "We will extend a hand if you are willing to unclench your fist." . . . So today, I've come to keep my promise and extend the hand of friendship. . . . *I, as President of the United States, make determinations that the military then carries out, not the other way around. . .[A] future where national security is strengthened by a military that serves under civilians and a Constitution that guarantees that only those who are elected by the people may govern.*" [Italics mine]

President Obama went to Burma again on 12 November 2014 to attend an Association of South East Asian Nations (ASEAN) conference, chaired by Burma. No other sitting U.S. President has ever visited the country. Ulysses

S. Grant made port calls in Rangoon and Moulmein after he left the White House. Herbert Hoover ventured to Burma in the early part of the twentieth century and made a fortune in silver mining. (Incidentally, his former home at 2300 S Street NW in Washington is now the Burmese embassy.)

THE STUDENT CAMPS

I started collecting money to take to the refugees fleeing Burma. The rebel students were suffering from malaria, including the severe encephalic strain that affects the brain. Those afflicted acted insane. Some students baked charcoal from fallen tree branches and sold it for fuel. Riri and I first visited the Burma–Thailand border in August 1983. In December 1988 we visited them at four different locations along the border: Thaybawbo; the Pai River near Mae Hong Son in northwest Thailand, bordering the Shan State; Manerplaw in the Karen State; and Three Pagodas Pass in the south. We took medicines, medical supplies, rice, *nga-pi* [fermented fish paste], clothing, agricultural implements, money—and above all, we gave them encouragement.

At Mae Sot, Riri and I visited the police lockup where many Burmese student refugees were held prisoner. They were swept up in a Thai police round up of the city and held in a cell packed like sardines, with little space to move about. We gave some money to a few of them to bail themselves out, which in actuality amounted to bribes to get out of the hellhole they were put into. Outside the lockup, revelers were serenading them in celebration of *Sonkram,* the Thai and Burmese New Year that falls in mid-April each year. We also brought them some ready-to-eat food.

Manerplaw, headquarters of the Karen National Union and its Karen National Liberation Army (KNLA), was bursting at the seams with the influx. General Bo Mya was overwhelmed. The students were city slickers not accustomed to jungle living. The majority were Burmans with a sprinkling of Arakanese, Indians, Kachins, Karennis, Karens, Mons, Shans, and other ethnic minorities among them.

We also visited a camp at Tennasserim in the Three Pagodas Pass area in the south. We took them a pickup truckload of relief supplies. While I was in conference with the Mon General Htaw Mon, a funeral procession approached the little hut on its way to the burial ground several hundred feet away. I excused myself and joined the procession.

The body, wrapped in a blanket, was borne on a bamboo gurney carried in turns on the shoulders of pallbearers. The young man had succumbed to malaria and died for lack of medical care—there in the jungle in the shadow of the Dawna Range, far away from hearth and home. It choked me up. At the freshly dug shallow grave, a monk chanted Buddhist rites in Pali, the sacred language. Afterward a student stepped forward and read the release. The release, which absolves all transgressions the deceased may have committed and releases him from all duties and obligations, is customary at Burmese burials. Superstition holds that until the deceased is "released," his spirit will hover about in this existence. The reading over, he ignited a lighter and put the flame to the document held in the other hand. The blackened embers floated gently down into the grave in farewell to the departed. Another student stepped forward and placed a token of money called *ga-doh-gah* [ferry fare] for the deceased to cross the river to his next existence. A volley of three shots, one for each of the jewels of Buddhist tradition—*pha-yah, ta-yah, thanga* [the Englightened One, His Teachings, and the Ecclesiastical Order]—fired from an M-16 rifle pierced the still air. Mourners then each took a handful of earth and gently tossed them into the grave. It was their final farewell to a fallen brother.

The rites over, they solemnly filed away. It was the young burying the young, a scene etched into my memory, which I pray never, ever to witness again.

In Mae Hong Son we bought hoes and fishing nets for the student refugees, as well as cameras, radios, mosquito nets, and tarps to shelter them from the elements. They planted crops, but the Thai authorities wouldn't let them settle down, and the Burmese army burned down their camps. One incident that was satisfying but also sad was when we fed several of them at a sidewalk eatery in Mae Hong Son. Among them was Pascal Khoo Thwe, who was later rescued by a Cambridge University don and taken to England to attend Caius College, from which he graduated in 1995. (In 2002, his memoir *From the Land of Green Ghosts: A Burmese Odyssey,* was published.) They ate ravenously, and it was obvious that they were starving in the camps. They would forage daily for whatever was available in the jungle: mushrooms, bamboo shoots, birds, snakes, even crickets.

We visited the barbed-wire-fenced holding camp, adjacent to the runway at Tak airport that held Burmese student escapees. The commander of the camp, a Thai major general, was amiable and chatted in halting English. He was full of praise for the queen, and repeatedly said: "My queen is helping these young people. She wants them to be comfortable here." On a tent we saw a graffiti reading, "We can't go home." A Burma air force plane stood ready on the tarmac to fly them back to Burma. They naively believed that America would come to their aid, only to be sorely disappointed.

It was at the home of Lydia Tamlawah, a Karen schoolteacher, who had become a refugee leader in Mae Sot, where we met a soft-spoken, unassuming young lady who was determined to bring medical care to the refugees from Burma. Her name was Cynthia but she later added Maung as her "last name" to facilitate the "Western" form of first and last name. Karens, like in some other Asian cultures, go by only one name. Cynthia herself had escaped the army crackdown. She had been working in a multi-ethnic village called Eain Du, situated between Pa-an and Myawaddy in Karen State. At twenty-nine she was already a practicing physician.

The Karen National Union had rented a dilapidated house on Asia Highway, the road from Mae Sot to the Moei River, which forms the boundary between Burma and Thailand, for her to use as a clinic. The wooden floor of the barren hallway in the house was covered with bamboo mats on which patients slept. The landing strip for flights into Mae Sot was right behind the house.

I met Thi Thi Khin, a young mother, who was occupying a tiny spot on the clinic's floor, tending her sick infant. A graduate of Mandalay University (chemistry), she was also called "Joy." She was very bitter at the Burmese army for the atrocities it had committed against the students who were peacefully protesting the military junta. In December 2004, Riri and I visited Joy and her family. She had since remarried to Jay Burleigh, an Australian, and had had another child. Now debilitated by multiple sclerosis, she lives in Launceston, Tasmania, with her family.

Dr. Cynthia used cooking pots to boil water to sterilize needles and other instruments. Soon after our visit, she began to receive funding and other help from outside. The clinic has since grown into a large facility with maternity care, family planning, eye surgery, orthopedics and manufacture of prosthetics for the victims of land mines, as well as treatment for gunshot wounds and the endemic diseases of dysentery, malaria, malnutrition, and tuberculosis.

Dr. Cynthia's clinic, officially known as Mae Tao Clinic, now enjoys the support of *Médecins Sans Frontières* (Doctors Without Borders). Handicap International, and other non-governmental organizations (NGOs), and foreign governments. Patients receive treatment free of charge and, in cases of surgery and serious illness, their families sleep on the floor in the clinic under their beds. Dr. Cynthia herself is a Karen, but the clinic's services are available to anyone. Her early work was predominantly among students fleeing the regime's crackdown. Mae Tao Clinic is still being called the "student hospital" by many patients who come from as far away as Rangoon.

Dr. Cynthia also oversees orphanages and schools and trains health care workers and sends them back into Burma to work. When I first met her in December 1988, there was nothing about Cynthia to indicate all that she would go on to accomplish. She was quiet and unpretentious. When Riri asked her what she intended to do here, she said simply she wanted to help the students. Dr. Cynthia has received many international prizes and honors, including the Ramon Magsaysay Award, often dubbed the Asian Nobel Prize. One person can make a big difference. (Ironically, the reopening of Burma beginning in 2011 has had an effect that Dr. Cynthia had predicted: Aid is being diverted into Burma, resulting in the hundreds of thousands of refugees still languishing along the Burma–Thailand border receiving less.) Former First Lady Laura Bush visited Mae Tao Clinic on 7 August 2008 and was visibly moved.

Throughout this period, I was also active on another front, writing letters to congressmen, newspaper editors, and national leaders worldwide—anyone I thought might be able to influence the situation for the better. *The New York Times* published a letter of mine on 2 May 1988. In the letter I had asserted: "No amount of military aid given to the much-hated, corrupt dictatorship will restore tranquility." On 5 September 1988, Riri's and my thirtieth wedding anniversary, I sent identical letters to several world leaders and members of the United States Congress, saying:

> After 26 years under General Ne Win's iron-fisted rule, the people of Burma are now marching for freedom, democracy, economic freedom, human rights and more rice on their tables. They seek the dissolution of the military's tyrannical Burma Socialist Program Party, the only legal political organization in their once prosperous land. In recent weeks, security forces have fired upon unarmed peaceful protesters killing an estimated 3,000 students, monks, workers, government employees and others. Thousands have been wounded and many languish in prisons.
>
> Since 1975, the United States Government has provided $65 million worth of military aid in the form of helicopters, fixed wing aircraft, the herbicide 2,4-D and the training of pilots and other support personnel. Part of this aid has been used in suppressing the tribal people on the fringes of the Golden Triangle where opium poppies are grown, causing untold suffering to innocent villages. This is in violation of the terms of the assistance. According to DEA sources, Burma's opium crop this year is nearly 1,250 metric tons. It was 25 metric tons in 1975. The situation there has the potential of becoming another Lebanon. The Burmese Government must immediately address itself to find solutions for economic reforms, human rights violations and peacefully end its 40-year-old civil war against the ethnic minorities. I urge you to urgently call for opening congressional hearings on Burma before Burma becomes the Lebanon of Asia.

Any threat to regional peace and security in Southeast Asia has the potential of spreading into other countries there. Also, a resolution similar to S.R. 464 should be passed in the House.

On 10 April 1988, I had appealed to Prime Minister David Lange of New Zealand for his government's help to mediate peace talks among Burma's warring factions. He wrote saying he had carefully read my letter, but his government was unable to respond positively. That was another disappointment.

I had earlier in 1973 appealed to the Archbishop of Canterbury, asking him to reach out to the Burmese junta to bring about peace in that land. The response from his Lambeth Palace staff was that the Anglican leadership in Rangoon was not receptive to this request because it would not augur well with the junta and do more harm. My appeal to Pope Paul VI, for help to facilitate Burmese Buddhist children resident abroad, accompanied by their mothers, in going back to Burma to perform religious rites during the Buddhist Lent also bore no fruit.

A HOUSE DIVIDED

Anger and recrimination were thick in the air. It was impossible to be neutral. The students and others inside Burma and along the border faced deprivation and danger every day and night. Even those of us living far away in exile could not avoid the fallout. An incident I was involved in stands out as emblematic of what we were up against—one of which was each other.

In the winter of 1989, Riri and I went to Arizona to visit friends. Five families lived in various towns around Phoenix. Their army colonel brother from Burma was coming, and they were having a party. Riri and I joined them because we wanted to hear news about our family and the church in Burma.

Our families had been closely linked since the early beginnings of Methodism in Burma. The eldest, Maung Yaw, joined the navy during colonial times. Number two was a sister, Khin Khin Aye. Number three, Maung Maung Khin, also joined the navy. During the insurrections of 1949, his gunboat was commandeered by the Communists, and he was killed in the Irrawaddy Delta. (I was the last of the kith to be with him; he walked me back to St. Paul's from his family home on the way back to his gunboat in the Rangoon River.) Maung Maung Aye, number four, joined the army, rose to the rank of colonel, and was appointed a deputy minister in the junta. Even though General Ne Win was his patron, to whom he gave all his loyalty in exchange for the privileges and perks that went along with it, including the freedom to travel abroad, he was prevented from rising above a colonel's rank because of his allegedly Manipuri (*ponna,* Brahmin priest) lineage.

The colonel was now visiting his four sisters and three brothers living in Arizona and the fifth sibling, Maung Maung Tin, in suburban Washington. Over the years the colonel had visited his relatives in America several times. U Ba Khin, head of the family, traced his roots to Manipur in northeast India. He was a practitioner of native remedies who compounded and dispensed herbal preparations from his home. He was a strict patriarch who presided over the whole clan. He sired six children with the first wife and eight more with the second. When four daughters with the second wife immigrated to America in the 1960s, the patriarch told them to marry white American men. He felt all along that Americans of "white genre" were of a superior race. This may be attributable to his earlier contact with, and conversion to Christianity, by American missionaries. The children all obeyed.

I was already in the home of a half-sister when the colonel walked in with his wife, Rose, a Karen, and a younger half-brother. He knew I was going to be there, and he was spoiling for a fight. "You are a *pyay byay* [absconder]!" he shouted. In Burmese, *absconder* is a derogatory term, implying disloyalty to one's roots. To add insult to injury, he also called me a traitor.

Fuming, I returned his "salutation" and yelled, "You are the traitor!" This exchange happened even before he had crossed the threshold. The confrontation continued, "Who is the government?" I challenged him.

"The *Tatmadaw* [armed forces]—the *Tatmadaw* represents the people," he said. This was not only offensive, of course, but self-serving since he was an active army officer.

"Who appointed the *Tatmadaw* the people's representatives?" I yelled, and quoted Oliver Cromwell, "The king is not England, and England is not the king!" for him to draw the analogy between Burma and England. In one of my editorials in *The Burma Bulletin*, I had challenged Ne Win's legitimacy by writing, "Ne Win is not Burma and Burma is not Ne Win."

Tension in the living room rose rapidly. There were at least a dozen family members assembled. It was an acrimonious prelude to the evening. I cooled my heels when his wife, Riri, and others injected some nervous non sequiturs. I also retreated, for the colonel was a pillar of the Methodist Church in Burma. When tempers cooled, the youngest half-brother gently escorted me to my car. A few days later, another younger half-brother said to me, "You walloped him good. He needed to hear that."

On a subsequent trip to America, he visited us in California. I have the feeling that his elder sister, who was living in Long Beach, had reined him in. She took care of me when I was little. I delivered the eulogy when she died in June 2002. I took him and his wife to show them the *Queen Mary* docked in Long Beach (a tourist attraction), and to Forest Lawn Cemetery in Glendale, where we paid our respects to the Rev. Clarence E. Olmstead at his grave. Rev. Olmsted was a Methodist missionary in Burma before the war whom we both knew as youngsters.

I also took them to hear a symphony orchestra concert in which next-door neighbor Peggy Sauerwald was a violinist. It was their first ever Western classical symphonic experience, and they enjoyed it thoroughly. When I went back to Burma in 2001 after having been exiled in America for forty years, he was most helpful offstage. He had by then retired from the army, but still enjoyed some residual clout. Political differences aside, we still remained kith. He died in 2011.

The economic and political situation in Burma became so stifling that whoever could, would leave by any means available. Many who made it to America took advantage of loopholes in U.S. immigration laws, by making false claims that they would be imprisoned or tortured if they returned to Burma because they had "participated in anti-military dictatorship" activities while in America. A thriving mini-industry of asylum seeker enablers sprouted up like mushrooms. On their lawyers' advice, these opportunists would appear at protest demonstrations or rallies and were photographed with well-known activists bearing placards or passing out anti-military leaflets—and then use the photographs to support their claims. Many were economic opportunists whose claims were as phony as a three-dollar bill. Unscrupulous lawyers who aided these opportunists were in abundant supply. Business for them was brisk and lucrative.

When Aung San Suu Kyi was released from house arrest and the generals seemingly loosened their grip a bit, these opportunists became nervous. They were concerned that their petitions, which were in the pipeline for approval, would be jeopardized. The Burmese diaspora has scattered Burma's sons and daughters to the far corners of the globe: to Australia (Tasmania), Denmark, Finland, Germany, Japan, Korea, Netherlands, New Zealand, Sweden, and beyond.

There was a lot going on around that time all over the world. Oppressed people as far away as Haiti, Nepal, and South Africa, were emboldened by the fall of the Berlin Wall and the Communist dictatorships in Eastern Europe. Clearly, SLORC understood the events, because when the Romanian uprising overthrew the dictator Nicolae Ceaucescu in November 1989, and he and his wife were executed on 25 December 1989, the tightly controlled Burmese media made nary a mention of it. The flip side of the same curse was that events in Burma rarely got mentioned in the international press. Something atrocious elsewhere always seemed to overshadow the situation in Burma.

Burma was never on the international community's front burner. Still, all of that said, the bottom line was that the 1988 uprising failed because Burma's pro-democracy leaders themselves could not get their act together. They blew it. If only U Nu, Aung Gyi, Aung San Suu Kyi, and the ethnic leaders had spoken with one voice, Burma's political landscape since 1988 would have been very different.

On 20 July 1989, Aung San Suu Kyi was placed under house arrest. My take is that she had grievously deflated Ne Win's ego by openly blaming him for the failures of his regime. Furthermore, adding insult to injury, she had asserted that her father had not trusted him. This was a rebuke to his boast that her father had tapped him as his right-hand man when the "Thirty Comrades," who had sided with the Japanese, re-entered Burma at the vanguard of the Japanese army in 1942. It was a slap on Ne Win's face, a grievous humiliation. In truth, General Aung San's trusted right-hand man was Bo Let Ya.

Suu's house arrest and the Burmese community's anger gathered momentum, and need for publicity spurred it to launch a "Free Aung San Suu Kyi" campaign. In December 2004, I took the campaign to Antarctica where I had myself photographed holding a hand-drawn *Free Aung San Suu Kyi* poster. The campaign took its inspiration from the "Free Mandela" campaign that had been integral to the movement against apartheid in South Africa. The difference was that South Africans were fighting a white minority government that was oppressing the black people. Many Americans saw parallels in that to their own country's civil rights movement.

Free Aung San Suu Kyi campaign in Antarctica. Photo by Gandasari Win.

Burma was less known to the Western world, and its political problems were seen as internal and not perceived as obviously racial—whites against non-whites. Another difference was that, unlike that of South Africa's, Burma's democracy movement did not enjoy the support of neighboring governments. South Africa's neighbors were eager to support opponents of apartheid. Burma's neighbors, like Indonesia, which had a military government of its own, had their own issues with democracy and they were intimidated by the Chinese dragon.

So, at least at first, the cause of democracy in Burma did not present a romantic appeal to the American public. The average American did not even know where Burma was, any more than they had known in the 1960s where Vietnam was. A measure of romance did come later, as the movement grew and Westerners began falling in love with Suu, thanks to her pulchritude and Oxford-refined eloquence. Celebrities like members of the rock band U2 and the actress Sigourney Weaver jumped on the Burma bandwagon. There was even a song, composed by the Rev. Wrightson Tongue, Jr.: *"Free-ee—Free-ee Aung San Suu Kyi-i!"* The song's Burmese version was popularized by Yuzana Khin, a remnant of the 1988 uprising.

In the winter of 1990, Physicians for Human Rights sent Dr. Howard Hu, a physician-scientist professor at the Harvard School of Public Health, and me to Mae Hong Son, Manerplaw, and the Three Pagodas Pass to document accounts of atrocities. I paid my own way for the mission. (In 2012, Howard became the inaugural Dean of the Dalla Lana School of Public Health at the University of Toronto.) We published a depressing summary of our interviews in the 1 June 1991 issue of *The Lancet*, a British medical journal:

> Credible eye witnesses gave us first-hand accounts of how the Burmese military hampered emergency medical care during demonstrations in the past 3 years—by blocking transport of the injured by ambulances; by denying medical workers access (sometimes by physical restraint) to the wounded; by closing main hospitals serving areas where there had been large-scale shooting of demonstrators; and by removing from clinics the red cross insignias marking them as emergency medical care centres. . . . Community health workers have been imprisoned for providing medical care "to insurgents."
>
> Most interviewees reported being kicked, punched, and beaten during the interrogation that preceded their 3–6 month confinement, with 120 to 150 other prisoners, in a cell measuring approximately 4 x 12 metres. The only toilet was an open trough, and some prisoners reported receiving only three mugs of water for cleaning after going without a bath for over a month.
>
> Requests for medical attention often took hours for a response or were simply ignored.. . . The long conflict between the minority ethnic peoples in the border areas and the Burmese Central Government have contributed to the lack of basic public health and health-care services in those areas under disputed control. . . . Malaria, including cerebral malaria and black-water fever, are very prevalent. Few children are vaccinated.

AUNG SAN SUU KYI AWARDED NOBEL PEACE PRIZE

The cause received a major boost when Aung San Suu Kyi was awarded the Nobel Peace Prize in absentia. I took my family to Norway for the ceremony, held on 10 December 1991, International Human Rights Day. It was extremely cold in Oslo, but I wouldn't have missed it for anything. Our hosts were Dr. Petter Eldevik, a physician- scientist, and his family. At the award ceremony we were dressed in formal Burmese attire. I wore a long *taung shay p'soe* and had a challenging time keeping it up—it kept coming undone. Wearing a formal Burmese *taung shay p'soe* was difficult for me. It was the first time I had worn the three yards of silk and, to my embarrassment, but relief, the venerable monk Dr. U Rewatta, noticed it slipping down before it hit the floor. Riri once joked that Burma's rebel soldiers don't win, because they wore *longyis* instead of trousers. There was also an inherent dislike for what Andrew Marshall called Burmese soldiers: "the trouser people."

My family of four was among more than a hundred Burmese exiles living in Europe, Japan, and North America whom the Norwegian Nobel Committee had invited to the ceremony. There were three Buddhist monks, from England, the Netherlands, and the United States. The Venerable Dr. U Rewatta Dhamma was the senior one among them. Those were the only three I could muster at Michael Aris's request.

Dignitaries and invited guests filled the 1,000-seat City Hall auditorium to capacity. The first to proceed to the front rows included the Nobel Peace laureates Archbishop Desmond Tutu and former President Oscar Arias of Costa Rica. Next were Michael Aris and his and Aung San Suu Kyi's sons, Alexander and Kim, escorted by members of the Norwegian Nobel Committee. The audience rose in tumultuous applause as they proceeded to the stage. After the applause faded, Norway's King Harald V and Queen Sonja and their party were escorted to the front of the center aisle. Professor Francis Sejersted, chairman of the Norwegian Nobel Committee, and another committee member took the end seats on the stage.

Led by Dame Iona Brown, the Norwegian Chamber Orchestra played Edvard Grieg's "Prelude" from the *Holberg Suite*. Professor Sejersted spoke in Norwegian, which was translated simultaneously into English. After that, Professor U Mya Maung of Boston College, accompanied by U Tun Aung on the *saung gauk* [Burmese harp], sang *Loving Kindness and the Golden Harp*, in Burmese. They were dressed elegantly in formal Burmese attire, and they bowed to the audience with their hands clasped, before and after their rendition. Professor Sejersted then asked Alexander and Kim, accompanied by their father, to come forward to receive the gold medal and diploma of the Nobel Peace Prize. There was a long, standing ovation after which Alexander delivered his speech.

"I stand before you here today, to accept on behalf of my mother, Aung San Suu Kyi, this greatest of prizes, the Nobel Prize for Peace. Because circumstances do not permit my mother to be here in person, I will do my best to convey the sentiments I believe she would wish to express," he began. I published his speech in the November/December 1991 issue of *The Burma Bulletin*. Alexander went on to say that it was his

> . . . deepest hope that it will not be in the face of complete economic collapse that the regime will fall, but that the ruling junta may yet heed such appeals to basic humanity as that which the Nobel Committee has expressed in its award for this year's prize.

I know that within the military government there are those to whom the present policies of fear and repression are abhorrent, violating as they do the most sacred principles of Burma's Buddhist heritage.

This is no empty wishful thinking but a conviction my mother reached in the course of her dealings with those in positions of authority, illustrated by the election victories of her party in constituencies comprised almost exclusively of military personnel and their families. It is my profoundest wish that these elements for moderation and reconciliation among those now in authority may make their sentiments felt in Burma's hour of deepest need.

The audience gave Alexander another prolonged standing ovation. Alexander was only sixteen. His father later told me he had written the speech himself. The chamber orchestra then played Johann Pachelbel's *Canon in D.* The violin's repetitive strains of the melodic backdrop made me emotional. Riri patted my back and held my hand. I was overcome by the haunting sounds of the strings, which saddened me because of Suu's glaring absence on the stage. She was being held prisoner in her own home halfway around the world in Rangoon.

In the evening, my family was among several thousand who congregated in front of the old railway station to walk in a torchlight procession through the streets. It wound its way to the front of Grand Hotel from whose balcony Michael and the two sons waved to the crowd, along with Dora Than É, a longtime family friend who was famous in Burma's colonial days as the recording artist widely known as *Bee-lat-pyan* Than, [England-returned Than]. Zali and Alexander vowed to march into Rangoon together one day. Zali had befriended Suu's family when they lived in Oxford when he was attending King's School in Worcester in 1976–1978.

In 1992 I ceased publishing *The Bulletin* because I ran out of steam. A staffer at the UC-Santa Barbara library telephoned and asked, "Aren't you going to publish *The Burma Bulletin* any more?"

I told her, "No, I'm tired." But also, other periodicals were starting to give more extensive coverage to Burma. They were doing good journalism. The reason for *The Bulletin* in the first instance was to encourage others to speak up, and now they were doing that.

Still there was a lot that needed to be done. I began turning my attention to health and education and continuing to help the refugees who were pouring into Thailand and India. I began attending gatherings of Burmese expatriates around the United States to discuss how we from the outside could best help the people in Burma. In the 1990s and 2000s we held symposia at Orange Coast and Golden West Colleges. The authors Bertil Lintner and Edith Mirante spoke at both, as did former American ambassador to Burma Burton Levin. Other members of a panel included the actor Mike Farrell and Eric Sandberg of the State Department. Congressman Dana Rohrabacher was the luncheon speaker. Mr. Rohrabacher was very supportive, even personally delivering to my home one hundred copies of the United States Constitution that I had wanted to distribute among the students and freedom fighters.

I went around to doctors' offices in southern California, collecting medical supplies and instruments to distribute to the refugees. Except for Dr. Aung Khin, Burma-born physicians in Southern California distanced themselves. My primary care physician, an Argentine-born American, asked what all the brouhaha was about. According to him, Burmese physicians that he met never mentioned the unrest in Burma.

Every chance I got, I was on a flight to Bangkok. In December 1992 I took photojournalist Gail Fisher of the *Los Angeles Times* and writer Jane Stevens to the Burma–Thailand border. I remember that we flew from Chiang Mai to Mae Hong Son on Christmas Day—and the pair published an excellent series of three articles in the *Los Angeles Times*, the *San Francisco Examiner*, and the *Deseret News* of Salt Lake City, in February 1993.

I spoke at Occidental College on a panel with the State Department's diplomat-in-residence there. Everything I was doing now was the same work that I had done for nearly two decades through *The Burma Bulletin*, only now in different forms, mostly face to face. I traveled around the United States talking about Burma. I got press coverage in Galveston, Texas, and in the *Kansas City Star*. At the University of Texas-Brownsville, Lara, a pretty Latina journalism student, asked, "How do you know about these things?" That was an excellent question for a budding journalist to ask. I spoke at Bucknell University and UCLA, and I spoke to an adult forum of more than eighty at First United Methodist Church in Williamsburg, Virginia, and at another one in Kansas City, Kansas. I spoke to all the service clubs: Kiwanis, Lions, Optimist, and Rotary. I went to lots of other places, but got very little press coverage. Nevertheless, I never passed up an opportunity to talk about Burma's struggle. We launched a campaign to persuade cities and universities around the United States to divest from companies doing business in Burma. We hit hard on Pepsi-Cola, which did eventually pull out; and on the oil companies Unocal and Total, which did not.

I spoke to the city councils in Boulder and Los Angeles, and others did the same around the country. Zarni, the student who had founded the Free Burma Coalition, did yeoman's work organizing some of these events. He also organized a core group of activists, who met at a hotel on a ridge overlooking the confluence of the Shenandoah and Potomac Rivers at Harper's Ferry on a very cold weekend in January 1999; at *Bukit Tinggi*, my home in the Colorado Rocky Mountain foothills in January 2002; at the estate of Professor Scott Thompson of Fletcher School of Law and Diplomacy on the Civil War battlefield at Manassas, Virginia, in July 2003; and again at his resort on the Indonesian island of Bali in January 2004. A series of meetings and demonstrations were held in Washington and California throughout the 1990s and 2000s.

Activists meet at Manassas.

Activists meet at Win's Rocky Mountain home.

We chanted in front of the Unocal building in Los Angeles, "Un-o-cal, out of Burma! Out of Burma, Un-o-cal!" And on a cold April day in downtown Denver, we demonstrated in front of Total Oil Company's regional office, distributing leaflets urging people not to buy gasoline from Total. Zarni Nyunt Aung, Naw Louisa Benson, Dr. Aung Khin, Ko Latt, Usman Madha, U Nyunt Maung, Taw Myo Myint, Yé Myint, Frank Thaung Oo, Dr. Myat Htoo Razak, Dr. Carol Richards, Inge and Tad Sargent, Jocelyn Seagrave, U Hla Shwe, Khin Maung Shwe, U Sein Tun, David Wolfberg, Peggy Yang, and several others whose names I do not recall, participated in these campaigns.

A woman from Total Oil's Denver office talked to us on the sidewalk. "You people are demonstrating at the wrong place, we're not involved in Burma," she said. We told her, "Your parent company in France is," but she denied knowledge of it.

Former President Jimmy Carter invited me to a symposium on Burma held by the International Negotiation Network, at the Carter Center at Emory University. Distinguished statesmen, lawyers, and diplomats from many countries were among the speakers and panelists. Ted Koppel of ABC-TV presided over a plenary session. Andrew Young, former Atlanta mayor and American ambassador to the United Nations, was also among the participants. The Association of South East Asian Nations sent its Secretary General, Arjit Singh, to share its views on Burma. His worthless spiel was "constructive engagement" with the pariah state. Nigeria's General Olusegan Obasanjo cut an impressive figure in his dignified robes.

I found President Carter himself deeply interested in helping bring democracy to Burma, but I was disappointed overall in the symposium, because I had come hoping that it would accomplish more than just talk. I had hoped, too, that President Carter himself would more actively enlist his prestige and that of the Carter Center to communicate with the regime in ways that would be concretely helpful. I made a point of approaching him directly, in a private moment as he was seated on the dais with other panelists, to ask him to go to Burma. His blue eyes made a striking impression up close. I was hoping he might do something like build homes in Burma through Habitat for Humanity. "I won't go to any country uninvited," he told me. I felt that, as a private citizen, he should feel free to travel anywhere he wanted. Being invited by the military regime was a pie in the sky.

Former UN Secretary General Javier Perez de Cuellar was sitting on President Carter's right. He overheard us and said, "I would like to go there too, but I can't get in." The only person at the whole symposium who could go in and out of Burma was ASEAN's Arjit Singh, but his "constructive engagement" mantra was hollow. Another ASEAN buzzword was "dialogue."

Both terms were euphemisms for traipsing around the Burmese regime but doing little else while letting its brutality continue unchallenged.

Also at the meeting were representatives of several of Burma's exiled ethnic communities, including the Kachin (Col. George Seng and Dr. Manam Tu Ja), the Karen (Saw Ba Thin), and the Mon (Nai Shwe Kyin). They invited President Carter and Perez de Cuellar to visit their areas from Thailand or China, but their invitations were not taken up. The BBC sent Oung Myint Tun, chief of its Burmese Language Service. (Oung Myint Tun and I played together as children in Thongwa before the outbreak of World War II.) Stephen C. Lipman, Unocal's vice president for business development, was there too. His company was concerned that its offshore natural gas pipeline might be imperiled. Their worry turned out to be unfounded. Lipman was warm and friendly. He invited me to share his limousine ride to the airport. Jointly with Total, Unocal had a big investment in Burma. I politely declined, because there were others I needed to talk to. All that came out of the symposium were the usual slogans and platitudes: "Patience, Understanding, Sensitivity." I left feeling flattered, but futile.

BEYOND RANGOON

One day in August 1993, I picked up the telephone to hear, "Dr. Win, we're making a film about Burma. We'd like to talk to you. When can we meet?" Never in my wildest dreams had I entertained the thought of doing anything Hollywood. On a slow afternoon in my office, the voice on the other end sounded suspiciously like a prank from an old high school buddy.

"Sure," I responded. "And where are you?"

Sounding somewhat peeved, "In Beverly Hills; I'm the executive producer," said the voice.

"Beverly Hills is out of my range," I said, "besides I dread driving the freeways and shy away from the L.A. basin as much as I can." I felt certain I had ensnared the prankster.

"All right, we'll come to you," the caller said. "I'll call back to arrange a mutually agreeable time."

I immediately phoned Riri and told her, "I just got a strange call from someone who claims to be a Hollywood film producer." I felt sure the culprit was Ken Bonham, a classmate from Woodstock School days in India. Ken was noted for pulling pranks on his classmates.

"Why don't you just let it slide and relax?" Riri said. "Everything will fall into place. If it pans out, this will be a good opportunity to tell the truth about what is happening in Burma."

And so, on a bright and bushy day in September, the director John Boorman, his executive producer, and an aide came to our home in Laguna Hills. We talked at length about Burma. Boorman asked many questions. He had an interest in Burma because his father had served there during colonial times. He was most interested in the religious, cultural, and social aspects of Burmese life—and of course we discussed the political situation, above all the military era. Riri served a lunch of carefully prepared Indonesian and Burmese dishes, making sure that the spices embellished the dishes just enough to whet the palate.

By now, reassured that it was not a prank, both of us had warmed to this opportunity to be part of a large endeavor that would tell the world about Burma. I described to Boorman the then-recent incident in which Aung San Suu Kyi had been confronted by a squadron of soldiers but escaped danger by the way she made her courageous stand. After lunch I showed him and his aides into my study. They were fascinated by the literary and art collections in our home. It was a stimulating afternoon spent with a British filmmaker, even if it took on the air of an inquisition. But I was thoroughly up to the mark.

Not being a moviegoer, film directors were of no moment to me. I knew nothing about John Boorman, but I learned quickly. Debbie Webb, a librarian at the college dug up reams of information about the British filmmaker. John Boorman's intense commitment to just causes, as revealed in his biography, struck a sensitive chord with me.

At parting, the executive producer turned and said, "I'll call you next week." He called sooner than that and asked, "Would you be willing to join the film crew as special advisor on location in Malaysia?" I had never been on a movie set, and this once-in-a-lifetime diversion from academia would involve being away from campus for a semester. I consulted my colleagues, including those in the film department, along with the dean and college president. The resounding answer from everyone I asked amounted to, "You'd pass up an exciting opportunity if you didn't go."

On a muggy tropical December afternoon in 1993, I arrived on the island of Penang, off the west coast of Malaysia. The next morning I bumped into John Boorman in the elevator. Coming from Ireland, he had checked into the Equatorial Hotel the day before. We had breakfast together. "I want to go over your duties with you," he said. "You'll work closely with the art, props, costume, make up, and casting departments and generally look around before we shoot to make sure that what's being done is authentic."

I went to work immediately. The work was fascinating. Here I was, doing something for which I had absolutely no training, but knowing exactly what questions to ask and what needed to be done. I supervised the painting of hundreds of signs to be used as props. The artists came from Sri Lanka and none of them knew Burmese, but they did a marvelous job reproducing the curlicues of the Burmese script. In the process, I learned a useful Singhalese word, *ah-ing-karang*, which means "take it down" or "erase it." One particular sign, which was subcontracted out, escaped my inspection and appeared on the set just prior to shooting. Hurried attempts to remedy the error failed.

To my distress, the sign slipped in before the camera, though it was seen for only a few seconds. Acquisition and arrangement of props, construction and decoration of sets, and sundry other details were most interesting parts of the job. I provided pictures and photographs from my personal collection to help them make the background look like authentic Burmese scenes, especially the village ones.

There was a Buddhist temple in Penang that Boorman wanted to use, and I was assigned to negotiate with the temple's secretary. "Don't do anything to denigrate the religion," he insisted. It was a Chinese temple, different from Burmese style, so the company planned to add things and make some architectural changes. Then, after a lot of work and preparations, Boorman decided not to film at the temple after all.

Boorman also told me, "There's a village whose inhabitants are of Burmese descent. They're Muslims now." He wanted me to check it out. I looked at their weaving and noticed that their *sampans* were Burmese style, with an elevated double fin-like stern. I spoke to them in Burmese, but they didn't understand. But the men tied their *longyis* the Burmese way, into a knot, rather than the Malay or Indian way, and their features were very southern Burmese.

The village was called Tanjung Dawai, and I figured that *Dawai* was Daweh or Tavoy in Burma. It was on the west coast of the island, several miles north of Georgetown, the main city on Penang Island. We were trying to get some villagers to appear as extras in the movie, but they were reluctant because the film was about Burma, which was not a Muslim country, and the scenes were around Buddhist temples, and the women would have to appear without wearing headscarves.

Lots of extras whose features looked plausibly Burmese were needed. Most of the people in Georgetown are Chinese or Indian; the Malays live in *kampungs* [villages] outside Penang. You could have hundreds of people milling about for hours to shoot a five-minute scene. The company had to build its own villages for the sets; portable toilets for the crew were brought in. There was plenty of catered food and drink. When no one was watching, a lot of it was pilfered. The villagers would just help themselves. A Malay man was in charge of security, but he was part of the problem. The Singhalese crew cooked their own food, and they invited me to eat with them. Their food was more agreeable to my palate.

The few Tamil words, such as, *Tambi, inge-re wa-re* [Little boy, come here] and *kasih il-le* [I don't have any money], that I had learned as a child thrilled them. They were artists, carpenters, electricians, mechanics, and set decorators. For some scenes the shooting was done deep in the jungle. Motorcycle taxis from the villages had to be hired to move the cast and crew from the staging areas to the shooting locations. The Malay taxi drivers enjoyed a sensual feast ferrying the white female crew in tight shorts.

When scenes along the Perak River were shot, there had to be a helicopter standing by in case anyone was injured and needed to be evacuated. It was parked on land connected to the Perak sultan's palace. One of the extras, who was dressed like a Buddhist monk wearing a saffron-colored robe with a shaven head, was a well-known Malay game show host named Hani Mohsin. A newspaper and some politicians made an issue with that and challenged the government, "Why did you let these foreigners come here and do this? Muslims don't do these things." They accused the crew of trying to proselytize by turning their villages into Buddhist scenes. Apparently they could not differentiate between real life and acting. There was an election coming up, and it provided political grist for the campaign mill.

The Burmese military regime was not pleased that a movie about Burma was being made in Malaysia. It tried to pressure the Malaysian government to stop it. Boorman flew to Sri Lanka in an executive jet to try to find another location, but that didn't pan out. The logistics of moving would have been a tremendous expense, not to mention the delay. Malaysian authorities told him to change the film's story to be about a fictitious country. The compromise was to change the working title to simply *Beyond*.

There was always someone from a Malaysian government's intelligence unit present on the set to spy on us. The officer asked me who the various members of the cast and crew were. We also had occasional guests who came to watch the shooting, such as the British High Commissioner to Malaysia. Another was the Sri Lanka High Commissioner. The Malaysian spook wanted to know who these men were. (*High Commissioner* is the appellation by which members of the Commonwealth of Nations accredit their envoys to each other. The Commonwealth consists of fifty-four members, all former British colonies).

During the early pre-shooting phase, film location sites had to be reconnoitered. I went along on these scouting trips with Boorman, first assistant director Mark Egerton, production designer Tony Pratt, art director Errol Kelly, director of photography John Seale, props master Eddie Fowlie, executive producer Sean Ryerson, and production supervisor Chandran

Ratnam. We flew in an eight-seater aircraft to Ipoh to scout jungle locations around the royal city of Kuala Kangsar on the Perak River.

I was dispatched to the Burma–Thailand border to obtain props and Karen artifacts. Attempts to recruit Buddhist monks and Karen villagers to be used as extras only partially succeeded, due to inability to obtain travel documents. I spent many hours with Tony Pratt, who sketched every set before it was built. Once built, we checked them thoroughly, correcting or embellishing for authenticity. I also worked with sound engineer Gary Wilkins, costume designer Deborah LaGorce Kramer, and the make-up crew. We were assigned individual vehicles that transported us to the shooting sites. I shared a van with Bill Rubenstein, the script writer/still photographer; Hillary Helstein, Patricia Arquette's stand-in; and Desiree Bertasso from the production department.

In addition to the principal actors and actresses, the cast consisted of more than 2,500 Malay extras who were dressed and made up to look as authentically Burmese as possible. They were recruited from the *kampungs* and schools in and around Ipoh, Kuala Kangsar, and Penang. I was consulted to rule on whether a particular face resembled a Burmese one. I coached some Burmese lines to front liners, who had difficulty with the tri-tonal language on short notice. Yé Myint and Cho Cho Myint were the only two Burmese supporting actors the Malaysian government would allow the company to bring from America to Malaysia. They were students who escaped from Burma during the 1988 uprising.

The crew ran into difficulty obtaining Malays willing to shave their heads and don yellow robes to appear as Buddhist monks, and eventually Thais from across the border had to be imported. Someone in casting held the notion that I had the face of a Buddhist monk, so I got drafted for a tiny walk-through part. Boorman afterward was gracious enough to call my "acting" convincing, but my line as an uncharacteristically agitated monk did not survive the editor's cut.

An amusing incident took place while rehearsing the scene of students escaping across the river. I was on the eastern bank of the Perak River when the crew physician's radio crackled with the call, "We're out of condoms. Send us more." What's going on? The call was from Special Effects, in the bushes preparing the extras to cross over the bridge that had been built for the scene.

There was to be a lot of small arms fire at the "escapees"—both boys and girls—by the pursuing Burmese army. Blood was sure to flow. Special Effects needed condoms to do the job. The condoms are filled with corn starch kneaded to a sticky consistency and dyed red. These "blood-filled" condoms are taped to escapees' chests, waists, arms, and thighs. When gunfire and explosives erupt, the "escapees" would squeeze the condoms to squirt the "blood" to give the appearance of being wounded.

I learned of this other creative use of the condom in the Malaysian jungle. Malaysia is good country in which to shoot bloody movie scenes, because the country happens to be the world's largest producer of this *appliance d'amour.*

Ten trucks loaded with equipment, generators, grips, water, food, and wardrobe had to be driven to each location and returned to the staging areas after each shoot. There were some 100 crew present at every shoot. Everyone had an assigned task, and they worked as a tight, well-focused team. A scaled-down replica of Rangoon's Sulé Pagoda was built on a bus parking lot at Penang jetty. It was made of fiberglass, painted gold and supported by a steel frame. It looked so real that later friends in Burma who were shown a photograph of me standing in front of it asked how I got into Burma. It was a magnificent structure that took three months to build, but it was torn down after the filming.

A huge reclining Buddha, measuring 26 feet from the tip of the nose to the top of its forehead, was literally built into the foliage along the Perak River. I was the monk in that scene when the tour party "*ooohed*" and "*aaahed*" at its serenity while "Professor Jeremy Watt" (Spalding Gray), tried to impart some Buddhist philosophy about the Buddha's *"sole."* The sculptor, Mansell Rivers-Bland, did a superb job with this and dozens of other sculptures appearing in the film.

Altogether, four villages were built into the jungle and one existing village were used in the filming. One bridge, which spanned the Perak River, and another suspension bridge across a ravine were also built. All except the existing village were destroyed after filming. The preparation and expense that went into construction of the sets and props was staggering.

One day before shooting began, Boorman asked me to call Michael Aris. He wanted to be introduced to him. It was early morning in England, and when Michael answered the phone, he was irritated. "Call back later!" he said.

Michael thought the movie was going to be about his wife. He was displeased. In his life as a scholar of Tibetan culture, he had enjoyed a contemplative life as an academic. Suu's celebrity had thrown him into the limelight. "I'm violently opposed to making any movie about Suu!" Michael said.

"It's not about Suu," I told him. Adelle (Bonnie) Lutz as Suu had only a walk-through part. (Bonnie was made up so well that a Burmese woman who was watching the shooting called me aside and asked, "Uncle, has Daw Suu Kyi been released from house arrest?") Michael was concerned that his wife was being used. But she had become a public person.

Before 1988, Suu and Michael had lived a private life. One could almost say that their lives in Oxford, revolving around his academic career, had been so private as to be cloistered. Even many Burmese living in England did not know she was there. When the demonstrations erupted in 1988, the students had called for Aung San Oo, Suu's elder brother who lives in America, to return to Burma. They weren't even thinking about Aung San Suu Kyi until she appeared and spoke at the rally on 26 August.

Although I remembered seeing the teenager Suu as a student at Methodist English High School in Rangoon, I properly met her for the first time on Christmas Day 1984, when she had invited Riri and me to their apartment at 15 Park Town in Oxford to celebrate Christmas. It was a traditional English Christmas, complete with celebrants wearing cute decorative hats, exploding Christmas crackers, and relishing Christmas pudding. Suu was a gracious hostess and she cooked the meal herself—very English food. After dinner we took a stroll across the university campus with the boys and Puppy, their pet. Suu and Michael were aware of my activism against the regime, but we didn't talk politics; it was purely a social occasion. But what was curious was that, on our way out at departure, Michael said to me, "Uncle, we are neutral."

In July 1987 I visited Suu and her family when they were lodged at Rashtrapati Niwas, the former British colonial vice-regal lodge in Simla, where Michael and Suu were visiting fellows at the Indian Institute of Advanced Study. I had taken the family a box of pastries purchased along the way as I walked from Oberoi Hotel on the far end of the mall to their home for dinner. Apparently Indian spooks monitoring the family spotted me bearing the box. They mistook me for a Bhutanese separatist agitator because I was dressed in an Indian outfit topped by a colorful sequined waistcoat I had acquired at Ladakh. After I left Suu and her family, Indian Intelligence agents came to their quarters and literally turned their study inside out looking for bomb-making or other seditious material. Although Suu tells about this incident with hilarity, it was no laughing matter at the time.

Michael has an identical twin, Anthony. I once said to Anthony, "Why don't you go to Rangoon?" He answered, "You must be joking. I would be marched straight to Insein Jail!" Anthony has a sense of humor. Michael was prickly about privacy; he was not amused by my taking pictures of his family. I was invading their privacy. Michael died of prostate cancer in Oxford on 27 March 1999, his fifty-third birthday. The Burmese regime offered to allow Suu to travel to England to see him before he died, but she declined fearing it would be a one-way ticket to exile.

Shooting for *Beyond Rangoon* began in Penang on 12 February 1994 and ended on the Perak River on 25 May 1994. The work was tedious and hard—long hours in humid heat. When things did not go smoothly or props weren't ready, the crew got snappy. They worked under a lot of stress. Practically everybody chain-smoked. The tropical weather got hotter and wetter as the weeks progressed. It was hard on Riri to remain home alone in California for this long a stretch. She did visit me on location twice, and Zali and Dewi once each.

On my sixtieth birthday, Riri telephoned to tell me that Mike Copp, my buddy at Orange Coast College from day one, had died of cardiac arrest while playing tennis. The news shattered me. He was so athletic, well loved by colleagues and students alike. John Boorman personally offered me his condolences. I appreciated that. I was asked to write a eulogy, which was faxed to the college that same day. It was read by another colleague, Gerry Sjule, at the packed memorial service held in the Robert B. Moore Auditorium on the campus. Mike was my loyal friend through thick and thin. Zali and Dewi clung to him and he loved them very much. Mike and I had planned to travel the world together upon retirement.

Beyond Rangoon is the story of a young American physician, Laura Bowman (Patricia Arquette), whose husband and young son were murdered in a home robbery. Grieving her loss, she joins a tour group with her sister Andy (Frances McDormand), who is also a physician. One night after the group had called it a day, she goes on a solo outing in the streets. She encounters a massive rally where the character Aung San Suu Kyi (Adele Lutz) is to appear on the stage, but soldiers attempt to prevent her. "Aung San Suu Kyi" signals her escorts to remain behind. A tense confrontation fraught with danger develops when the captain orders his troops to open fire. The soldier directly in front of her trembles and cannot shoot. She gently pushes his weapon aside and slowly proceeds to the stage.

Laura is overwhelmed by "Aung San Suu Kyi's" courage. In the morning at the airport when the group leaves Rangoon, Laura's passport is missing—lifted by a pickpocket at the rally the night before. She stays behind to obtain a new one at the U.S. embassy. On her way out of the embassy Aung Ko, a tour guide, approaches her. He promises to show her the sights beyond Rangoon. Aung Ko is a former physics professor who was imprisoned, then fired from his job for aiding students who were being hounded by the army for participating in an earlier anti-government protest. The army pursues the anti-military demonstrators. There is a lot of gunfire. Many are wounded, many killed.

I was the one who tried to restrain the Aung San Suu Kyi character from moving forward when the troops obstructed her path. My heart was so burdened when rehearsing the scene that I had to turn away from the set several times to regain composure. Not sensing my emotion, Boorman called me aside and said, "You seem to be disinterested. Let's try that scene again."

The rest of the story is a suspenseful one. In the end Laura is helped through the jungle to Thailand. Witnessing "Aung San Suu Kyi's" courage reinvigorates Laura to pick up the pieces and continue her own life in the wake of personal tragedy. She is inspired by the Buddhism that has permeated Burmese life and by her guide Aung Ko's own phoenix-like history. Aung Ko uttered the most memorable line when he reins in the students who are pummeling a Burmese soldier, "If we do to them what they have done to us, we will become what they have become," he counsels. The movie is about a crushed spirit coming back to life and moving forward.

While *Beyond Rangoon* did not make a hit at the box office in the United States, it did well in France. It also earned Burma some much needed attention. American students from elementary to college levels were doing projects on Burma for their schoolwork. Columbia Pictures had tried hard to release the movie while Aung San Suu Kyi was still under detention, hoping the Burmese junta would free her *after* it was released. But the junta jumped the gun and freed her before it was released, all to the good.

Before the movie's release in August 1995, John Boorman invited Michael Aris to a screening in London. I heard that he liked it. But for my part, I was disappointed with the reception it got from American movie goers. "I speak here and there, at colleges, churches, service clubs and other civic organizations," I told a writer for *The Chronicle of Higher Education*, for an article she was writing about my part in the making of the movie. All these little things put together are nothing compared to the impact of this film.

At the pre-release screening that I attended with some members of the film's crew at Sony Studios in Culver City, we looked at each other as we walked out afterward, not quite sure what to say. We were "underwhelmed."

There was a film called *Z* released in 1969, directed by Costa-Gavras, about the fall of the Greek colonels. It was a powerful movie. I wished *Beyond Rangoon* had done the same for Burma. I had hoped that its release would be a godsend. The film's promoters failed, in my estimation, to approach or engage human rights activists. Even the Burmese expatriate community was cool to it. "So much money was spent to make the movie," they said, "it would have been much better if the money had been spent on the movement." I think *Beyond Rangoon* failed also because it tried too hard to be a political movie.

An executive from Castle Rock Entertainment called me and Yé Myint, a supporting actor who portrayed a student in the party escaping to the

Thai border, to a meeting and asked us to rein in Burmese expatriates from demonstrating at showings. We told him we had no control over them. His concern was for naught, because there were no demonstrations whatsoever against the movie. In fact, dissidents who had been in the thick of events said its portrayal of the massacres did not go deep enough, that the actual events of 1988 were much worse.

Regardless, clips from the movie have been shown in media coverage of the situation in Burma. If people in Burma got caught with a pirated video of the film, they were sentenced to seven years in jail. Seven years was the minimum for everything. Even so, some enterprising people were making money by secretly showing the film. They obtained pirated copies from Malaysia and Thailand.

BURMA AND BEYOND

In the winter of 1995, with Riri and two friends, I traveled to Pajau in Burma's Kachinland. We flew into Mangshi from Kunming where we were fetched by David Zau Baum of the KIO and a young Kachin driver who was fluent in Chinese. Early the next morning, the pair drove us on the Burma Road to Ruili. We stopped by the road side to eat at a tribal noodle stand. All along the route we saw many tribal people dressed in their native attire clearing the jungle, gathering firewood, or tending to their livestock. The actual Burma Road, which was built in record time in 1938, linked Lashio in Burma with Kunming in China. My father traveled on it when he went on a goodwill mission to China in 1939, beginning in Rangoon, as described earlier in this memoir. Portions of it were being rerouted or repaired when we traveled on it.

At Ruili, I saw a large mural of Chinese Prime Minister Zhou En Lai welcoming Prime Minister U Nu in 1957. U Nu had come to Kunming to discuss mutual concerns with his Chinese counterpart and cement Sino-Burmese friendship. We were driven north from Ruili along the Burmese border on the Chinese side and smuggled into a Kachin village called Sima, which is inhabited by Kachins on both sides. As the car approached Pajau gate, I asked the driver to let me out. I wanted to walk into my homeland. It was pitch black, but the stars were shining. We were in cold Pajau for three nights. I held discussions with General Zau Mai, Commander in Chief of the Kachin Independence Army (KIA). I visited the schools and medical clinic and attended a worship service.

The people were delighted to view the videotape of *Beyond Rangoon* that I had brought. I also visited the northern branch of the ABSDF camp, which was situated on a hill at Pajau, away from the KIA headquarters. The Kachins received us with open arms. The Kachin Independence Organization (KIO) had recently signed a ceasefire with the Burmese military junta. I had been skeptical of the deal and the KIA's Vice-Chief of Staff, General Tu Jai, tried to convince me that it was the right thing to do. I found the headquarters well organized; I was impressed by their determination and motivation. After being entertained at a sumptuous banquet that featured a recently slaughtered cow, we were smuggled out of Kachinland in the dark of night, just as we were smuggled in.

At the airport terminal in Mangshi, I encountered a group of students from Reed College led by a faculty member. They were entering Burma by bus at Ruili, the entry point across the river of the same name, but called Shweli in Burmese. I gave them a piece of my mind over their going into military-ruled Burma. Why were they going there to see destitute people who were being ground to poverty by the regime? Were they not lending legitimacy to the junta by spending their dollars, which invariably lined the pockets of the ruling military clique?

On 10 July 1995 Aung San Suu Kyi was released from house arrest. Riri said it could not have been a better birthday present. At first it seemed as if Aung San Suu Kyi and her National League for Democracy might have some space for political initiative, but the military restricted her movements and played cat-and-mouse games that stunted NLD supporters. By 23 September 2000, the regime had put her back under house arrest again. All hope that the Burmese student generation of 1988 and its supporters abroad had invested in the democracy movement seemed to be coming to naught. It was a Sisyphean blow. If any progress was being made, it was at glacial speed.

The military threw out a carrot in the form of a National Convention whose purpose was to draft a new Constitution. The restrictions placed on the sequestered delegates were onerous. They were forbidden to discuss the proceedings among themselves or with anyone outside. It was also punishable by imprisonment for ordinary citizens to discuss the Convention. No one outside was allowed to draft any version of the Constitution—an exercise that a class in political science at an American college might be assigned to do. The Convention dragged its feet. It went on and off for eighteen years. The National League for Democracy boycotted it, although some within the party took exception and participated in the proceedings. Suu called the Convention what it was: "a farce."

The regime was determined to ignore the results of the 1990 elections. It was done very cleverly. First it said the candidates' bona fides had to be checked. After that it scrutinized their funding sources. Finally, it announced that none of the candidates was qualified, and that was that. The official who declared the election null and void was the commander of the Rangoon military district.

Part of the role I assigned myself in the movement in America was to lobby universities to award an honorary degree in absentia to Aung San Suu Kyi. My purpose was that, even if her movements were restricted, it would put Burma on the map, and she could send a message. I approached American, Bucknell, Indiana Universities, Kenyon College, and The College of Wooster. Bettyjane (BJ) Champlin, a lawyer, human rights activist, and colleague in the movement for Burmese democracy, took on the task with Chapman University, which awarded Suu an honorary Doctor of Humane Letters degree in absentia. (BJ died on 13 January 2014 of cancer.)

I thought Indiana University would be receptive, but a senior administrator there told me: "We've never awarded an honorary degree in absentia." I pointed out to him that Suu was not free to leave and return to Burma. The faculty chairman at Kenyon College made the same excuse. Bucknell did not award honorary degrees at that time, but in lieu of one it honored her with an Award of Merit. Bucknell's Burma connection predates the American Civil War. Burma's first ever student to study in America, Mong Shaw Loo, came to Bucknell in 1858. He was Bucknell's first student from abroad. Several Burmese students have since attended Bucknell. Suu's commencement address was read by former American ambassador to Burma Burton Levin. At American University, I had the help of two trustees, Methodist Bishop James K. Mathews and attorney Betty Jane Southard Murphy, who were long time friends. They successfully pushed Suu's candidacy for an honorary Doctor of Laws degree, in absentia. American University enlisted the help of the United States chargé d'affaires in Rangoon to get its formal invitation delivered to Suu. The United States dealt diplomatically with the regime at the chargé level after it withdrew its ambassador in rebuke over the 1988 uprising. Kent Wiedeman was the chargé d'affaires at the embassy.

The invitation went via David Young, Burma Desk Officer at the State Department, to Wiedeman in Rangoon and on to Suu, in November 1996. Connecting with Suu was a challenge. She was blocked from receiving any mail at her home. David Taylor, AU President Benjamin Ladner's assistant, and I were getting nervous. He tried several times to reach her on the phone, but it was all in vain. By a stroke of luck, I got through to her one morning. "Have you received American University's invitation, Suu?" I asked.

"No, Uncle, I haven't received anything. Nothing," she said. I told her, to stay right there, and immediately called David Taylor, asking him to call her right away. He was so relieved and happy to be speaking with her for the first time. He asked her to fax him her commencement address. When Suu's speech arrived, David e-mailed me and said, "The smartest move I made all week was to tell my secretary at closing to leave the fax machine on with plenty of paper in it."

Armed guards kept her house tightly sealed. A big stretch of University Avenue where her house is located was blocked off, open only to residents. She received the formal invitation later. I don't know how the American chargé Kent Wiedeman got it delivered to her.

When Suu asked, "Uncle, what shall I say in the speech?" I told her to be sure to include two things: "One, call upon American University and by extension all other universities, to divest from companies doing business in Burma. Two, tell the audience that the purpose of freedom is for those who enjoy it to create it for others who are shackled." I got the latter from the Prophet Isaiah, "I have given you as a covenant to the people, a light to the nations, to open the eyes that are blind, to bring out the prisoners from the dungeon, from the *prison those who sit in darkness* [italics mine]." The sender's name on the faxed speech was *Naga Min* [Dragon King].

Michael Aris delivered the speech on Suu's behalf at the commencement on 26 January 1997. I was seated on the very front row between Marie T. Huhtala, a State Department official, and Dr. U Sein Win, Prime Minister of the exile National Coalition Government of the Union of Burma. I introduced the California-born Marie Huhtala of Salinas to Michael at the reception that followed. She was later posted to Malaysia as ambassador. Whitney Stewart, a friend and author of several books for young adults including a biography of Suu, was seated on Sein Win's left. In her speech read by Michael, Suu said in part:

> Of course we all hope that our tomorrows will be happy. But happiness takes on many forms. Political prisoners have known the most sublime moments of perfect communion with their highest ideals during periods when they were incarcerated in isolation, cut off from contact with all that was familiar and dear to them. From where do these resources spring, if not from an innate strength at our core, a spiritual strength that transcends material bounds? My colleagues who spent years in the harsh conditions of Burmese prisons, and I myself, have had to draw on such inner resources on many occasions.
>
> Nobody can take away from us the essential and ultimate freedom of choosing our priorities in life. We may not be able to control the external factors that affect our existence, but we can decide how we wish to conduct our inner lives. We have to live in a society that does not grant freedom of expression, but we can decide how much value we wish to put on the duty to

speak out for our rights. We may not be able to pursue our beliefs without bringing down on us the full vengeance of a cruel
state mechanism, but we can decide how much we are prepared
to sacrifice for our beliefs. Those of us who decided to work for
democracy in Burma made our choice in the conviction that the
danger of standing up for basic human rights in a repressive society was preferable to the safety of a quiescent life in servitude.

Ours is a non-violent movement that depends on faith in the
human predilection for fair play and compassion. Some would
insist that man is primarily an economic animal interested only
in his material well being.

This is too narrow a view of a species, which has produced
numberless brave men and women who are prepared to undergo relentless persecution for the sake of upholding deeply
held beliefs and principles. It is my pride and inspiration that
such men and women exist in my country today.... You who are
gathered here to celebrate the opening of the doors of hope and
opportunity might wish to assist our fight for a Burma where
young people can know the joys of hope and opportunity.

Part of our struggle is to make the international community
understand that we are a poor country not because there is an
insufficiency of resources and investment, but because we are
deprived of the basic institutions and practices that make for
good government. There are multinational business concerns,
which have no inhibitions about dealing with repressive regimes.

Their justification for economic involvement in Burma is
that their presence will actually assist the process of democra-
tization. Investment that only goes to enrich an already wealthy
elite bent on monopolizing both economic and political power
cannot contribute towards egality and justice, the foundation
stones for a sound democracy.

*I would therefore like to call upon those who have an interest in
expanding their capacity for promoting intellectual freedom and
humanitarian ideals to take a principled stand against companies which are doing business with the military regime of Burma.
Please use your liberty to promote ours.* [italics mine]

I was highly pleased that Suu did incorporate both my points into her
speech. "Please use your liberty to promote ours" has become an iconic
quote of hers worldwide. In September 2012, she spoke in person at American University.

PERSONAL STRUGGLE AND TRIUMPH

In May 1997, I was diagnosed with prostate cancer. The diagnosis frightened me. I broke down. The "C" word was like a delayed death sentence. I didn't know how much time I had remaining, especially after the open-heart surgery in 1982 to unblock four arteries. I wondered whether my body could withstand another assault. Once again, Riri, my mainstay and my rock, stood firmly by me. "We are going to pray and fight this together," she said. After a year of being injected monthly with Zoladex, I underwent brachytherapy, a procedure where little seeds of slow-release radiation are injected into the prostate. I was told not to go near pregnant women for at least six months. That was the least of my concerns. The treatments left me feeling weak as well as worried. In 2009, another cancer assaulted—it was the bladder this time. That unwelcome invasion has also been conquered, although it continues to be monitored annually.

Maung Zarni, the activist-founder of the Free Burma Coalition, graduated from the University of Wisconsin with a PhD in May 1998. (Coincidentally, the Dalai Lama was awarded an honorary degree at the same commencement.) I went to Madison for the occasion. I was in pain but I was glad to be there to honor my young friend.

In December 1998, I retired from Orange Coast College. The school offered an attractive golden handshake, so I took it. I was sixty-five and wanted to use my remaining active years in other ways. At the exit interview, the human resources administrator told me the average OCC employee dies within fifteen years of retirement. My fifteen years are up. I hope to be above average for several more years.

Riri and I spent the next two years battling the Boulder County Commissioners over land-use issues on the dream house we wanted to build, and did build, in the Rocky Mountain foothills of Colorado. The county wanted to micromanage where we could build, and the spot it chose for the site on our 35-acre parcel was unacceptable. They say you can't fight City Hall. We did, and we won. But that's another story that need not be told here. After we moved into our dream home and started getting adjusted, I began the tedious job of collecting information and sorting out documents to write this memoir. There were three years in the research and writing, with several false starts, but now I can finally see the finish line.

In 2000, Riri and I established an endowment to fund a scholarship for a Burmese student at Bucknell University. I also helped raise a substantial sum for the Shaw Loo Memorial Scholarship there. The first Win Scholar was a Karen girl named Naw Khee Htu. I am so happy that Thet Hein Tun, another recipient, graduated *magna cum laude* with the class of 2014 and was initiated into Phi Beta Kappa. He majored jointly in engineering and humanities. Riri and I were happy to meet his parents in Rangoon in January 2014.

In Boulder I participated as actively as I could in my local church's activities. In 2000 I was honored with the Peace Maker Award by the Rocky Mountain United Methodist Church Conference. We chose to retire in Boulder, a college town that offers many stimulating intellectual and cultural activities. Among them is the annual Conference on World Affairs where scholars, journalists, statesmen, and sundry experts from the world over come together to the University of Colorado for one week and engage in exercises that advance the frontiers of knowledge, and share their humanity.

We met Kerry Meyer, when she first came from New Hampshire to pursue graduate study in engineering at the University of Colorado. Kerry and her bosom pal Anji Hamilton visited an orphanage and a school in Mae Sot on the Burma–Thailand border in 2002, and raised money for the school.

Anji Hamilton was one of six American young people included among a total of seventeen activists from Indonesia, Malaysia, Philippines, and Thailand who distributed leaflets written in Burmese and English with the message: "We are your friends from around the world. We support your hopes for human rights and democracy; 8–8–88 don't forget, don't give up." They did this on 9 August 1989, standing in front of Rangoon's Scott Market and other central Rangoon locations, in remembrance of the horrific massacre of the year before. According to a personal communication I had from Anji, they were arrested and detained for six days at a police station and a government guest house before being deported.

After she earned a master's degree, Kerry Meyer decided to make Colorado her home, to our delight. We more or less "adopted" her as our own and have enjoyed her parents whenever they have visited. She sequestered herself in the guest suite on the east wing of our home when she was preparing for the final master's and professional engineer's examinations. We were so happy to share the joy when she earned the designation of a Professional Engineer (PE). Of course we take some credit even though she did all the hard work. She has been a joy to us, filling in for our own daughter who lives far away in New England. The two women share the same passion: lecturing me on the "correct" way to live. It is good to have her working and living in Denver with Lucy, her canine companion, even if she is a pain sometimes.

For forty years I had wanted to return to Burma. There were many places in my own country that I had never seen. Beginning in 1969, though, I had felt compelled to become politically active, which made it all the more unlikely that I would have been allowed into Burma. So, for many years Riri and I worked hard to make ends meet while raising a family in America. We are happy that our son Zali graduated from Kenyon and Babson Colleges, and daughter Dewi from Bryn Mawr and Harvard. She was the youngest in her graduating classes in high school and at Bryn Mawr, where she majored in mathematics. She did not get that from me.

We moved into our dream home, named *Bukit Tinggi* (Indonesian for "high hill"), in April 2001. We have been blessed indeed. For the open house we had our pastors, Reverend Carolyn Waters and Reverend Trevor Potter, and Reverend Travis Kendall from Phoenix, join in the blessing. (Travis Kendall died on 25 June 2015.)

The previous September, *Sayadaw* U Pyinnya Wuntha, the missionary Buddhist monk I had befriended in Penang during the filming of *Beyond Rangoon*, visited us while the house was under construction. He stayed a week in the cabin, our former home next door. Riri and I showed him the sights in western Colorado and Arches National Monument in Utah. He really enjoyed the fall colors. At my request, he blessed the house and left an inscription on a wooden structural member, since built over, and wrote in our guest book, "May Mr. & Mrs. Win and family be well, happy and successful by the grace of the Enlightened One!"

After he returned to Malaysia, Dr. Rewata Dhamma, the abbot of the Birmingham, England, temple, visited him in Penang, while he was en route to Rangoon. U Pyinnya Wuntha asked him to speak to General Khin Nyunt to request that he grant me a visa to Burma. The general respected him very highly and wished to be blessed with a good karma in the next life. Apparently General Nyunt wired the Burmese embassy in Washington to expedite a visa for me. It was one small step the junta was taking in the hope of polishing its tarnished image.

In October 2004, General Khin Nyunt was ousted from office. For the first time, on 28 December 2015, I came face to face with the once-feared mighty general, now shorn of all power and ozymandiazed. I found him to be a friendly seventy-seven-year-old, who exuded warmth as he escorted me through his garden and tenderly explained the characteristics of its flora. He was particularly proud of his success in growing durian trees in his patch and offered me some saplings, but I had to politely decline due to the prohibition of un-quarantined vegetation entering the United States. "I am being watched," he told me. I found the remark pathetic, coming from one who presided over a brutal institution which watched those whom it perceived to be a threat to the junta—and meted out untold pain and suffering to millions. A month later, I saw him again, alone, in his ornate living room. He did most of the talking for an hour. I almost felt like I was a Catholic priest listening to a confession. He said the military is all about orders and he

followed them. He was proud of the seven-step road map to peace he
initiated.

**Win, at left, with Gen Khin Nyunt in the general's home, 28 Jan 2016.
Photo by Tin Tin Cho.**

I arrived in Rangoon on 3 November 2001 and stayed in Burma for
a fortnight. I had already made plans to attend the fiftieth anniversary reunion of my Woodstock class in October, so the timing worked out perfectly for me to enter Burma. There was no direct flight from New Delhi to
Rangoon, so I had to fly over to Bangkok and stay there overnight to make
the connection.

The Bangkok Christian Guest House is the lodging of choice for travelers because it is relatively inexpensive and conveniently located just off
Silom Road. The night in Bangkok allowed me time to "review the situation"
and decide whether or not to enter Burma. So I said to myself, "Here I am in
Bangkok. I have a ticket and a visa. So go, I will."

I went back again in 2003, this time with Riri, and I had wanted to
continue going back. But for eight years after that I was denied another visa.
Why? Because I had been with Aung San Suu Kyi. That was unpalatable to
the military junta. But how in the world did they find that out? General
Khin Nyunt was no longer in power. He was ousted in October 2004. In
2003, Vicky Bowman was the British ambassador in Rangoon who arranged
for Riri and me to meet Suu at her residence on 20 January.

Suu was meeting with some visitors from England when we arrived at the British ambassador's residence. While waiting for our turn to see her, I chatted with U Myint Thein, her aide, who gave me a fighting peacock lapel button. I treasure that memento. U Myint Thein's death a few months later saddened me. Vicky came and got us when Suu's guests had gone and left us alone with her. As soon as Riri laid eyes on Suu, she started to cry. "Don't cry, Aunty," said Suu.

"But you've suffered so much, Suu!" Riri said.

"There are others who have suffered much more," Suu told her.

I asked Suu, "Where are your flowers?" Suu is known for wearing flowers in her hair. She turned her head to show fresh orchids; I was sitting on her left, and the flowers were pinned in her hair on the other side.

She said, "Uncle, I'm surprised they let you in." I had not seen her since our last meeting, in July 1987, in Simla. We exchanged news about our families, and we talked about our elderly mutual friend Dora Than É, whom we affectionately called Auntie Dora, who was in declining health. Suu called Dora her "emergency aunt." She said whenever she needed to cry on someone's shoulder, it was Auntie Dora's. After Auntie Dora had a fall and lay supine on the floor in her Oxford apartment, she wrote to tell me she had an "excellent view of the ceiling." What a lofty view!

Auntie Dora passed away on 17 June 2007—eight months shy of her 100th birthday. It was a reunion of sorts when Riri, Zali, and I joined Anna Allott; Alexander and Kim Aris; U Nwe Aung; Vicky Bowman and her husband, the artist Htein Lin; Ken and Marion Freeman; Patricia Herbert; Martin Morland; Win Win Nu; Tin Htar Swe; Pascal Khoo Thwe; Justin Wintle; and several others, to bid Aunty Dora farewell at an Oxford crematorium, followed by a reception at St. Hugh's College, Suu's alma mater.

The situation in Burma had become truly dismal at this point, and people were pessimistic. We asked Suu for her assessment. "I am optimistic," she said.

"But it has been so long, more than thirty years," said Riri.

"The longer it continues, the sooner it will end," said Suu. She was expressing a Buddhist attitude, as if the destiny were already written. However, she was the only one we met who was optimistic about the country.

We were with her for about 45 minutes, until she had to go to her next appointment. Vicky took a photograph of us. We left Burma the next day. At the airport, after we had gone through Customs and Immigration and while waiting in the departure lounge, a uniformed officer approached me and asked, "May I see your passports?" He took them and disappeared into an office for what seemed like an eternity. Riri was getting nervous. I was not. But eventually he returned them without any explanation.

Upon our return to Boulder, I e-mailed the photo of the threesome to a friend in Rangoon. She answered cryptically, "Uncle, I'm not involved in politics." I suspected something sinister underlying her remark, as this was an uncharacteristic message. I was certain she was ordered to do this by the military. Later I learned that Military Intelligence agents had indeed come to her and showed her the intercepted photograph. They recognized me and Suu, but not Riri. "Who is this lady?" they wanted to know, pointing at Riri in the picture.

"She's Uncle Cho's wife," answered the young friend.

"No, his wife is Indonesian," they said. "This lady is Burmese." In the picture, Riri was dressed in a Burmese outfit. I cannot identify this young friend, for the military is still venomous.

Later I talked to U Lin Myaing, the Burmese ambassador in Washington. "I cannot help you anymore," he said.

"Why?" I asked.

"They saw the picture of you with Aung San Suu Kyi. They did not like that." I told him that Suu is a personal friend. "I understand," he said, "but they don't."

Ambassador U Lin Myaing was ousted from his position in 2004. On a subsequent trip to Burma, I tracked him down because I felt I owed him a courtesy call. He was working for an investment company owned by Serge Pun, a Burma-born Chinese. "How did you find me?" he asked. I told him that June, his sister-in-law, had given me his home phone number. I had met June when she was visiting California a few years before. We Burmese can't get away from each other. People like U Lin Myaing are entangled in their own oppressive web.

Back in Boulder, I kept talking about Burma whenever I was invited. Riri and I remained active in retirement, especially in our community. We also continued traveling to Indonesia and the Burma–Thailand border in alternate years, teaching English to Burmese refugee children and to Indonesian children in Pariaman (West Sumatra), visiting orphanages, and doing social work in both countries. When we visited Indonesia in 2004, we sought out the former foreign minister, Ali Alatas, who was Riri's schoolmate at the Academy for the Foreign Service in the early 1950s. Alatas went to Burma as the Association of South East Asian Nations' (ASEAN) emissary to help bring Burma out of its self-imposed isolation. These emissaries go in, they greet each other, they smile and receive the red-carpet treatment, but nothing substantive happens. I asked Alatas to do whatever he could to help free Aung San Suu Kyi, who had been briefly imprisoned at Insein and then placed under house arrest once again after the infamous Depeyin ambush of 30 May 2003. There is no doubt in my mind that the attempt to assassinate her that night got botched. It happened on the road near a little village called Depeyin, north of Monywa, up country. "I sit down and have a discussion for twenty minutes—what can I do?" said Alatas. "Please talk to the foreign minister," he advised me.

He meant Dr. Hassan Wirajuda. That was an excellent suggestion! We hit gold because one of Riri's many relatives is married to Dr. Wirajuda's daughter. In their tightly knit Minangkabau matriarchal system, Riri and Hassan are related, even if distantly. Riri went to work right away and we got an appointment with the foreign minister. We were instructed to enter the foreign ministry by a private entrance. Surprisingly, there was no metal detector or any security check. The door keeper directed us to the elevator to the second floor. A neatly dressed protocol officer met us when we exited the elevator. She showed us to the reception hall; said, "Silakan duduk" [please sit down]; and took off. It was closing time and she wanted to go home. We waited, twiddling our thumbs, wondering whether we had been forgotten. Suddenly Minister Hassan and an aide popped in. The minister's wing was by now deserted. It had been a long day. Hassan spent forty-five minutes patiently telling us of his efforts talking to the generals in Rangoon of Indonesia's desire to rekindle the once close relationship Indonesia had with Burma and for Burma to rejoin the community of nations, and, of course, to have Aung San Suu Kyi freed.

In its nascent days, Burma had supported Indonesia's struggle against the Netherlands for independence, and Prime Minister U Nu even sent a planeload of weapons to assist in the fight against the Dutch. It was also Indonesia that had hosted the Asian-African Conference of April 1955, widely known as the Bandung Conference. I expressed my appreciation to Minister Hassan for his personal role in having Burma admitted to ASEAN and asked his aide to take a photograph of us "before we got any older." I also thanked him for the vital part he had played in softening the Burmese military junta to get relief delivered to victims of Cyclone Nargis, which devastated the Irrawaddy Delta in May 2008.

In 2005, Burma's military regime abruptly moved the seat of government to a new capital constructed in central Burma, called Naypyidaw. To be precise, the move took place at the auspicious moment prescribed by astrologers—6:37 a.m. on 6 November 2005. They had been secretly building it for about ten years. North Korean engineers had designed and built the tunnels at Naypyidaw, presumably to shelter from attacks. This was not what Burma needs. What Burma needs are reconciliation, peace, schools, roads, healthcare, housing, electricity, and clean drinking war. Senior General Than Shwe's paranoid justification was that Naypyidaw was remote from any possible attack. How absurd! Doesn't he know about drones? Burma's

enemies are not from abroad but from within. The new capital's name itself reflects his megalomania: Naypyidaw, officially written Nay Pyi Taw in
the Constitution, means "abode of royalty." (In Burmese, a monosyllabic
language, each syllable is spelled out.) But, sad to say, there is continuity:
Burmese kings of yore held the custom of moving their capitals when they
ascended the throne. So Than Shwe was aligning himself with the glorious
past—reflective glory—by continuing the tradition. Lee Kuan Yew, Singapore's elder statesman, minced no words, calling the move "dumb."

In September 2007, Buddhist monks by the thousands paraded
through the main streets of Rangoon leading to the Sulé Pagoda, chanting
the *Mingala Sutta*, prayer for compassion and loving kindness. The regime
had nearly doubled the price of gasoline, which had the domino effect of
rendering consumer goods prohibitively expensive. Veterans of the 1988 student-led uprising had protested in August, and to everyone's astonishment
the monks followed suit a month later. In their saffron-robed thousands
they paraded, many of them holding alms bowls turned upside-down—a
powerful gesture signifying refusal to accept offerings from members of the
military and their families—and chanting a Buddhist mantra: "Let everyone
be free from harm. Let everyone be free from anger. Let everyone be free
from hardship." Civilians locked hands and lined the streets to protect them.

Author Andrew Marshall, in a powerful account published in the 11
October 2007 issue of *Time* magazine, described the monks' collective action as having an "electrifying" effect on Rangoon residents:

> They pour south from the Shwedagon, the immense golden
> pagoda that is Burma's most revered Buddhist monument, in
> an unbroken, mile-long column—barefoot, chanting, clutch-
> ing pictures of Buddha, their robes drenched with the late-
> monsoon rains. They walk briskly—if you stick to the city's
> crumbling pavements it is almost impossible to keep pace with
> them—but when they reach Sulé Pagoda they stop awhile to
> pray. Soon they're off again, coursing through the city streets in
> a solid stream of red and orange, like blood vessels giving life to
> an oxygen-starved body.

Millions of Burmese, wrote Marshall, had "glimpsed what life was like
without their hated rulers," but even as he looked on, soldiers opened fire on
the crowd, and he was left to ask: "Are the protests that took place over 10
days in late September over, or merely dormant?"

In Burma, monks are the pulse of the community. So things begin
in the monasteries, and the so-called "saffron revolution" of September
2007 could have been important. But alas, nothing much came of it. "We

mustn't retreat," a young monk said bravely to Marshall. "If we retreat now, we fail." What nobody expected was what actually happened: For the first time in Burmese history, the regime's soldiers invaded monasteries across Rangoon, beating and arresting monks, leaving pools of their blood on the floors, piercing the thin walls of the monks' dormitories with what in Burma are euphemistically called "rubber bullets": potentially deadly 40-mm cartridges thinly coated with rubber. The regime's willingness to brutalize monks enraged ordinary Burmese. As one Rangoon resident accurately explained to Marshall, "A devout Buddhist will not even step on the shadow of a monk."

"What's happening?" Marshall asked a Burmese friend he reached by telephone.

"They are hunting us," his friend replied. Indeed, not even foreigners, not even journalists, were safe from the ire of the Burmese military. A Japanese cameraman named Kenji Nagai was shot dead by a soldier at point-blank range. Marshall was fortunate to survive to publish his eyewitness account.

With the monks preaching tolerance and peace, and the military demanding obedience at gunpoint, "these protests pitted Burma's most beloved institution against its most reviled," he wrote. The reviled institution prevailed, at least in the short term, because they were willing to shoot to kill. In Burma it is the army that keeps anything from changing for the better, because they are the ones that wield the sword. It's as simple as that, sadly. Soldiers sealed off the entrances to the Shwedagon and Sulé pagodas and drove through the city, clearing the streets. "For more than a week—for most of their lifetimes—Burmese have called peacefully for dialogue," wrote Marshall. This is the closest the junta gets to it: "screaming at its people through loudspeakers from a truck surrounded by men with guns."

On my trip in 2012 to the Burma–Thailand border I went to the garbage dump on the edge of Mae Sot, within sight of Burma's Dawna Range across the Moei River. I took enough knee-high boots for everyone there. There dwelt about fifty families who eked out an existence collecting recyclable plastic and other leftover items for re-sale. The stench was overwhelming. A pregnant woman told me she was going to have her fourth child delivered right there, by a masseuse. These people had nowhere else to go, but despite their dire circumstances, they seemed resigned to their lot. I was with an Australian volunteer, a retired aerial photographer named Fred Stockwell who does the work of a one-man Peace Corps without any fanfare. Fred was building a tank for clean drinking water. He was also repairing the roof of a shack that had been blown away. He brought rice and medicine for these destitute people. One man felt very happy when he caught a small fish and two snakes for his family. Other Burmese living in Mae Sot did not bother to visit or to help. To many, the garbage-dump dwellers were considered pariahs, to be stigmatized. It was their bad karma.

Garbage dump dwellers, Mae Sot, Thailand, 2011. Photo by U Kyaw Win.

In May 2008, the Irrawaddy Delta was devastated by Cyclone Nargis. An estimated 135,000 people perished and many more were left homeless. Uncounted numbers of rice fields were inundated with sea water. The regime's callous and cruel response, preventing outside help from delivering relief to the victims, clearly constituted a crime against humanity. United States, French, and Royal Navy warships stood by offshore with aid, but they were not permitted to deliver it.

It was during this time that the regime rammed its deeply flawed Constitution down the people's throat and proclaimed victory at the polls with a huge margin. It was flawed because it enshrined the military's hold on the country by reserving 25 percent of the parliamentary seats to themselves; prohibits anyone married to a foreigner or have children who are not Burmese citizens from enjoying the rights of full citizenship; and authorized the *Tamadaw's* commander in chief to be the final arbiter who can take over the government if, in his judgment, the country's security is at risk. The Constitution of 2008 also reserved for the military the ministries of Border, Defense, and Home Affairs. There are several other unjust provisions, but these are the salient ones. The paperback edition of the Constitution weighs 1 pound, 10.3 ounces (746 grams).

There were moves by the international community to take the generals to the U.N. Security Council to form a committee of inquiry, a first step in establishing culpability in the International Criminal Court for crimes committed against humanity. But any such attempt would have been dead on arrival, as China would have exercised its veto, so the matter is now quietly shelved.

There is a principle dubbed R2P—responsibility to protect—which is also referred to as the Rome Statute. It allows the international community to intervene in a member country's internal affairs when its government is unwilling or unable to protect its own citizens. While the Burmese military junta's unwillingness to permit the international community to come to the aid of Cyclone Nargis victims clearly constitutes culpability under this statute, action against the junta has no chance of going forward against China's veto.

Crimes against humanity are large issues that must be brought to justice. Throughout its harsh rule, the military committed many acts of murder, rape, arson; performed extrajudicial executions of innocent citizens; confiscated real and personal property of citizens; deprived many of their livelihoods; imprisoned thousands; and exiled untold numbers of citizens, including educated and skilled people sorely needed to develop the country. The ones who perpetrated these acts should be brought to trial in the International Criminal Court, and those found guilty should receive their due punishment. There is no statute of limitations for murder.

Riri and I visited Burma in November 2011, after I had been shut out for the second time for eight more years. I visited my alma mater, St. Paul's High School. Like all other private schools, St. Paul's was nationalized in 1963. When I told the principal that I had been a student there in 1946–1950, he instructed a staffer to escort me around the ground floor and the quad between the two wings of the main building. When I pointed out to the young man a lab on the second floor, he said there is a piece of heavy machinery in that room whose purpose is not known to school officials. I told him it was a compressor that generated gas for the Bunsen burners. "Oh, that's what is!" he exclaimed. St. Paul's was the first high school in Burma that had a science laboratory.

A few months earlier, we had written to Suu that we would like to see her. She had been released a year earlier, on 13 November 2010, and was relatively free to receive guests. She was taking a conciliatory stance towards the military regime, especially General U Thein Sein, and was getting a lot of attention from the international media. When we learned that Hillary Clinton was to visit her the following week, we held out little hope of seeing her. But two days before we were due to leave the country, we received confirmation that she would indeed receive us. "For fifteen minutes only," her scheduler had e-mailed us earlier. We were happy, nevertheless.

Suu had told our son, Zali, when he visited her a few weeks before, that she wanted some poetic works. So in New Delhi we purchased a few, including those by Rabindranath Tagore. When I told the salesman that we were making the purchases as gifts for Suu, his face lit up. He gave us a couple more books. "Please take these to Daw Aung San Suu Kyi as my gift," he said.

Another telling and touching little incident took place on our way to her home. I flagged down a taxi on Lower Kemmendine Road, but did not give the driver the address because one could never be sure whether he was MI or an informant. Riri was dressed in a light blue *htamein* with floral designs topped by a pinkish blouse and wore a shawl over her shoulders; I wore a *longyi* of Arakanese design, topped by a collarless white shirt and a white Burmese *taik pon aingyi* [jacket]. I told the driver, a thirty-something: "Enter University Avenue from Prome Road. Just before you reach the intersection with World Peace Pagoda Road, make a quick U turn, and drop us off at the iron-gated house on the right that has plenty of banners flying atop. And speed off." He studied me and nodded to signify that he knew the house. "*Beh laut lehh* [how much]?" I asked.

"*Yah bar deh' A Ba, M'pay bar neh* [It's okay, father, please don't pay]." This, coming from a worker whose day's labor barely covers food for the family, if at all, touched me deeply.

Taxis in Burma do not use meters; you have to negotiate the fare when you engage them. The incident showed how much love taxi drivers in Rangoon hold for Suu. I paid him the customary fare and added a handsome gratuity. When I related this incident to an NLD member I met in Thailand, she told me Rangoon taxi drivers often don't charge those visiting Suu at her home.

We entered through a small opening in the gate and were asked to wait. The dog that her son Kim had given her a few months earlier was there; a big sign cautioned that it bites. Later Suu told us that only she could come close and that it was a protective guard dog. I asked whether she felt safe in the house. She said there was nothing for her to fear. I kidded her that she should dig a moat outside the front gate and put some crocodiles in it. She chuckled. Preparations were being made for Hillary Clinton's visit, and the garden was abuzz with workers sprucing it up. Chairs were being arranged overlooking the lake. Suu was happy to see us and presented us with a lovely lacquer tray. "I cannot give you much," she said. "This is a souvenir from Burma." In return we presented her with a Kashmiri shawl and the few Indian poetry books we had obtained in India.

"We have to work with the army," she said. "We have to work together."

Impulsively, I asked, "What are you going to tell Hillary?"

"I can't tell you, Uncle," she said.

"You realize that Christian missions have had an impact on education in Burma," Riri said to her. "Please give the schools back to us. We will educate the children."

"It was the army that took over the schools," Suu said.

I mentioned the grave of King Thibaw in Ratnagiri, which Riri and I had visited before coming to Rangoon. The grave was in a disgraceful state and the former residence locked, but a caretaker showed us in and we went from one empty room to the next. The mansion was totally devoid of furniture. When we came to a hallway between two rather substantial bedrooms, I asked the caretaker, "*Yay kamara, kun ka hai* [this room, whose is it?]"

"Sir, the king had two misses," he replied.

"And you?" I quipped.

"Only one, sir, only one," he assured me.

I stood on the balcony where King Thibaw himself had stood, to fix his gaze at the Arabian Sea, which is in the opposite direction of Burma. According to Amitav Ghosh, the author of the novel *The Glass Palace*, Thibaw acted as the unofficial weatherman for the local fishermen, who would come to him to inquire about approaching storms. The king had a telescope, which gave him an edge.

King Thibaw's exile palace, Ratnagiri, India. Photo by U Kyaw Win.

It would mean something profound, if nostalgic, to the Burmese if King Thibaw's remains were exhumed and properly re-interred in Mandalay. When I made that suggestion to former deputy Prime Minister U Kyaw Nyein when he visited us in Laguna Hills, California, in January 1984, he pounced on me, saying, "What, you want to restore the monarchy?" Of course not, but I would like to see King Thibaw's remains returned, because his exile was a humiliation by the British to the Burmans' psyche. I would also like to see a three-dimensional model of his exile residence and grounds built and displayed in a museum within the walls of the restored Mandalay Palace.

Thibaw was no angel. Nor was Henry VIII a serial killer, as a young lady docent at Castle Howard in Yorkshire, once told me. Now, to Suu, I said, "Please ask for his remains to be returned to Burma."

"Or at least ask the Indian government to take good care of his grave," added Riri. She suggested I try to interest Amitav Ghosh about this. I'm pleased to note that President U Sein Thein visited the former residence and gravesite a few months after we did, and that interest in re-interring King Thibaw's remains has once again rekindled in some quarters. Media reports noted that President U Thein Sein became emotional when he visited the exile residence.

King Thibaw's grave, Ratnagiri, India. Photo by U Kyaw Win.

When U Kyaw Nyein and his wife, Daw Nwai Yi, were with us in America, we discussed the situation in Burma. He asked penetrating questions, and wrestled with how to deal with the multiethnic militias once the civil war came to a close. He wanted to know how the National Guard in America interfaced with the U.S. Army. I took them to Sea World in San Diego and to the border crossing at Tijuana, which we watched from a bridge above it. I asked if they would like to go across. They both declined. They feared the consequences once they got back to Burma because the military junta had not authorized them to visit countries not endorsed in their passports. (Burmese passports of the day were valid for travel only to the countries designated therein. In 1952, when I came to America for the first time, my passport was endorsed as valid for travel to the United States and Hawaii.)

Before they left us, I asked if he would carry a letter from me to General Ne Win. He said he couldn't do it, because the general would be very offended. In my letter I was going to appeal to the general to extend *metta* [loving kindness] to the people of Burma and to rule with compassion. Just as they were boarding the plane, I asked him to reconcile with U Ba Swe, a former prime minister and his colleague when the Anti-Fascist People's Freedom League split into the "clean" and "stable" factions in 1958. He said, "We have been distant." I was in New Zealand in June 1986 when I read in the paper of his passing, which saddened me greatly. His death was a great loss to Burma.

We had some photographs taken in Suu's living room beneath the large painting of her father. As she walked us out of the grand mansion, the sun was shining over the lake at just the right angle. Workers were putting away their tools at the end of the workday. Here was a good opportunity for another photograph. I grabbed a worker and asked him to shoot a photo. That photograph was the best one of the afternoon. Suu walked us to the gate, clutching Riri's arm tightly.

Riri, Suu, Win in Jan 2011

It was almost 5:00 p.m., and we were her last callers of the day. Once again, she had given us almost an hour from her extremely crowded schedule. Riri said to me afterward that she felt a special bond with Suu at that moment, as if Suu were expressing her inner loneliness. The accolades she has received, the adulation of the public, and the honors that have been heaped on her are but a small consolation for her inner longing for the deceased husband whom she could not even kiss goodbye. During those years she also missed being with her two sons and seeing them grow into maturity. She was caught between her ideals for a free Burma and the personal suffering she had endured.

Only a mother can feel such loneliness.

5

My Song

"Exile is strangely compelling to think about but terrible to experience. It is the unhealable rift forced between a human being and a native place, between the self and its true home: its essential sadness can never be surmounted."

EDWARD SAID, *REFLECTIONS ON EXILE*

TERRA FIRMA (BHUMI IN Sanskrit) gives firmness of place to those who dwell on Earth. From the moment a newborn inhales a first breath, that person's roots are implanted in the soil that nourishes and nurtures. In Burmese tradition, "home" is where the umbilicus is buried. To be uprooted from that soil, one's native land, is grievous to the core of one's being; it is tantamount to being condemned to death. I am such an exile, and this book is born of the pain of being exiled from my native land.

Civilizations rise and fall. Many have become extinct: the Aztecs, Chaldeans, Mayans, Orang Asli of Indonesia and Malaysia, Pyus of Burma, Sumerians, the ancient peoples of China, to name but a few. The people of

Burma have to face the possibility that in the fullness of time they too will perish— unless they choose a path forward for all of Burma's peoples that is open, just, and free, making it a land where its exiles can go home.

THE PRESENT CHALLENGE

Desire for freedom is a natural instinct. From the moment of birth, the child lets out a cry for the chance to breathe free. Fortunately, the biological composition of the human body necessitates that longing, because the newborn's lungs require oxygen to live. What better way to let life flow in than to let out that cry?

The cry of Burma today is such a cry. It is worthy of a Greek tragedy; Sophocles could tell the tale of Burma's suffering. "Civilizations die from suicide, not by murder," wrote Arnold Toynbee. And so it is with Burma. Dwellers of the earth have farmed, hunted, fished, gathered, manufactured, and traded with each other, but the notion of nationhood and its formative processes emanate from within. It is from within that Burma faces its challenge. While tribalism gives cohesion and strengthens the bonds within the tribe, the impetus for nationhood arises only when individuals within the tribe are willing to go beyond the constricting impulses of ethnicity to the vision of a larger, inclusive social reality. *E pluribus unum* ["out of many, one"] is the apt motto of the United States. So may it one day be said of Burma.

SEPARATISM

The British left the country in disarray when they departed in 1948. Ethnic peoples, speaking different tongues and expressing their desire for freedom in their own ways, felt they had been left to fend for themselves in the midst of conflicting opinions and forces. There was one common denominator: They all wanted autonomy as understood and defined by themselves. When I lived in Kalaw in the Southern Shan State, shopkeepers in the towns and local markets proudly insisted that the wares on their shelves were products of *Shan Pyay* [Shan Country], and not *Bamar Pyay* [Burman Country], so deeply was ethnocentrism entrenched among the common Shan folk of 1959 and before.

General Aung San, the founding father of what was meant to become a Union of Burma, was cut down by assassins, together with his cabinet-to-be, six months before the country attained independence. He was the leader with a vision. He courageously advanced the idea of a federal union when he convened the Panlong Conference in 1947.

Then followed a period of fourteen years when a nascent parliamentary democracy tried courageously to navigate the ship of state. Sadly, the twigs of national unity were never allowed to be bundled together into a solid core. The failure paved the way for the army to usurp power and, by its utter misrule, drive the otherwise richly resourced country into penury. It was then that the centripetal forces of division gained momentum.

The separatist aspirations of Burma's minority peoples are man-made. They arise in large measure due to the arrogant presumption held by the majority Burmans. They assume that it is their right, if not their destiny, to rule over others. Recognition that such a presumption is false, that it has no future in a just world, is the challenge the Burmans face. The Kachins, Karens, Padaungs, Palaungs, Shans, and all other ethnic peoples must be allowed to emerge in their own right, unhindered in the pursuit of their own happiness. They must be given the opportunity to live in peace and in harmony among themselves and with others without the majority Burmans exercising hegemony over them.

On their part, however, the minority peoples must also shed the debilitating feeling of inadequacy when dealing with the Burmans and with other ethnic peoples. "No one can make you feel inferior without your consent," said Eleanor Roosevelt insightfully. That consent must not be given; the ethnic people must courageously stand their ground and claim equality with the Burmans. "Concept of self" is the term social scientists use to explain this feeling of one's worth. It is a learned behavior, and the feeling of lack of worth permeating so many ethnic groups can be unlearned. The human psyche is re-programmable. Pride of self is a burgeoning cultural phenomenon across America in recent decades: women, blacks, the disabled, the mentally challenged, gays, and so on. That pride can infuse the ethnic groups of Burma as well.

A simple homily on solidarity I recall from childhood goes like this: An old man approaching the twilight of his days gathered his sons around him and gave each one of them a twig and asked them to break them. One by one the sons broke their twigs with ease. The old man then brought out another set of identical twigs and tied them into a tight bundle. He then passed the bundle around to the sons and asked each one to break it. None could. The bundle was as solid as a rock. The simple lesson: band together or perish separately.

HONOR WHERE HONOR IS DUE

I honor the sacrifices the Karens have made over the decades. Not only did the movement for a Karen State permeate to the masses, but many educated leaders have fled to the jungles to pursue the dream of freeing themselves from Burman hegemony. Many Karens have been killed. Likewise, untold numbers of soldiers and innocent civilians on all sides of the civil war in Burma have perished. Burma Army soldiers have committed horrific atrocities against the Kachins, Karens, Karennis, and Shans, raping their women, torturing their men, burning down their dwellings, destroying their fields and livestock, and forcing their youth into mine-laden frontlines as cannon fodder. Burmans have not been spared in the pogrom. Brutal acts have been committed by all sides.

The Mons are justifiably proud of the kingdoms their forebears established, including the building of Rangoon's magnificent sacred Shwedagon Pagoda.

The Rohingyas, generations of whom have settled on Burma's remote fringes, have been subjected to persecution. They have been branded the world's most discriminated-against people. Their fragile homes have been torched, their people beaten and corralled into concentration camp-like dwellings bounded by barbed wire. It is alleged that because they do not speak Burmese, their claim to Burmese citizenship is suspect and that they illegally dwell on the lands they occupy. However, there are many other ethnic peoples in Burma who do not speak Burmese. Many Rohingyas have found life so intolerable that they have taken to the sea in unsafe boats. Untold numbers have perished before reaching unwelcoming shores in neighboring lands. How can we remain indifferent to such an assault on human dignity?

The Shans are rightfully proud of their verdant highlands and the civilization they have nurtured. I have stood against the Ne Win regime's and the Burmans' overbearing attitude all these years. I am proudly descended from a Karen mother and a Burman father. Humiliating ethnic epithets such as *Kayin-boke* [rotten Karen] or *tah ta paw* [a roasted rice gumbo favorite of Karens] were hurled at me as a youngster.

We can and must celebrate our differences and cherish them as we move forward to live in peace and harmony on the soil that has been bequeathed to us by our ancestors.

We need to move forward. More Karens now live beyond the boundaries of their ancestral homelands. Kawthoolei [Land of Flowers], as the Karens like to call their homeland, should never be only for the Karens. Likewise, Kachinland should be open to any and all the inhabitants of

Burma to live and work there. Kachins are scattered throughout the country. Many Shans live in the Kachin highlands. Many Chins have been forced to forsake their hills. Many are now resettled in America, longing for their lost homeland. We should strive for a sovereign Burma where equality of all its peoples is guaranteed and justice for all is a fact of life. States established on geographic features and not on ethnic or religious lines must be given the right to govern themselves, save for those functions reserved for and shared by all, to the federal government. Diversity is a creation of God, or, to the Buddhist, of evolutionary consequences. Whichever definition one holds, a garden grows flowers of many hues and colors—all are beautiful.

LINGERING EFFECTS OF PRIMITIVISM

Although traditionally and predominatly Buddhist, animism is deeply rooted in the mind of ordinary Burmese. Lacking widespread literacy, the populace has for generations been susceptible to the irrational appeal of superstition and folklore. Hearsay and legends take the place of an independent and trustworthy press.

A legend that has been incorporated into many a Burman's psyche is that a Burmese person educated to a high level in the West would free the people. That person was thought to be Sir Ba U, who studied at Cambridge University and earned a law degree in 1912. Knighted in 1947, he shed the "Sir" when he was awarded an honorary doctor of laws degree by Rangoon University. When he became the second president of Burma, a ceremonial head of state, the Burmans found an answer to their self-fulfilling prophecy in this knight in shining armor. The legend continued, there will be no peace in the land until human remains have been piled high at the foot of Rangoon's Shwedagon Pagoda. As General Aung San and his colleagues were laid to rest on the western slope of the Shwedagon Pagoda, soothsayers said it was the opening act of that terrible legend. More were to follow.

The Karens have their own legend, which says that a teacher from the West would bring them a book whose message would liberate them from oppression. So here came Adoniram Judson, the American missionary-scholar, a graduate of Brown University, holding a Bible in his hand. He preached the gospel to the Karens. To his scholarly credit, Judson mastered the Burmese language, translated the Bible, and authored the first Burmese dictionary, all within seven years of his arrival in Burma in 1813.

Somehow, in each of these legends, the messiahs have come from the West. Why? Is it because white-skinned people are perceived to be of a superior race in the psyche of the Burmese peoples? Or, if one wanted to be poetic, is it simply because it is Shelley's west wind that portends a promising spring that can give longed-for peace? India is on Burma's west; did it not matter?

The proclivity to rely on legends, myths, omens, and pronouncements of soothsayers has, to the astonishment of the educated class, been accorded far too much primacy in the affairs of state by Burma's rulers. While the stars may have guided ancient mariners, modern navigation instruments have superseded them; similarly, the stars, omens, and soothsayer pronouncements cannot be the compass used in navigating the modern ship of state. Building a democratic state requires an educated citizenry. The ability to think critically is essential.

WHO IS A BURMAN?

A question that must be candidly answered is: *Who is a Burman*? Ne Win's father was Chinese. Khin Nyunt, who at one time was the second most powerful general in the junta, is half Chinese. Is Burma only for Burmans who walk the Buddhist path?

The idea of "foreignness" and its attendant feelings must be deleted from the vocabulary and the psyche. Missionaries brought Buddhism from India to Burma's fields, forests, rivers, mountains, and valleys eons ago. Siddhartha, the prince, whose enlightenment blessed him to Buddhahood, was born in today's Nepal. Animism, Christianity, Islam, and other religions and philosophies all came to Burma from elsewhere as well. People bring their customs and traditions with them when they move from one place to another in search of greener pastures. Regardless of how our DNA is constituted, all of us who inhabit *Suvarnabhumi*—the Golden Land, as Burma and adjacent lands were called in antiquity—came from somewhere else.

In Mongolia, I rubbed shoulders with people whose features were no different than mine. At a theatre in Ulan Bator in 2005, I spied a petite young usher whose beauteous high-cheek-boned innocence resembled that of the teen-aged Aung San Suu Kyi. When I tried to find her at the end of the performance to photograph her, she had melted into the night. Again, in Kyrgyzstan, where Riri and I have done volunteer work in an orphanage and taught English to children, I found people whose features resembled the many races of Burmese people. We do share common genetic roots. Many summers ago, in a Native American village in northern Arizona, when I was doing field work in anthropology, I was asked by a Navajo brave what tribe I belonged to. It flattered me: He mistook me for a Native American. What an honor to be thought one of them.

My own ancestors probably came from Tibet or Mongolia by way of Yunnan in southwestern China. Others came from India. The people who call themselves Burmans tend to be darker-complexioned and probably have more Indian than Mongolian blood flowing in their veins.

When it comes right down to it, a "Burman" is any brown-skinned person, or one with any brown shade and speaking Burmese, who (for expediency) claims to be one. So much for anyone claiming to be a "pure" Burman or pure anything else for that matter.

A STATE RELIGION?

Religion is another challenge to the development of a modern state. What is to be made of U Nu's passion for Buddhism as a state or national religion? Is that an ideal to pursue? Is to be Burmese not only to be Burman but also Buddhist? In a political democracy, the religion one follows is not subject to legislation.

Brewing now in Burma is a dangerous fundamentalist movement in the name of religion. This movement is led by a young firebrand Buddhist monk who has unabashedly claimed to personify the Osama bin Laden of the land. His misguided mission is to "purify" religion and race by legislating how humans should live in matters of faith and love. Under this twisted, self-serving interpretation of the teachings of the Enlightened One, marriage between Buddhist women and men of other faiths is now circumscribed by legislation that was passed by Parliament and signed into law by the president on 2 September 2015. He would go a step further by urging his adherents to boycott commerce with citizens of the land who express their humanity in the Islamic tradition, depriving them of their livelihood and choking them off the land.

Adolf Hitler did the same thing in Germany at the time of my birth. In 1977, I walked the former concentration camps of Auschwitz in Poland and Dachau in Germany. I viewed with horror the defunct gas chambers and the skeletal remains of crematoria. I was simply mortified, and could only ask myself, "How could such barbaric deeds be inflicted by educated men on their fellow men? Have they become totally bereft of all their humanity?"

THE PLACE OF RELIGION

Something that should be emulated is the leadership by example of individuals like Dr. Cynthia Maung of the Mae Tao Clinic, and U Kyaw Thu of the Free Funeral Service Society. Earlier in this memoir, I maintained that the Buddhist religion does not collectively tend well to social needs. U Kyaw Thu and his associates have proven me wrong by starting something out of the ordinary. His organization also performs other social services, like caring for the aged and operating orphanages—things heretofore kept at a distance by Buddhist clergy or even monasteries on institutional scale. These are the good works U Kyaw Thu is doing now.

While it is true that Buddhist teachings urge the individual to seek his or her own inner peace, its clergy can lead by extending their sacred order to collectively reach out to the community in social services. I am pleased to honor the Venerable U Nayaka, abbot of Phaungdaw Oo Monastery in Mandalay, who together with his brother monk U Zawtika, have led the way by operating a fully developed secular high school, complete with a medical clinic and the care of orphaned and poverty-stricken children. The monastic education center has schooled 8,000 children of both sexes.

I can think of another orphanage at a monastery in Taunggyi that operates a community health clinic. I doff my hat to U Ohn Maung, a Kingswood School alumnus and a former political prisoner, who has lit a candle in his corner. There are undoubtedly others whose names escape me.

The Christian Church, through its various denominations, has in its outreach addressed these issues for centuries. Christian missions were doing excellent work reaching out to the people, addressing their health, education, and welfare needs. The Christian Hospital in Moulmein, the Seventh Day Adventist Hospital in Rangoon, the leprosaria in Mandalay and Moulmein, the Old People's Home in Kandawgalay, and the school for visually and hearing impaired children in Rangoon are examples.

Other faith communities have operated health care facilities, like the Ramakrishna Mission Hospital in Botataung (East Rangoon) established by a Hindu missionary sect and the Islamic community's Free Clinic in Rangoon.

There is plenty of need to be met. The facilities taken over by the *Tatmadaw* should not only be restored to these faith communities, but encouraged and helped. Healthy minds and bodies are essential for the people to free themselves of anger and live harmonious lives.

NEED FOR SOUND EDUCATIONAL SYSTEM

I published *The Burma Bulletin* for nineteen years. In 1975, when few were interested in what I had to say, I demonstrated on the sidewalks of San Francisco and outside the White House gates. Later, with many more, I paraded around the *Los Angeles Times* building and outside City Hall and the Federal building in Los Angeles and outside the regional office of Total Oil in Denver, and UNOCAL in Los Angeles, holding placards in my hands. I helped organize political action against the military junta in Burma and did relief work for refugees after the bloody events of 1988.

Throughout the 1990s, I traveled around the United States, telling any audiences that would have me about the situation in Burma. I worked behind the scenes for American University to award Aung San Suu Kyi an honorary degree in absentia in 1997. My purpose was to give her a forum, through the commencement address read by her husband, which would amplify her voice for democracy in Burma. I consulted on the making of the movie *Beyond Rangoon*, in the hope that the film would tip the scales against the current regime.

All of the above happened in my lifetime and before. What is going to happen in the twenty-first century and beyond? The "curse of independence," as Shelby Tucker calls it, is that struggling against colonialism is not the same as building a nation. We're all in this together—but only if we want to be. The Kachins, Karens, Mons, and Shans have all struggled for autonomy. They have defined *autonomy* as being left totally alone to run the affairs in their own space. However, if Burma is ever to be united, they must accept that each and every state in a federal republic is for any and all citizens, regardless of ethnicity or the religion they espouse (or the absence of it). In their pursuit of "autonomy," the ethnic peoples have sustained untold pain and suffering. Surely, that path has no future. We all share the same space, breathe the same air, and drink the same water. We are interdependent. We need each other.

The ethnic peoples feel, and justifiably so, that if all authority resides in the central government seated in Naypyidaw, then it is colonial divide-and-rule all over again. In such a scenario, everything right down to the placement of a street sign in some remote village is decided by the central government. A recent demand by the people in the Chin Hills, where there have been an influx of tourists, is for the government to allow homeowners to accommodate these visitors. There is a dire shortage of approved lodgings in those hills not earlier frequented by tourists. Why should the government seated in distant Naypyidaw micro-manage the matter of local people taking lodgers into their homes? A state cannot be based on ethnicity or religion, certainly not in Burma. And it must be democratic; military rule leads to tyranny. A maxim in political science maintains that the best government is one that governs least.

My father's nationalistic pride hurt me. He failed to see, or to admit, that the military regime that took over from the British colonial powers had simply become the new masters. I speak more in sorrow on this issue than in anger. The British used repressive nineteenth-century laws to govern Burma, purportedly "to bring civilization" to its people, yet Britain itself never had a constitution to which all the people had subscribed. In truth, colonial rule was designed to subjugate the native peoples. Many of the laws left behind by the British after their departure, especially the oppressive ones, are now being used by the junta, such as its right to do midnight inspections of homes in order to do a head count, prosecuting households that shelter persons not on the "midnight roster." Such laws must be banished from the books.

The eventual healing of Burma's tragedy will be slow and difficult. What is most certain, though, is that it will be brought about only by the creation of a federal republic in a form acceptable to all. This can be achieved with the establishment and allowance of local governments that include the preservation of ethnic languages and cultures. Jurisdiction must fall to separate but equal states, at all levels down to the tiniest hamlet. In a federal republic, the constituent states and the federal government work in partnership: everyone is a citizen of the republic and must be allowed to live and work in any of the constituent states in pursuit of personal happiness, regardless of ethnicity or religious faith. In a political democracy, the majority rules, but respect for the minority is maintained and celebrated. Citizens of the land are not the property of the government—state or federal. They work in partnership with the government and not as its subjects.

Another thing that would help is for the inhabitants of Burma to break out of their boxes and treat each other with dignity and respect. Prejudice is a learned behavior. It must be unlearned if we are to move forward to tolerance.

Acting alone in coalition with my conscience does not make me a kook. What it does make me is a loyal son of my father, who in 1947 wrote, in his book *Burma Under the Japanese*:

> Democracy is not a form of government, not even government by a majority. The statement that its purpose is to secure the greatest good for the greatest number is, like most simplifications, wholly inadequate and misleading. True Democracy is much more than that. It is an inner spirit, an attitude to life. It implies a spirit of toleration, an inborn hatred of oppression, the readiness to grant equal rights and equal opportunities to all. The ends of the earth are so linked together that mankind has become, in a sense, one family. . . . Extreme and narrow nationalism is a danger.

PROPOSALS

It would be noble to have King Thibaw's remains at Ratnagiri exhumed and properly re-interred next to his father King Mindon's grave within the Konbaung Dynasty's last palace in Mandalay. This would be an honorable healing act. It would unburden the present and future generations of Burmans, if not all Burmese, to know that their last sovereign, exiled to foreign turf, has finally been brought home to rest in eternal repose. (By the same token, the Burmese authorities should offer to have the remains of the last Mogul Emperor of India, interred in Rangoon, returned to India.)

Public donations should be sought to rebuild the Rangoon University Students' Union building, foolishly and unthinkingly dynamited by the army on 8 July 1962 with the loss of many young lives. It was in the hallowed halls of that university and in this particular edifice beneath the majestic shade trees that Aung San and his associates sounded the clarion call to rid Burma of its colonial rulers.

The University of Rangoon must be restored to its pre-eminence of an earlier era as a temple of higher learning. Having spent my entire working life as a college teacher, I hold the beauty of a college campus in the tight corner of my heart "where seekers and learners alike, banded together in search for knowledge will honor thought in all its finer ways, . . . welcome thinkers in distress or in exile," as England's Poet Laureate John Masefield said.

Nationalizing all the schools, followed by banning the teaching of English, was very short-sighted and bereft of logic. It would be a benevolent act if the faith-based and other private schools taken over by the army were returned to their rightful owners. A rejuvenation of institutions like Judson College would augur well for a nation trying to re-make itself, where educated people are sorely needed. Farmlands and other real estate confiscated by the army should be returned to their rightful owners.

These gestures, small and simple, speak from the heart. They would be first steps in a long journey to heal the wounds of the past. To allow Burma's sons and daughters who have been exiled to the far corners of the globe to come home would be another giant step forward.

One day in 1944, when the Second World War was still raging, Judge Learned Hand stood in New York's Central Park and made a few remarks before swearing in new American citizens. These were his words:

> I often wonder whether we do not rest our hopes too much upon
> Constitutions, upon laws and upon courts. . . . Liberty lies in the
> hearts of men and women; when it dies there, no constitution,

no law, no court can save it; no constitution, no law, no court can even do much to help it.

MY SONG

My hope now is that, by telling my story in this memoir, I will help educate those who know little of Burma's suffering and motivate others to take up the mantle. I have written this book as part of my lifelong effort to brighten the corner where I am. Those words are from an old Sunday School song that I learned as a child. I still remember the melody and some of the words:

> Do not wait until some deed of greatness you may do
> Do not wait to shed your light afar
> To the many duties ever near you now be true,
> Brighten the corner where you are.

Peace in my homeland has eluded my parents' lifetime and now my own. My father and many others of his generation struggled first against the British, then against the Japanese, then once more against the British. And now we are fighting among ourselves. The multi-ethnic skirmishes continue unabated to this day. They have been going on in various forms for more than six decades. The end of these internecine wars is long overdue.

On the eve of India's independence, Pandit Jawarhalal Nehru exhorted his compatriots with these soul-stirring words:

> Long years ago we made a tryst with destiny, and now the time comes when we shall redeem our pledge. . . . A moment comes, which comes but rarely in history, when we step out of the old to the new, when an age ends when the soul of a nation, long suppressed, finds utterance.

It is my fervent hope that Burma's long nightmare has seen its midnight hour and we can "step out of the old to the new" dawn. Heed our plea, you who wield the sword. Seize the moment and let *metta* [loving kindness] and *garuna* [compassion] rule your hearts. Give no haven to hatred. Let us together in sisterhood and brotherhood rebuild our beloved homeland. History will smile on those who can turn Burma into a land of peace and prosperity.

"Let there be peace on earth and let it begin with me," intones a familiar refrain. Younger generations must realize that the future belongs to them. Let the torch be passed on.

This is my song.

A disciple asked:

"How can I know when the dawn has broken, when the darkness has fled?
Is it the moment when I can know a sheep from a dog?"

The holy man answered:

"No."

The disciple asked:

"Is it then that moment when I can know a peach from a pomegranate?"

The holy man replied:

"No, none of these. Until the moment when you can gaze on the face of a man
or a woman and say, 'You are my brother, you are my sister' until then there is
no dawn, there is only darkness."

In Memoriam

Naw Louisa Benson Craig

Mike Jendrzejczyk

A. B. Aung Khin

Ko Latt

Rusty Than Lwin

U Nyunt Maung

Bishop James K. Mathews

Ko Phone Maw

Taw Myo Myint

Ko Soe Naing

Frank Thaung Oo

Win Maw Oo

Ida Pay

David Rettie

U Hla Shwe

Eugene Thaike

U Yé Kyaw Thu

U Tin Maung Win

"This story shall the good man teach his son.
From this day to the ending of the world,
But we in it shall be remembered."

WILLIAM SHAKESPEARE
HENRY V, ACT 4, SCENE 3

Appendix 1

What's in a Name?

Throughout the memoir I have used the anglicized place names as they existed in 1948. In 1989 the Burman dominated junta "changed" the country's name to Myanmar. The reason, the generals claimed, was that Myanmar encompassed all the inhabitants of the polyglot country. It does not! It merely entrenched the Burmanization of the country deeper.

Portuguese traders who set foot in the land in the sixteenth century interacted with inhabitants of the western coastal plains who called themselves *Bamar lumyo* (Burman people) speaking *Bamar zagar* (Burman language). Hence *Birmania* came into Portuguese usage from which derived the universally anglicized *Burma* adopted by the British who followed centuries later.

It is not unusual for early tribal states to be called by universally pronounceable names introduced by Europeans, mainly the British. China, from Qin (Chin) Dynasty, became the name for Zhongguo (Middle Kingdom), which the Chinese have always called their country. Other examples are India (from the River Indus) for Bharat; Japan for Nippon; Finland for Suomi, and so on.

The Burmese language has two forms: *bamar zagah* (colloquial) and *myanmar barthar* (formal). Both mean the same, but *bamar* and *myanmar* respectively qualify the colloquial and the formal. Hence, *myanmar* is an adjective in the Burmese language. It is therefore incorrect to "rename" the country by its corrupted adjective.

The nation's founding Constitution of 1947 (Burmese edition) and the 2008 edition, which the junta rammed down the people's throat in a referendum while the country's plains were being devastated by Cyclone Nargis, correctly called the country *Myanmar Naingngan.* The gallery of activists the regime targeted in 1989 as "treasonous minions and traitorous cohorts," also correctly called the country *Myanmar Naing-Ngan.*

Several rivers, cities, towns, and streets were also renamed. Rangoon reverted to its traditional name by which the Burmese people have always called their former capital. Non-native speakers have difficulty with the tritonal language in which each and every sound or syllable takes on a different meaning. A word can be embarrassing or offensive when incorrectly pronounced.

The grand Irrawaddy was renamed *Ayeyarwaddy.* In Pali, *Ayeyar* (from the Sanskit *Irra*) means big, and *waddy,* a body of water. The Burmese have always called the river *Ayeyarwaddy* because the consonant "r" is alien to their tongue, but not in the Pali of their sacred scriptures. The river's name would have been best left unchanged from its original classical Pali even though the Burmese will continue to call it by its Burmanized name. And they will continue to speak in Burmese, a member of the Tibeto-Burman group of languages, not "Myanmarese."

Kawthoolei is the Karen name for their state. Its origin is shrouded in mystery and its meaning a matter of debate among the Karens themselves.

BaSaw Khin, my geologist friend of more than a half century, maintains that *thoolei ploh/bloh* is a stalk three-eighths to five-eighths inches in diameter and one- to one-and-one-half-feet tall, which bears a small whitish flower with a mauve petal fringe that disintegrates at harvest time. The stalk resembles asparagus but differs and is segmented but with an absence of any hard bark, thus tender for consumption. The plant is ubiquitous in Karen land. So *Kawthoolei* could be translated as *Flower Country* or *Land of Flowers. Kaw* means country in Karen.

Zoya Phan, the author of *Undaunted: My Struggle for Freedom and Survival in Burma,* on the other hand, translates it as *Land of No Evil.* In s'gaw Karen, *thoo lei* literally means "devoid" or "completely blacked out," thus *Land of No Evil.* Whichever translation one subscribes to, it is a beautiful name, but I vote for flowers because God alone can create a flower.

APPENDIX 2

Manassas Call for Worldwide Solidarity for a Democratic Burma

Let's Build Unity in Diversity in Our Diaspora and Beyond!

Dear Compatriots:

On July 12 and 13, 2003, about thirty compatriots from Burma of diverse backgrounds convened in the shadow of Virginia's Manassas Battlefields of the American Civil War, to reaffirm our support and commitment to the people's freedom struggle in our ancestral homeland. For two days, we explored ways to build a worldwide solidarity movement for Burma's freedom and deliberated our resolve.

Although we presently reside thousands of miles away from our troubled birthplace, we are in solidarity with our fellow peoples inside Burma and throughout the democratic resistance-controlled areas of the country. We hereby pledge our unwavering support for our people's struggle to regain their inalienable rights to live as free, dignified citizens in a nation governed by the rule of law and founded upon principles of democracy, respect for universal human rights, and appreciation for our country's cultural, ethnic and religious diversity. In this, we share a common noble goal.

We are unanimous in our belief that we must pursue all means necessary to free Burma from the ruinous yoke of oppression by a handful of military elite, which for more than four decades have blatantly disregarded the manifest desire of our peoples to live under a representative government.

In the unending waves of popular pro-democracy uprisings since 1962, Burma's peoples have made this indestructible democratic aspiration known to the country's military rulers and to the international community, culminating in the 1990 multi-party elections in which the peoples gave the National League for Democracy and Daw Aung San Suu Kyi an overwhelming mandate to usher in a new, democratic era for Burma.

To date, the military rulers have blatantly disregarded this popular aspiration—and demand—for freedom, democracy, the rule of law, and fundamental human rights in our communities throughout the land.

Let us be reminded that we are indeed a nation blessed with diversity—diversity of ideas, cultures, beliefs and talents. But almost half a century of the oppressive military rule has amplified our differences and historical grievances toward one another and wrought divisiveness in our midst, instead of unity and strength from our diversity.

We must undo the deep impact of the regime's divide-and-rule policy and practice. We know that our country's problems are the creations of the mind and they can—and must—be solved only through our determined and coordinated efforts, dynamic and visionary leadership, and a democratic process. We hereby pledge to build solidarity and draw strength out of our rich diversity.

Basked in "grace under pressure," we are Burma's peoples noted for resilience, resourcefulness, kindness of heart and generosity of spirit toward neighbors and strangers alike.

It is they, the military dictators, who have made any and all attempts to crush our strengths and potentials, our desire and efforts to live as free and dignified peoples. They have robbed us of our right to freely associate with our compatriots of kindred spirits; to assemble freely; and to deliberate and decide upon the Common Good of our neighborhoods, our communities and our nation. We the peoples of Burma must not allow this destruction to continue. And we will not. As a nation, we are fit to meet the challenges attendant in a democratic nation building.

As we strive for freedom and democracy in Burma, each and every one of us must contribute to the urgent mission of building an effective, dynamic, and democratic leadership in and for our diaspora which in turn is capable of mobilizing our strengths and potentials in the service of Burma's freedom struggle.

We call upon all compatriots, and our friends, the world over to descend on Washington, DC and participate in "Global Solidarity Rally for Burma's Freedom" and/or organize and coordinate similar rallies in the world's capitals on December 10, 2013, the International Human Rights Day.

Let the whole world know of our peoples' epic struggle for our inalienable rights articulated in the American Declaration of Independence, demanded by the French Revolution and enshrined in the Universal Declaration of Human Rights.

Our immediate goal is to get a rally of 500–1,000 expatriates from Burma in Washington, DC.

Our long term goal is to establish an expatriates' forum and a fair and democratic process for all compatriots who care about Burma and her future.

Please heed this call and join hands with us.

Burma needs each and every one of us, wherever we may be. And she needs us NOW!

Burma will be free.

Signed:

Aung Kyaw Oo	Moethee Zun
Aung Saw Oo	Naing Soe
Aung Thu Nyein	Nyi Nyi Than
Bo Bo Kyaw Nyein	Phone Myint Tun
Bush Gulati	Ronnie Thoung Nyein
Chan Min	Sein Myint
Henry Soe Win	Show Ei Ei Tun
Ko Ko Lay	Than Aung
Kyi Win	Tun Kyaw Nyein
Mahn Robert Ba Zan	U Kyaw Win
Maung Maung Than	Victor Win
Min Zaw Oo	Win Win Nu
Moe Chan	Zar Ni

APPENDIX 3

Supplemental Illustrations

Allotted to Burma Office.
Copies to:
Sir A. Carter.
Depy. US.
Asst. US's.
US. for Burma.
Asst. US. for Burma.

PS. to SS.
PS. to US.
PS. to Parly. US.
Mr. Joyce.
Resident Clerk.

2289

B/C
1496
1947

CYPHER (SIMPLEX).

From	Governor of Burma
To	Secretary of State for Burma
Dated	Rangoon, 11.45 hours, 2nd August 1947
Received	13.35 hours, 2nd August 1947

IMMEDIATE.
No. 337 E/S.   SECRET.

Personal from Governor. The first part of this telegram relates to an amusing incident last night.

1. At about 5 p.m. yesterday evening as the sun was shining for the first time for many days I determined to get a little exercise in an attempt to reduce my figure to within the limits ordained by my tailor when he built my clothes. I accordingly took some golf balls and clubs on the front lawn and was enjoying myself immensely when at a few minutes to 6 McGuire informed me that Tyaw Nyein wanted to see me on a matter of great importance and would arrive at 6 P.M. in about ten minutes time with some other Ministers. My heart sank and I was left wondering what further catastrophe had occurred. I was awaiting the delegation in my study when at about 18.18 hours my A.D.C. reported that the whole Cabinet had arrived and were awaiting me at my office. I proceeded as quickly as possible to the office assured now that something frightful must have happened and there I met Thakin Nu dressed in his best clothes with a gaungbaung on his head. Nu then told me that it had been discovered that Sunday 20th July when the majority of the new Cabinet were sworn in was a most inauspicious day. The Cabinet therefore tendered me their resignations individually and in writing. I was then asked to re-swear the Cabinet immediatel as Friday 1st August between 18.20 and 18.25 hours was most suspicious. The time was then about 18.21 hours and the chap that held the key of the office containing the form of oaths and the regalia could not be found. Tin Tut reminded me that the oaths were in Government of Burma Act 1935 and that book luckily I had with me. The Cabinet stood up and with their right hands lifted repeated after me the oath of allegiance. I then discovered that the oath of secrecy was not included in the Act so while the remainder of the Cabinet stood strictly to attention with right hands lifted Tin Tut hastily scribbled out an oath of secrecy which was duly repeated after me. The ceremony was over by about 18.27 hours and I then called for drinks which were enjoyed by all so much so that at 19.00 hours I had to remind them that the curfew was now on and it was almost dark. There was an immediate scurry. It is incidents like these that make us love the country and the people so much.

2. Thakin Nu after the ceremony gave me the following fresh information on the assassination.

   (A) one person arrested has confessed that he was detailed by Saw to kill Nu if the plot at the Secretariat were

/successful

Governor Rance's telegram to Lord Listowel, 2 Aug 1947.

218

successful. The assassin to be was instructed to act as a look out man at the Secretariat and immediately he knew that the plot was successful he was to go to Nu's house and kill Nu. He went to Nu's but luckily Nu was not at home when the killer arrived.

(2) Saw told his followers that it was certain that when the leaders of AFPFL were removed H.E. would send for Saw and ask him to form a Government. This sounds incredible and all I can suggest if this information is true is that Saw anticipated that suspicion for the crime would fall on one or other of the Communist parties.

3. The new Cabinet consists of 14 members including Counsellor for Frontier Areas. Tin Tut returns to his old appointment as Finance Minister. The complete list will follow in a succeeding telegram and it will be noted that PE Khin and Win are not included. The former is to be the Government of Burma Representative with Pakistan and the latter with India. These two appointments I expect to be confirmed today.

4. It is proposed that Sir Maung Gyee should be High Commissioner in London but he has not yet been approached.

5. A place in the Cabinet has been reserved for Mrs. Aung San who must firstly contest a bye-election.

Page 2 of Governor Rance's telegram.

U Nu with Burmese students at the Liberty Bell in Philadelphia on 3 Jul 1955.
U.S. Information Agency photo.

Win and Riri's wedding, 5 Sep 1958. Photo by Frank Williams.

USALS award for Win.

Col Richard Long presenting award to Win. U.S. Army photo.

Left to right: U Nu, Edward Law-Yone, Daw Mya Yi, Riri, James Dalton, Win, with
young Dewi Sita in front, 1970. Photo by U Aung.

Gen Kya Doe introduced me to Rangoon Ba Swe
at a River Kwai camp in Thailand 1972.

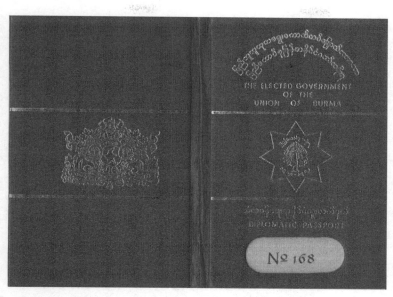

Diplomatic passport issued by the Elected Government of the Union of Burma.

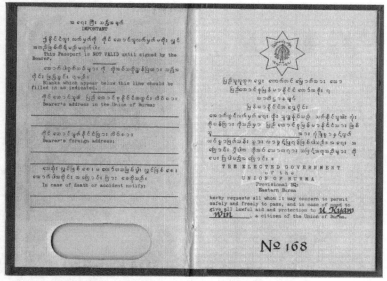

Diplomatic passport issued by the Elected Government.

Diplomatic passport.

Diplomatic passport.

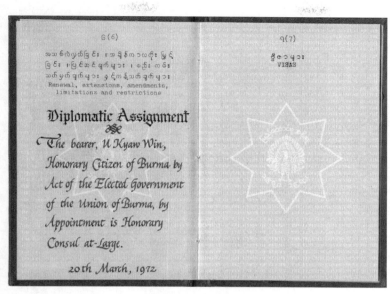

Diplomatic passport.

U Nu with Win's family, 1973. Photo by U Aung.

19 June 1973

His Holiness Pope Paul VI
Vatican City
Rome, Italy

Your Holiness:

    The Revolutionary Government of Burma, which assumed power after a coup d'etat on 2 March 1962, has pursued a policy of destroying the civil liberties of its citizens. One such policy is the exclusion of all Burmese citizens who have migrated to other lands from visiting their friends and relatives in Burma. Neither is it now possible for Burmese citizens to visit their friends and relatives abroad.

    On behalf of the several thousand former citizens who are now settled in foreign lands I appeal to Your Holiness to intervene by making representations to the Revolutionary Government of Burma through its Ambassador in Rome to permit children of former and present Burmese citizens presently residing abroad, under the age of eleven years, accompanied by their mothers, regardless of the travel document they may now hold, to visit Burma for a period of at least one month during the Buddhist lenten season which begins on 30 June 1973.

    For Your Holiness' perusal, I am enclosing a copy of the July 1973 issue of THE BURMA BULLETIN of which I am the editor, calling Your Holiness' attention to the editorial which appears on page 1.

    Peace.

                                        Sincerely yours,

                                        U Kyaw Win

Letter to the Vatican

SECRETARIAT OF STATE

                                FROM THE VATICAN, July 17, 1973

        The Secretariat of State acknowledges receipt of the recent communication addressed to the Holy Father and, regretting that it is not found possible to accede to the request made, has pleasure in communicating that His Holiness invokes upon the sender abundant blessings from God.

                                        E. Martines

Response from the Vatican.

                                                              7 May 1974
The Honorable William O. Douglas
Associate Justice
United States Supreme Court
Washington, D. C.

Dear Mr. Justice Douglas:

I was pleased to read in today's Los Angeles Times a review of GO EAST YOUNG MAN. Ever since I read your account of your visit to Burma in the early fifties, I have held you in high esteem.

After the military coup by General Ne Win on 1 March 1962 many Burmese citizens who left Burma have had to do so on condition that they never return to their homeland. Signing such an agreement was the only way, for many fortunate enough, to obtain a travel document known as a "Certificate of Identity." Many such immigrants to this country have become United States citizens but the Burmese Government has denied them even tourist visas to visit their homeland for seven days normally granted to American tourists of non-Burmese origin.

For those of my Burmese brethren of Buddhist faith, the initiation of their young male offspring into the faith of their ancestors is a very sacred and time-honored tradition. That practice has been denied to the Burmese now resident abroad.

Through an editorial in the July 1973 issue of THE BURMA BULLETIN (copy enclosed), I appealed to the rulers of Burma to permit young Burmese Buddhist boys and their mothers to visit Burma to observe this religious practice. My appeal fell on deaf ears.

In the name of humanity I appeal to you to undertake a mission of reconcialiation to Burma on behalf of our Buddhist brethren and speak to U Ne Win and his colleagues. I am a Christian but my feelings for my Buddhist compatriots run deep.

May you be blessed with peace of mind and body.

                                        Sincerely yours,

                                        U Kyaw Win
                                        Editor

Enclosures: clipping
            Bulletin, 4/74

Letter to Justice William Douglas.

Supreme Court of the United States
Washington, D. C. 20543

CHAMBERS OF
JUSTICE WILLIAM O. DOUGLAS   May 13, 1974

Dear Mr. Win:

I thank you for your gracious letter of
May 7th, for your kind comments, for the book
review.

I would gladly write the person you
mention regarding this humane cause but
my other friends from the area think it would
do more harm than good as the man in question
has a very low regard for me.

Yours faithfully,

W. O. Douglas

Mr. U Kyaw Win, Editor
The Burma Bulletin
P. O. Box 1891
Costa Mesa, CA 92626

Response from Justice Douglas.

THE
BURMA BULLETIN

U Kyaw Win, Editor   P.O. Box 1891   Costa Mesa, CA 92626

Volume 1, Number 1	Quarterly	April 1973

EDITORIAL   The Burma Bulletin, or The Bulletin, as we shall refer to ourselves when speaking in the third person, is an idea whose time has arrived. For the time being we shall publish quarterly, until our footing is sure. Our learned Mandalay bay-din saya (astrologer) has had some difficulty foretelling our reception and, "for there to be poets there must be audiences." Our pages shall be devoted to articles of interest to the Burmese community in the United States. Book reviews, undated news items, helpful hints for effective living, both culturally and economically, in a milieu that is not native to us, will make their occasional appearances. And, of course, we shall publish Letters to the Editor when their writers clearly identify themselves with their name and address.

To those who are uncertain of the definition of our being, let the word be heard that in personal terms we shall be friend to all and foe to none. We will turn the other cheek and even walk that second mile but we will not shirk from our commitment to the human condition when addressing ourselves against the actions and policies of those who seek the deliberate destruction of the dignity of man. We reserve the right to dissent but resolve to love.

For our masthead we have turned to Burmese mythology where a tale is told of an infant prince abandoned in the forest long years ago. A lioness who chanced upon this helpless infant human being took him to her lair and suckled him and took care of his needs for safety and protection. This symbiotic bond continued until the young prince grew into the estate of manhood when he began noticing the differences between himself and his foster mother. Finally when the day for him to strike out on his own in search of his kind arrived, he bade his foster mother farewell and swam across a wide river. The mother in her desire to give the young prince his freedom watched with a heavy heart until it burst and she died when he reached the opposite bank.

The thousands of chin-thay (lions') figures that stand sentinel at entrances to pagodas and other sacred places in Burma are placed in memory of the lioness' love for her human foster son. Myths are made by men, not men by myths. The myths a people pass on and on to posterity tell a good deal about the spirit of its ethos. A story of love more enduring and poignant than the lioness and her human foster son would be difficult to come by in a millennium.

Our beginnings are simple and parsimonious, perhaps, but like Einstein said: "The container should never be allowed to become more important than the contents."

****

HAPPY BURMESE NEW YEAR   Thin-gyan, the Water Festival, this year begins on 13 April. It ends on 16 April, the first day of the year 1335, Burmese Era. Let us be the first to wish you a Happy Burmese New Year. May you enjoy the blessings of good physical and mental health in the year to come. (See page 5 for Burmese New Year celebration in Southern California.)

****

This first issue of The Burma Bulletin is sent to you with the compliments of the Editor. If you wish to receive subsequent issues, send $1.00 cash or check payable to THE BURMA BULLETIN, P. O. Box 1891, Costa Mesa, CA 92626, for the next four issues.

1

First issue of *The Burma Bulletin.*

THE
BURMA BULLETIN

U Kyaw Win, Editor and Publisher   P.O. Box 1891   Costa Mesa, CA 92626

Volume 3, Number 1   Quarterly   January 1975

General Ne Win Should Resign   Editorial

Blood has once again stained the streets of Rangoon. Students, monks, and citizens demonstrating their anger at the   oppressive dictatorship under General Ne Win were ruthlessly mowed down by bayonets and bullets. The fact they held as hostage the remains of former UN Secretary General U Thant was grotesque, of course, but desperation drives crowds to the unimaginable. Just one year ago the ruling junta proudly proclaimed to the world that 99% of the people had supported its platform in a national referendum as they "shed" their military uniforms and continued doing whatever they were doing.

Unity among all the people of Burma was a professed goal when General Ne Win and his cabal of colonels usurped power forcefully in the small hours of 2 March 1962. The ethnic minorities are more splintered than ever. Resentment against their Burmese brothers has been building up to explosive proportions.

Rice, which used to be harvested and exported in abundance in bygone years, is now in short supply. Starvation among many is a reality while the ruling clique lives and eats well, going about the city in shiny Mercedes sedans. Shopping sprees to London are routine for the General and his entourage. In the dozen years that the country has been poorly administered, the country's population has increased while rice production has drastically declined. Family planning is opposed by the tyrants.

Martial law was recently declared in Burma, the country closed to external traffic in the aftermath of the imbroglio on the body. One Burma-born American citizen who left the country as a child several years ago was detained at Mingaladon for twenty-four hours and deported on the next plane out. Immigration officers explained that the Consulate had erred in issuing the visa because no Burma-born who left the country after 1962 was permitted back--even for a visit. What falsehood! Persons who left even before Independence have been denied visas.

Acting alone but in coalition with our conscience, we call upon General Ne Win to resign before the dawning of his thirteenth anniversary in power, which may well become his violent epilogue. A Council of Citizens from a representative spectrum, including those now in exile, selected for their administrative ability and genuine desire to reconstruct the land of their forefathers from the ashes should be appointed. The Council would serve for six months without remuneration and replaced by a provisional assembly elected by the people for a year, to be succeeded by a regularly elected parliament. Fifty percent of the military should be disarmed and the soldiers put to work rebuilding the dilapidated buildings, bridges, roads, schools, and hospitals. United Nations peace keeping forces should be requested to provide security during the transitional period. No amount of blood should be expended in securing one man in power. Ne Win is not Burma, and Burma is not Ne Win.

                                                              k.w.

A call for Ne Win's resignation in *The Burma Bulletin.*

Win, Bo Let Ya, U Thwin, and Gen Kya Doe, Bangkok, 1975.

Left to right: Win, Riri, Ko Aung. Demonstration at the White House, 18 Jul 1975.
Photo by James Moore.

Department of State **TELEGRA**

LIMITED OFFICIAL USE

AN: D750252-0147

PAGE 01   STATE   17144

73
ORIGIN EA-10

INFO OCT-01 ISO-00 SY-05 CIAE-00 DODE-00 INR-07 NSAE-00

PA-01 USIA-06 PRS-01 SP-02 /033 R

DRAFTED BY EA/TB - JAKLEMSTINE:MFG
APPROVED BY EA/TB - GBROBERTS
A/SY/I/PIB - MR. BENNINGTON
---------------------   015904
R 212236Z JUL 75
FM SECSTATE WASHDC
TO AMEMBASSY RANGOON

LIMITED OFFICIAL USE STATE 171441

E.O. 11652: N/A

TAGS: PFOR, BM

SUBJECT: ABORTIVE ANTI NE WIN DEMONSTRATIONS
1. THE DEPARTMENT WAS INFORMED BY THE BURMESE EMBASSY
JULY 18 OF PROPOSED DEMONSTRATIONS TO BE LED BY U KYAW WIN,
AN ACTIVE CRITIC OF THE NE WIN GOVERNMENT AND THE PUBLISHER
OF BURMA BULLETIN, AT THE EMBASSY, WHITE HOUSE, AND/OR
CAPITOL HILL. INQUIRIES AT THE DC POLICE INDICATED A
PERMIT FOR A DEMONSTRATION HAD BEEN GRANTED FOR JULY 18.

2. DUE TO LACK OF FOLLOWING OR INTEREST, THE INTENDED
DEMONSTRATIONS APPEAR TO HAVE FIZZLED. WE HAVE RECEIVED
A REPORT THAT ONLY A VERY SMALL DEMONSTRATION (5 OR 6
PERSONS) WAS HELD AT THE WHITE HOUSE. KISSINGER

DEPARTMENT OF STATE	IS/FPC/CDR 𝟙𝟜	Date: 5/18/95
(✓) RELEASE ( ) DECLASSIFY	MR Cases Only:	
( ) EXCISE ( ) D.CLASSIFY	EO Citations	
( ) DENY IN PART		TS authority to
( ) DELETE Non-Responsive Info	( ) CLASSIFY as ( ) S or ( ) C OADR	
FOIA exemptions	( ) DOWNGRADE TS to ( ) S or ( ) C OADR	
PA Exemptions		

LIMITED OFFICIAL USE

State Department telegram to US embassy, Rangoon, regarding demonstration.

Left to right: Saw Than Aung, Gen Bo Mya, Win, Aug 1983. Photo by Gandasari Win.

Win making a point to Gen Mya. Photo by Gandasari Win.

Christmas at Aung San Suu Kyi's Oxford home, 1984. Win at far right.
Photo by Gandasari Win.

Aung San Suu Kyi at Simla, 1987. Photo by U Kyaw Win.

"AND THE SUN COMES UP LIKE THUNDER, OUT OF BURMA 'CROSS THE BAY;"

Copyright, 1988, Los Angeles Times.
Reprinted with permission. 22 Sep 1988

Paul Conrad's cartoon in the *Los Angeles Times,* **1988.**

THE
BURMA BULLETIN

U Kyaw Win
Editor & Publisher

24941 Mustang Drive

Laguna Hills, CA 92653
U.S.A.

10 April 1988

The Honorable David Lange
Prime Minister of New Zealand
House of Parliament
Wellington
New Zealand

Prime Minister:

The recent call for a peace conference by Burma's National Democratic Front, to be convened in a neutral country, is an opportunity your government should not pass up. The civil war that has been consuming Burma for forty years has gone on far too long.

Chairman General U Ne Win's one-party military dictatorship has been firmly ensconced at the reins of a despotic regime since 2 March 1962 with no sign of relenting its grip.

Ethnic minorities, namely the Arakan, Kachin, Karen, Karenni, Lahu, Mon, Pa-O, Palaung, Shan, and Wa, have been engaged in armed struggle to gain a measure of autonomy from the Burman-dominated central government.

United States military aid given to the Ne Win regime, purportedly for narcotic interdiction in Burma's sector of the Golden Triangle, has been employed in the war against the minorities and other citizens who oppose its harsh rule. The economic policies pursued by the military rulers have reduced the country to the status of a Least Developed Country within the United Nations' definition of that designation.

Documented instances of murder, torture, rape, beatings, imprisonment, extra-judicial executions and genocide abound. Burning of villages, indiscriminate spraying of the US-supplied defoliant, 2,4-D, on villages and agricultural lands far away from the opium poppies of the Golden Triangle have exacted heavy casualties of innocent hill peoples. Men, women and young people have been forcibly removed from their homes and made to serve as porters for Burma army troops in the frontier regions. Innocent hill people have been herded into Vietnam-style "secure" hamlets and thus deprived of working their traditional farmlands.

Letter to New Zealand Prime Minister David Lange.

Page 2

I have conferred with National Democratic Front leaders, whose combined forces are capable of fielding 35,000 guerrillas. They have now disavowed their earlier goal to secede from the Union and would be willing to live in a reconstituted federal republic. Their calls for negotiations have fallen on Rangoon's unhearing ears. I can assure you that New Zealand's initiative would be enthusiastically welcomed by the National Democratic Front and other opposition elements within Burma.

New Zealand's best interests would be served if it would be willing to offer its good offices by mediating at peace talks. I have written to Prime Minister Robert Hawke of Australia to find out if Australia would be willing to host the conference on its soil.

The United Nations help in the form of a peace-keeping contingent to supervise the truce while negotiations are in progress would be most helpful.

No amount of military aid given to the much-hated, corrupt dictatorship will restore tranquillity to that once prosperous land.

Peace, freedom and the re-establishment of a democratic government in mainland Southeast Asia's largest country would deter the spread of Communism. Given a chance to peacefully develop its hinterlands would gradually eliminate opium poppies as a cash crop in the Golden Triangle. These twin goals must be in New Zealand's best interests. Clearly, New Zealand's future remains with Asia.

The purpose of freedom is for those who enjoy it to create it for others who do not.

Sincerely yours,

U Kyaw Win
Editor & Publisher

Office: (714) 432-5860
Home: (714) 831-2000
Enclosure

Letter to New Zealand PM, page 2.

PRIME MINISTER

MAY 2 6 1988

17 May 1988

U Kyaw Win
Editor and Publisher
The Burma Bulletin
24941 Mustang Drive
Laguna Hills
California 92653
UNITED STATES OF AMERICA

Dear U Win

Thank you for your letter of 10 April 1988. I have read it carefully. I do not wish to comment on the claims it makes about the situation within Burma and I am not able to respond positively to the request you make of the New Zealand Government.

Yours sincerely

David Lange

PARLIAMENT BUILDINGS WELLINGTON NEW ZEALAND

Reply from New Zealand Prime Minister Lange.

Mortally wounded Win Maw Oo, Sep 1988. Photo by Steve Lehman.

Congressman-elect Rohrabacher at LAX upon return from refugee camps, Dec 1988.

CRDB booth, Dr. Aung Khin. Photo by U Kyaw Win.

CRDB's Yé Kyaw Thu and Win at Manerplaw, 1989. Photo by Gail Fisher.

Forum on Burma. Left to right: Win, Mike Farrell,
Burton Levin, Josef Silverstein, Bertil Lintner, Eric Sanberg, 1992.

Win's family at Nobel ceremony for Aung San Suu Kyi, 10 Dec 1991.

Student warriors at Three Pagodas Pass, 1988. Photo by Gail Fisher.

Guerilla warfare country, Salween Gorge. Photo by Gail Fisher.

This Padaung girl's mother declined the offer from Win's surgeon brother to separate the girl's fused ring and middle fingers. "It is God's will," she said.
Photo by Gail Fisher, 1992.

Win with Anglican Archbishop Andrew Mya Han in 1992. Photo by Gandasari Win.

**Win with Kayaw refugee girl at Mae Hong Son refugee camp, 1992.
Photo by Gail Fisher.**

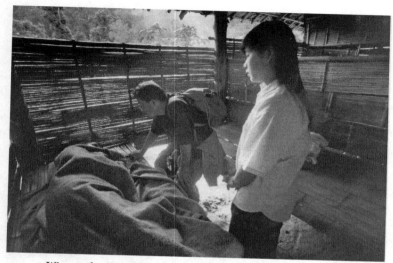

Win comforting a patient in Mae Hong Son refugee camp, 1992.
Photo by Gail Fisher.

Riri and Win with the KIO Central Committee, Pajau, 1995.
Photo by Mimi Forsyth.

Left to right: Riri, Win, Gen Bo Mya, Mahn Shah, 1995.

BENJAMIN LADNER
PRESIDENT

January 29, 1997

Dr. U Kyaw Win
24941 Mustang Drive
Laguna Hills, CA 92653-5730

Dear Dr. Win:

Thank you so much for your able assistance in helping to make our January 26 commencement such an important occasion for American University. I am fully aware of the countless hours that you invested behind-the-scenes for this historic event.

I am grateful that you, as an alumnus, worked with your alma mater in suggesting American University as the appropriate venue for Daw Aung San Suu Kyi's honorary degree and accompanying remarks. As you know, the values that she represents are ones that we embrace and that our students, faculty, and alumni embody. It is a privilege to help her communicate her ideals to the audience across the United States, and I hope that through this event we have achieved progress in the struggle for freedom and democracy in Burma.

Thank you for helping to make this day possible. I look forward to seeing you again in the future.

Sincerely,

Benjamin Ladner

4400 MASSACHUSETTS AVENUE, NW   WASHINGTON, DC   20016-8060   202-885-2121   FAX: 202-885-3265

American University President's letter to Win.

Peacemaker Award presented to Win by Rocky Mountain Conference of the United Methodist Church.

Win and Riri's fiftieth wedding anniversary, 2008. Photo by Ellen Scheffler.

Win teaching in Pariaman, W. Sumatra, Indonesia, 2011. Photo by Gandasari Win.

Demonstrating to girls at Phaungdaw Oo Monastic School in Mandalay, 2011.
Photo by Ellen Scheffler.

Win with Burmese refugee children, in a class at Mae Sot, Thailand, 2011.
Photo by Gandasari Win.

A class in critical thinking, Mandalay. Photo by Ellen Scheffler.

Win with orphans at Mae Sot. Photo by Gandasari Win.

Orphan girls and Win at Mae Sot, Thailand. Photo by Gandasari Win.

Left to right: Pascal Khoo Thwe, Win, U Htein Lin, Vicky Bowman, Martin Morland at Dora Than É's funeral, Oxford, England, 7 Jul 2007. Photo by Zali Win.

Bibliography

Abdoellah, Baginda Dahlan, "Indië voor de Indiërs. Rede, gehouden op het Congress der Indische studenten, te Leiden op 23 November 1917." *Indologenblad*, 7(1917) 95–99.

The Conspiracy of Treasonous Minions within the Myanmar Naing-Ngan and Traitorous Cohorts Abroad. Rangoon: Ministry of Information of the Government of the Union of Myanmar, 1989.

Dun, Smith. *Memoirs of the Four-foot Colonel.* Southeast Asia Program. Data Paper Series. Ithaca, NY: Cornell University Press, 1980.

Hu, Howard, U Kyaw Win, and Nancy Arnison. "Burma: Health and Human Rights." *The Lancet* 337 (June 1, 1991) 1335.

Khant, Maung Khine. 8888 *Democracy Revolution Record* (in Burmese). Rangoon: Kyi Hla Maung Literary House, 2013.

Kin, On. *Burma Under the Japanese.* Lucknow: Christian Publishing House, 1947.

———. *China as a Burman Saw It.* Rangoon: American Baptist Mission, 1939

———. *China's Freedom and the New World Order.* Rangoon: American Baptist Mission, 1939

———. *Cruising Down the Irrawaddy.* Rangoon: Thudhama, 1956.

Larkin, Emma. *Secret Histories.* London: John Murray, 2004.

Law-Yone, Wendy. *Golden Parasol: A Daughter's Memoir of Burma.* London: Chatto & Windus, 2013.

Marshall, Andrew. "Anatomy of a Failed Revolution." *Time* 170 (2007) 30.

———. *The Trouser People.* Washington, DC: Counter Point, 2002.

Maw, Ba. *Breakthrough in Burma: Memoirs of a Revolution, 1939–1946.* New Haven: Yale University Press, 1968.

Montefiore, Simon Sebag. *Speeches that Changed the World.* London: Quercus, 2005.

Myint-U, Thant. *The River of Lost Footsteps.* New York: Farrar, Straus and Giroux, 2006.

———. *Where China Meets India.* New York: Farrar, Straus and Giroux, 2011.

Nu, U. *Saturday's Son: Memoirs of the Former Prime Minister of Burma.* U Law Yone, trans. U Kyaw Win, ed. New Haven: Yale University Press, 1975.

Oung, Kin. *Who Killed Aung San?* 2nd ed. Bangkok: White Lotus, 1996.

Phan, Zoya. *Undaunted—My Struggle for Freedom and Survival in Burma.* New York: Free Press, 2009.

Said, Edward W. *Reflections on Exile and other Essays.* Cambridge, MA: Harvard University Press, 2002.

Seekins, Donald M. *State and Society in Modern Rangoon.* London: Routledge, 2011.

Swe, James Myint. *Cannon Soldiers of Burma.* Self-published, 2014.

Tucker, Shelby. *Burma: The Curse of Independence.* London: Pluto, 2001.

Win, U Kyaw, ed. *The Burma Bulletin.* 1–19 (1973–1992).

Win, Zali, ed. *Cruising Down the Irrawaddy and Other Writings by U On Kin.* Rangoon: Myanmar Book Centre, 2015.

Zan, Saw Spencer. *Life's Journey in Faith: Burma from Riches to Rags.* Bloomington: AuthorHouse, 2007.